Hitchcock and Philosophy

Popular Culture and Philosophy®
Series Editor: George A. Reisch
(Series Editor for this volume was William Irwin)

Popular Culture and Philosophy®

Hitchcock and Philosophy

Dial M for Metaphysics

Edited by

DAVID BAGGETT

and

WILLIAM A. DRUMIN

OPEN COURT
Chicago and La Salle, Illinois

Volume 27 in the series, Popular Culture and Philosophy®

The pictures on pages 62, 114, and 228 are reproduced by permission of Corbis.

To order books from Open Court, call 1-800-815-2280, or visit our website at www.opencourtbooks.com.

Open Court Publishing Company is a division of Carus Publishing Company.

Library of Congress Cataloging-in-Publication Data

Hitchcock and philosophy : dial M for metaphysics / edited by David Baggett and William A. Drumin
      p. cm. — (Popular culture and philosophy ; 27)
   Includes bibliographical references and index.
   ISBN-13: 978-0-8126-9616-5 (trade paper : alk. paper)
   ISBN-10: 0-8126-9616-6 (trade paper : alk. paper)
   1. Hitchcock, Alfred, 1899-1980—Criticism and interpretation.
 I. Baggett, David. II. Drumin, William A.
 PN1998.3.H68H53 2007
 791.4302'33092—dc22
                         2007000242

To Donald Spoto

Contents

Part III
The Reeling Mind   99

Part IV
Hitchcock's Ethical Dilemmas   157

Part V
What's It All About, Alfred?   213

Previews and Opening Credits

As we look at popular culture through the lens of philosophy, a familiar, portly figure ambles into view—the master of suspense, Alfred Hitchcock.

Hitchcock was a profound artist as well as a popular entertainer. His numerous classic movies engage the viewer through the elaboration of ideas, concepts, and humanist issues, deployed via the medium of compelling cinematic language, of images and sounds.

Hitchcock has long been recognized as a cinematic *auteur* whose films embody expressions of a personal vision of the world. The chapters presented in this volume address a range of issues, some raised by consideration of a single film (including one segment done for Hitchcock's TV series), some by a comparison of two or more movies, and some by an examination of a significant facet of Hitchcock's entire work. We aim to critically examine Hitchcock's approach and to uncover some of its philosophical implications.

Many viewers have observed that Alfred Hitchcock focuses on *ideas* in the construction of his films. The French director-critics Claude Chabrol and Eric Roemer, in their book, *Hitchcock*, claimed that each of his classic films is based on a sort of "formal postulate."[1] Hitchcock organized the dramatic

---

[1] Eric Roemer and Claude Chabrol, *Hitchcock: The First Forty-Four Films* (New York: Unger, 1979), p. x. The original French edition was published by S.A. Éditions Universitaires in 1958.

elements of the films around the expression and deployment of conceptual elements. Philosophical issues are thus proposed by the thematic motifs in Hitchcock's major films. Among conspicuous elements of Hitchcock's personal vision, we may discern the following:

1. A strong anti-utopian outlook that finds the human species, and indeed the universe itself, to be in a "fallen" condition with a disillusioning propensity for unleashing chaos and destruction.

2. A decidedly existentialist perspective that affirms the challenge of individual self-definition through the risk of personal choice and commitment.

3. A correlative construal of spectatorship as flight from commitment and authenticity, or an attempt to deny the primary reality of the subjective.

4. A remarkable anticipation of later viewpoints regarding the social roles of women.

This book explores the philosophical implications of these perspectives and other aspects of Hitchcock's artistic vision. The philosophical issues have their inherent interest and challenge and also deepen our appreciation of the movies.

Like the films it investigates, *Hitchcock and Philosophy* was made possible by a huge collaborative effort. Many thanks to all of our excellent authors. Their patience was Herculean and their philosophical talents and sincere regard for Hitchcock are obvious. The deepest thanks to our own masterful director and friend, the *auteur* Bill ("T-Bone") Irwin, whose vision for this book and the popular series of which it's a part guided all our efforts and whose influence can be felt on every page.

We appreciate all the good folks at Open Court for bringing the book to its final stage of completion, and special thanks go to Jaime McAndrew for offering some very useful editorial suggestions.

And now, kindly turn off your cell phones and pagers. It's time to dig in to your popcorn. Enjoy the show.

I

The Mystery of Everyday Life

1

Sabotage: Chaos Unleashed and the Impossibility of Utopia

WILLIAM A. DRUMIN

In Hitchcock's 1943 film, *Shadow of a Doubt,* a young woman discovers that the uncle she idolizes is a pathological killer. The confrontation with this horrific revelation engenders a profound identity crisis that forces her to abandon her naive insular view of the world as a domain for unlimited adventure, growth, and self-development, and compels her instead to recognize that the world is permeated with profoundly evil forces for chaos and destruction.

In this film, as in others, we can discern a strongly anti-Utopian element in Hitchcock's artistic vision, rejecting a view of the world as inherently good, rational, or perfectible. Chaos, destructiveness, evil are not mere temporary or eliminable obstacles to the perfect society. Attraction to chaos and destruction lies very deep at the heart of the individual and social psyche. So that while Hitchcock does not construe the world as inherently or predominantly evil, he warns that it does require constant and diligent watching: for it is perpetually at risk of "going crazy," like the psychopathic uncle of *Shadow of a Doubt.*

Ever since Plato's *Republic,* diverse visions of the ideal or perfect society have exercised a powerful attractive force on the imaginations of many philosophers and savants. Derived from the title of the visionary work by Renaissance philosopher Thomas More, the term *utopia* has come to signify the generic characterization of such reconstructive visions of the social order. In addition to Plato (427–347 B.C.), whose *Republic* has exercised perennial influence on human thought, the history of philosophy has seen the advocacy of utopian visions by such diverse thinkers as Francis Bacon (1561–1626), Thomas Hobbes (1588–1679), Thomas Campanella (1568–1639), Claude Henri de Saint-Simon (1760–1825), Karl Marx (1818–1883), Henry David Thoreau (1817–1862), and B.F. Skinner (1904–1990).

And no doubt one can find utopian elements in the thought of many other philosophers.[1] This is hardly surprising, as philosophers are especially proficient in detecting differences between the actual and the ideal order of things. In existing societies they all too readily detect such serious faults as crime, war, poverty, injustice, and exploitation. And some have come to believe that such evils can be effectively eliminated from human life through a more perfect ordering of society. They hold that the structure of an ideal society could be grounded on rational and moral principles, encompassing a full and comprehensive account of human nature and human personhood, which would enable a full reconciliation between social and individual needs. We may characterize the strong utopian position as one which holds that an individual person living in Utopia would be guaranteed maximal fullness and satisfaction in his or her life through participation in such a harmonious ordering of society. This viewpoint would regard both the individual and society as inherently perfectible through the application of rational and scientific methods of social reconstruction.

Yet there have also been many prominent anti-utopian thinkers, who expressly deny even the theoretical possibility of the social and individual orderings mentioned above. Such were Søren Kierkegaard (1813–1855), Fyodor Dostoyevsky (1821–1881), Friedrich Nietzsche (1844–1900), and Sigmund Freud (1856–1939). In *Notes from Underground,* Dostoyevsky argued that human passional will would inevitably resist and frustrate any rationally or scientifically designed utopian society.

Later, under the influence of Dostoyevsky's outlook, Sigmund Freud construed the human personality in terms of an often precarious balance between the chaotic, self-seeking drives of the Id and the restraining socializing forces of the Superego. The Superego originates from the socialization of the person and imposes a sense of obligation to put social interests

---

[1] For an informative study, see Ruth Levitas, *The Concept of Utopia* (Syracuse: Syracuse University Press, 1990).

ahead of selfish ones, while Id drives are inborn and know only the law of gratification and self-satisfaction.

Though the repression of these impulses through various kinds of education makes a stable social order possible, Freud nevertheless insists that the forces of the Id can only be repressed to a degree but never completely destroyed or eliminated from the psyche. It always will require effort and commitment from the individual to keep them in check. In the absence of such commitment, no society, no matter how scientifically or rationally planned, will be able to guarantee harmony just by the application of preset rules and structures. Given the difficulty of keeping our instinctive drives in check, society will always need to deal with the kind of self-seeking, atavistic outbreaks that constitute criminal or violent behavior.

The films of Alfred Hitchcock reveal an artistic vision strongly influenced by Freud's theory of the human personality. We need only recall that his 1945 film, *Spellbound*, was one of the first Hollywood films with a narrative centered on psychoanalysis (and in which a murder is solved through the Freudian interpretation of a dream). Psychoanalytic elements also play an important role in other works like *Rope*, *Psycho*, and *Marnie*. And, in fact, Hitchcock fully shares the anti-utopian outlook of Freud and Dostoyevsky, though with a significant twist. For in his view, it is not only the human psyche that is inclined to the unleashing of chaos; the very universe itself has a chaotic and destructive dimension.

Accordingly, a centerpiece of Alfred Hitchcock's artistic vision is the acknowledgement as a stark fact that we live in a profoundly flawed universe, one that embodies intractable evil, one in which the eruption of violence and chaos is a permanent possibility and live threat. Human societies provide security for their members through such institutions as the state, the church, the economic order, science, industry, and the family. But as several of Hitchcock's most powerful film works have illustrated, these institutions can prove fragile and ineffective against the threat of unpredictable outbreaks of chaos and destruction.

As a manifestation of the evil and flawed character of the universe, this threat has a bipolar character. The chaos may erupt upon a society or individual through the working of seemingly impersonal and accidental forces (as in *The Wrong Man, North by Northwest,* and *The Birds*). Or it may erupt as a consequence of a permanent forceful attraction exercised by chaos and destruction upon the individual human psyche. Hitchcock's anti-utopian vision of life mandates that, if the deep-seated attraction to chaos and destruction is not to issue in tragic consequences, individuals must keep careful, ongoing scrutiny against the promptings of this attraction. They must beware especially of the inclination to rationalize their agency for chaos by reducing its effects to stylizations and abstractions. This is exactly what happens to the protagonist of Hitchcock's 1936 British film, *Sabotage.*

Sabotage

Adapted from Joseph Conrad's 1907 novel, *The Secret Agent, Sabotage* was released during a time of mounting unease and fear of war on the international scene. Though the film was nei-ther a critical nor popular success, it reveals itself from a more distanced perspective as an extraordinary cinematic masterpiece in which Hitchcock creates and conveys powerful emotional states through the cinematic language of image and sound. A good part of its expressive power arises from its remarkable compactness; there doesn't appear to be a single wasted shot or line of dialogue in the film's seventy-five-minute running time. Hitchcock has formed the narrative of Conrad's novel into a striking depiction of the ease with which chaos and destruction can be unleashed upon the world through the most unlikely human agency of a quiet, seemingly inoffensive family man.

The enduring relevance of Hitchcock's vision received unex-pected confirmation in an occurrence sixty-five years after the film's release, when film critic, Michael Stragow reviewed the film in his syndicated column. Writing just three weeks after the terrorist attacks of September 11th, 2001, Stragow recommended the film as "a timely look at a terrorist," a revealing view of how a terrorist act can be spawned.[2] Yet the terrorist in the film is not a religious or political fanatic, like the September 11th terrorists, but a quiet, home-loving family man (as his wife explicitly

---

[2] As revealed by the dictionary definition presented in the film prior to the opening credit sequence, the then meaning of "sabotage" approximates what today has come to be called "terrorism." The definition reads, "Willful destruction of buildings or machin-ery with the object of alarming a group of persons or inspiring public uneasiness."

describes him). The film exhibits in sequential detail how appallingly easy it can be for even such a man to become involved with terrorism and to rationalize his involvement to the point where he becomes an agent for mass murder. In four key scenes, Hitchcock both prefigures the eruption of chaos and links it thematically to the film audience, forcefully reminding us that everyone has the capability to become an agent for such eruption. We will examine each of these scenes and retrace the route from seemingly innocuous rationalization to murderous outcome.

Thing with a Mustache

Karl Verloc is the manager of a neighborhood movie theater in a crowded, slummy section of London. With his young wife and her younger brother, he lives in an apartment adjoining the theater. Times are hard, and, without informing his wife, Verloc has been working for agents of a foreign country by staging destabilizing events in London. The film opens with Verloc's sabotage of an electrical generator that causes a brief blackout in the city. On the next day, he keeps an appointed meeting with his foreign controller at the municipal aquarium, where he anticipates payment for his accomplishment. But the agent refuses to pay him, instead showing him a newspaper report that the briefness of the blackout led to amusement rather than fear. ("Comedies in the Dark," reads one headline.) The foreign agent explains that his employers are not comedians; they didn't hire Verloc to make people laugh. To receive payment, Verloc will have to plant a bomb in the crowded Piccadilly section of London, during the upcoming celebration of a civic holiday.

At first Verloc protests that he will not become involved in any act that causes the loss of life. But he very much needs the money, and the agent shrewdly suggests that he can farm out the job to some underworld acquaintances. The agent shows he is a most perceptive judge of Verloc's character, as he discerns and appeals to the latter's capacity for abstraction. For if Verloc can get someone else to deliver the bomb, he can and will rationalize that the moral responsibility for the resulting loss of life and limb attaches entirely to that other person. If he is not physically connected to the site of the destruction, the outcome will appear to him as a basically harmless abstraction (say, a list of names of the victims in the next day's newspaper), and he will disconnect from it and imagine that he is free from moral responsibility. Reading the names of the victims, he will feel a tinge of regret at their misfortune, even while rejecting any suggestion of personal guilt for what happened to them. After all, he did not even know the victims; their deaths or injuries were due entirely to their bad luck in being at the wrong place at the wrong time. And if any blame is to be assigned, then surely it must devolve entirely on the person who physically delivered the bomb to the site.

The aquarium setting of this scene is especially significant for appreciating Hitchcock's thematic development in this film. The undersea creatures, prominently visible behind exhibition windows throughout the scene, symbolize "monsters from the Id," destructive chaotic drives and impulses that inhabit the Unconscious. Verloc's lack of watchfulness over these forces will allow them to be unleashed through his agency with catastrophic consequences that even he cannot fully realize. Hitchcock deploys this symbolism consistently in the scene. Not only do Verloc and the agent discuss their murderous business while gazing at one of the exhibition windows, but the agent makes specific reference to them in connection with his terrorist plans. The sight of a huge ocean turtle reminds him of the soup to be prepared for the upcoming public celebration of Lord Mayor's Show Day, and it is during this festivity with its prospective throngs filling the streets that he directs Verloc to place the explosive device. Earlier, when the agent casually pointed to a creature that he called "a thing with a mustache," Hitchcock was even giving us an oblique clue to the identity of the foreign country behind the terrorism. What leader of what country in 1936 could be accurately characterized as a monster from the Id and a "thing with a mustache"? Who else but Adolf Hitler, the fanatical Fascist leader of Nazi Germany, who already in 1936 was casting war-like shadows over Europe and the world? In a few years, this "thing with a mustache" would become a major agent for the unleashing of the most destructive war the world has ever known.

Most significantly, after Verloc has agreed to the agent's proposal, he projects the prospective destruction of Piccadilly onto the exhibition window, where the tranquil view of the sea animals is momentarily displaced by the image of the well-known

Piccadilly Circus neighborhood virtually melting away to destruction. Through visual juxtaposition, this shot explicitly links the unleashing of destruction both with the undersea creatures and with Verloc's conscious perspective. It thus serves an important function in the narrative in establishing for us Verloc's full moral responsibility for the consequences of his involvement in terrorism. It implies that when Verloc later rationalizes his participation in terror and denies personal responsibility, he will be in bad faith. He clearly understands the consequences of his proposed action. Despite all his elaborate rationalizations and denials, he will be morally culpable for the violence he helps to unleash.

Conspiring in a Bird Shop

The agent sends Verloc to a munitions maker to arrange for the bomb to be constructed and delivered to him. The man runs a bird shop as a front for his activities. He leads Verloc to his living quarters behind the shop, his "other department," where he keeps deadly explosives disguised as foodstuffs. He lives with his daughter and her young daughter, and during his discussion with Verloc he finds several of his granddaughter's playthings in the area where the explosives are stored. Indeed, there is almost a fatal accident when he removes the girl's doll from the food cabinet and displaces a jar of explosives that he just manages to catch.

We can recognize in this simple scene another prefiguration of a future outbreak of violence, one, in fact, which will take the life of Verloc's own stepson, Stevie. When adults play with dangerous "toys," it is only to be expected that innocent persons, including children, will be killed. It is significant how, in response to the reproachful stare of his daughter, the proprietor tells his granddaughter to slap him hard because he has been "naughty." (The little girl complies with gusto!) Unfortunately, the man does not realize the literal truth of his remark, as he shows by his threat to resist with violence any attempt by the police to shut down his terrorist operation. The proprietor is a true fanatic, a dedicated supporter of the terrorist cause, who even envies Verloc for getting to work in the "front lines" of the struggle. Verloc in no way shares the man's ideological commitment, being motivated exclusively by a desire for the extra income it will bring him. His pronounced nervousness at the appearance of a passing police officer is a manifestation both of his lack of personal commitment to the cause he is serving and an unacknowledged guilty conscience for violating the legal and moral code that is an integral part of his individual and social life.

As Verloc leaves the shop, Hitchcock's camera remains inside, and we watch a nervous Verloc wring his hands and move off, followed immediately by the Scotland Yard detective who has been assigned to shadow him. We know that Verloc is moving to arrange for a murderous act. Within the shop the soundtrack disgorges a crescendo of bird cries welling up to a near cacophony. In an eerie anticipation of *The Birds*, twenty-seven years later, the bird cries here signal not the attack of the birds themselves, but the impending unleashing of chaos from the depths of the Id through Verloc's human agency. In an artistic convention dating from the time of the Renaissance, Hitchcock here deploys birds, especially in their singing and crying, as emblems of erupting chaos, violence, and destruction.[3] Here the effect is most unnerving as the crescendoing outburst is linked visually to acts by Verloc that will lead irredeemably to terror. It imparts prefigurative force to the scene as a warning that the protagonists' designs for terror are fated to erupt in violence that will destroy the lives of many innocent persons, including young children. Not all children exposed to the threat of terrorist violence will be as lucky as the proprietor's grandchild. Playing in the midst of dangerous explosives, she escaped harm. With Verloc and the proprietor intent on their plans, it can only be a matter of time before children and other innocents will be killed or maimed.

Conspiring in a Movie Theater

The next day three men with underworld connections come to Verloc's apartment in the rear of his movie theater to see about a job he has for them. Police Detective Ted Spencer has been

---

[3] See Donald Spoto, *The Art of Alfred Hitchcock*, second edition (New York: Doubleday Dell, 1992), p. 59. Later, the bomb will be delivered to Verloc in the bottom of a bird-cage holding a pair of birds that Verloc is to give to Stevie. An accompanying note will warn that "the birds will sing at 1:45," reminding Verloc of the time set for the bomb to detonate.

working at an adjoining produce store in order to watch Verloc, and he recognizes one of the visitors. On the pretext of wanting to watch the movie currently playing, he gains entrance to the theater, where he must first walk through the darkened auditorium where the current film presentation is being screened. The film appears to be some kind of screwball comedy. There's a lot of struggle and upset among the characters, and the audience is laughing uproariously at their antics. In order to reach Verloc's apartment, Ted moves to a space behind the screen, where there is a transom looking onto Verloc's living room. Assisted by Stevie, he eavesdrops on the conversation between Verloc and his guests. As he strains to hear a possibly incriminating remark, the sound track prominently features frenetic action and dialogue coming from the screen, along with the appreciative laughter it arouses from the audience. As Ted opens the transom, a jump cut immediately takes us inside the apartment, where one of the guests is agreeing to do the job proffered by Verloc. The latter has agreed to the man's price, and he doesn't find a significant danger of detection. Hitchcock's camera presents him from a low angle to convey a "laid back" attitude, as, with a cigarette dangling from his mouth, he tells Verloc, "I don't see anything against it." It is Hitchcock's striking visual representation of a dead conscience.

The juxtapositions in this scene again powerfully further Hitchcock's prefigurative purpose, and connect it with a central theme of movie watching. In the Joseph Conrad novel, the Verloc character ran a tobacco shop. It was Hitchcock's idea to make him the manager of a movie theater, so that most of the narrative would be played out in and around the theater, where audiences are inevitably watching films, and, more often than not, finding them enjoyable and laughing at them. In this way, Hitchcock consistently links the narrative with the problematic of movie watching.

In this scene, there is chaos on the screen, and in the darkness of the theater, the audience *laughs* at it. Thematically, the film and the screen on which it is presented represent "appearance." The re-enactment of violence and chaos generates laughter, because, as appearance, it is stylized and "abstracted" from the real entity. The mere representation of violence is abstract in the sense that it does not impact our lives. It does not threaten us or our loved ones. At the same time, the expression of violence holds a positive appeal for our psyches. And so the audiences in this film find it amusing and enjoyable.

At the crucial time, Hitchcock cuts directly from the onscreen chaos to the conversation in Verloc's parlor where people are plotting the unleashing of *actual* chaos. Significantly, this room is located *behind* the movie screen, linking it to the cinema and its audience as reality to appearance. Here Hitchcock, as he so often does, employs a literal relationship to express a metaphorical one. The real violence unleashed by Verloc and his co-conspirators will not be "abstracted" by those affected by it, and it will provoke, not the laughter of the cinema audiences, but the pain and lament of those who have suffered grievous loss.

Before Ted can learn the conspirators' plan, the man who has agreed to plant the bomb for Verloc spots Ted's hand protruding through the transom. Immediately changing the subject to the harmless and legal topic of what to bet on the soccer matches, the man works his way over to the transom, grabs Ted's arm, and pulls him into the room. Ted pretends that he was only exploring how the films were shown, but one of the other men recognizes him as the police detective who once sent him to prison. The three hoods flee in panic, leaving Verloc with the problem of ridding himself of the bomb that tomorrow will be delivered to his home.

Ted's fate in this scene constitutes yet another of Hitchcock's prefigurations—here a forewarning of what is in store for the audience of the film. Like Ted, they will not be allowed to remain bemused spectators at the impending unleashing of chaos. Rather, they will be pulled *into* the narrative, forced to become engaged in the outcome and to relate personally to it. And unlike the audiences *in* the film, who laugh at on-screen chaos, the audience *of* the film will not laugh, but will instead be deeply moved and saddened by the resulting tragedy.[4]

Chaos in a Cartoon

Verloc is now under open surveillance by Scotland Yard, so he cannot deliver the bomb without being searched and intercepted. But he cannot simply leave the device in his home,

---

[4] A coded message sent to Verloc by the foreign agent warns, "London must not laugh on Saturday."

because it has been preset to detonate at a definite time. As a last resort, Verloc asks his young stepson, Stevie, to deliver the package (which he explains contains a "projector device," another link of violence to movie watching) to the Piccadilly underground station. He warns Stevie to be sure to have it there by 1:30, thinking to allow him enough time to get away from the area before the bomb explodes. But the thronging crowds celebrating the holiday hold Stevie up, and the bomb explodes while he is still in transit on a bus, killing him and most of the passengers.

Contemporary audiences were profoundly shocked at this development. They never expected that Hitchcock would let an innocent boy like Stevie be killed, not to mention the cute puppy held by a passenger sitting right next to him. Many people were profoundly angry at Hitchcock, causing the film to fare poorly during its initial release. People felt that Hitchcock had set them up, first getting audiences to relate positively to Stevie by presenting him as a typically insouciant pre-teenage boy, one who could be anyone's son, brother, or best friend, and then callously killing him off. The negative reaction was so strong that Hitchcock made a concerted effort in his next film to defuse the resentment and recover his audience. In that film, *Young and Innocent*, he allowed himself to become unusually sentimental in the narration of a love story with a decidedly gratifying ending.

In several subsequent interviews, Hitchcock repeatedly claimed he had made a mistake in first relentlessly building up suspense and then letting the audience down by a tragic and cruel outcome. But it is clear that in this regard Hitchcock was talking primarily in his function as an entertainer. It is dangerous to antagonize one's audience if one hopes to keep them loyal. But the death of the boy is an essential element of this film as a masterpiece of cinematic artistry. It is the centerpiece of the narrative. Every element of plot and characterization leads up to or devolves from it.

In killing off Stevie, Hitchcock accomplished in an unusually stark way what he was to do in several of his other films in a more palatable manner. He punishes his audience for its impure motives for watching—in this instance, for watching a film about violence and murder. For like the rest of humankind, the audience is under the influence of a deep-seated attraction to chaos and destruction. It had sought to gratify this interest in the secure and comfortable darkness of the theater through the screen's display of violence that they may enjoy without fear of personal engagement. Hitchcock raises audience consciousness by forcing it to confront the effect of violence as something personally experienced, rather than rendered "abstract" from the viewpoint of disinterested spectators. The attitude of the audience is in an important sense likened to that of the Verloc character. Both tend to rationalize violence through the process of abstraction by which the sting of its tragic aftermath is removed.

Consider as an illustration the attitude of the audience during the suspense scene, when Stevie is carrying what we know to be a bomb. Everyone is intensely rooting for him to get to his destination, deposit the infernal machine, and get far away from the site of the impending explosion. Now suppose Stevie had managed to do this and had gotten away from Piccadilly "just in the nick of time," as occurred inevitably in the cliffhanger serials of the day. We would all have been immensely relieved and gratified, and, with the subsequent arrest of Verloc and the exoneration of his wife, we would have rejoiced in a happy outcome. But what about all those other people who would inevitably have been killed or maimed by the blast? To the audience they would not matter. They would be mere abstractions, represented perhaps by a list of names in a newspaper account, worthy of no more than a brief twinge of regret. And in the same event, that would have been precisely Verloc's reaction! Both he and the audience are ready to benefit in their own way from the release of violence as long as it remains abstracted and does not touch them personally.

Mrs. Verloc has known nothing of her husband's terrorist activities. In response to Ted's efforts to plant suspicion in her mind, she has all along insisted that her husband is an utterly harmless home-loving man. But now, when she learns of Stevie's death, she is forced to confront the appalling truth that she has been living with a terrorist. When she confronts him, he justifies himself through his standard strategy of abstraction: He didn't mean for the boy to be hurt; he would have taken the bomb himself if the police hadn't been watching him; the agent forced him to do it. None of his rationalizations can stand up to the stark fact of Stevie's death, and Mrs. Verloc now realizes that she has been living with a man she does not know. When at length her husband suggests that he might give her a child to make up for Stevie, his utter callousness drives her out of the apartment and into the adjoining movie theater. It's Saturday afternoon, and as usual in those times, the audience is composed primarily of children, who are laughing heartily at the antics of the characters in a Disney cartoon. Laughter is contagious, and Mrs. Verloc, still in a state of shock, momentarily forgets her trauma and joins in the laughter at the antics of the cartoon characters. The cartoon is titled, "Who Killed Cock Robin?", and suddenly the title character is killed with an arrow by an avian rival. Mrs. Verloc immediately stops laughing, as the violent act on the screen brings her back to reality.

A cartoon is an especially stylized mode of cinema, which allows for the representation of violence impossible to more realistic modes. A character can be demolished in an explosion, flattened by a steam roller, crushed under a huge boulder, and return good as new in the next scene. (Just think of the *Roadrunner* cartoons, where virtually every scene issues in the demolition of the hapless coyote.) The stylization of chaos and destruction facilitates the suspension of belief and the attendant enjoyment of the violence. In effect, the violence is almost totally abstracted out of its real context, like the dictionary definition of "sabotage" that opened the film. The inevitable "sting" of real violence is removed, and the audience can yield to its fascination for it in complete safety. For Mrs. Verloc, however, this is no longer possible, even in watching a cartoon. Followed by the haunting refrain of the cartoon song, "Who killed Cock Robin?" she goes back into the living room to confront her husband.

Violence Against Utopia

In *Sabotage*, we encounter already in Hitchcock's British period a potent expression of his anti-Utopian vision, in which he discerns the dark destructive forces latent in the human psyche and challenges the notion that they can be tamed or conditioned out of existence through social planning. For ultimately, as happened with Mr. Verloc, the responsibility falls upon the decisions and choices of the individual. Only through the firm vigilance of each individual can destructive impulses and attractions be kept in check. The greatest danger lies in the inclination to rationalize one's readiness to indulge in the impulses and to neutralize the sting of conscience by conceiving their destructive impact in abstract and stylized modes. This is precisely what Verloc does in *Sabotage*, and the result is a major act of terrorism, resulting in the death or maiming of twenty or more people.

Verloc is not an ideological fanatic like the perpetrators of the September 11th terror attacks. He is indeed presented as the very opposite—a non-political, quiet, introverted family man, who desires nothing more than to be left alone to enjoy the better things of life with his family. His sole motive for abetting in the terrorist cause is to earn extra money to obtain a little more "margin" in his life. In many ways, he's a typical member of society. How did he become a mass murderer? Simply by failing to keep a constant watch against his capacity for unleashing violence. Even if a utopian society might anticipate the breeding of fanaticism, and devise programmatic means to eliminate it, how could any social ordering reasonably anticipate and control a potential for violence that is an engrained component of the psyches of all its citizens? Such is the basis for Hitchcock's anti-utopian vision.

2

Shadow of a Doubt: Secrets, Lies, and the Search for the Truth

ANGELA CURRAN

Everybody in the World Ain't Honest

As fans of Hitchcock know, things are seldom what they appear in his films. In a cameo role in *Shadow of a Doubt* (1943), one of Hitchcock's personal favorites, he acknowledges this reputation for pulling the wool over the eyes of the audience.[1] Early in the film, Hitchcock plays one of the passengers on a cross-country train that the villain, Charles Oakley (Joseph Cotten), is taking in order to avoid capture. Oakley is pretending to be seriously ill so that he can hide away and elude detection from the police. A woman (Sarah Edwards) urges her husband (Vaughan Glaser), who is a physician, to help the "poor soul" on the train who is so sick. We see the back of a man—Hitchcock—playing bridge with the doctor and his wife. The doctor says to their bridge partner, "You don't look so well either." We see that the gentleman, Hitchcock's character, is just putting on the proverbial "poker face," for he has thirteen spades, a grand slam in hand!

This minor scene is an illustration of a major recurring theme in *Shadow of a Doubt*: people sometimes deceive us and things are not always in reality what they appear to be. Deception involves the projection of a false image that does not correspond with reality. Philosophers share Hitchcock's interest in deception. *Epistemology* is the area of philosophy concerned with the questions: "What can we know?" and "How can we tell

---

[1] See the chapter on Hitchcock cameo appearances, Chapter 17 in this volume.

the difference between appearance and reality?" The film also raises philosophical questions regarding the *moral* implications of gaining knowledge: Is it wrong to lie? Is there a morally relevant difference between lying and failing to divulge the truth? Philosophers often take the search for truth to be a fundamental goal, and *Shadow of a Doubt* poses a challenge to the *value* of truth: Does truth trump other concerns or are other things more important?

As the Hitchcock cameo suggests, misleading speech is not the only way to deceive. Hitchcock famously said, "The camera lies, you know." Oscar Wilde praised art for its ability to fool an audience, and the ancient Greek philosopher, Plato (427–347 B.C.E.), was critical of art's capacity for deception. Plato denounced the ancient Greek playwrights, for example, for producing plays that mislead viewers into falsely thinking that the actions of the gods are immoral or improper. Because of this capacity to lie to the audience, Plato concluded that imitative art has no place in a proper society. *Shadow of a Doubt* examines this debate about the role of truth in art, though Hitchcock's view on this question is not what it at first might seem.

Family Ties

The film opens with a mysterious, kaleidoscope image from the Gay Nineties, splendidly dressed men and women dancing to the tune of the "Merry Widow Waltz." On its surface this picture is a pleasant reminder of a grand, bygone era. Yet through its repeated association with the antagonist, Charles Oakley, the image will take on another, darker meaning. Oakley, to all appearances an elegantly dressed, refined business man, is in reality the "merry widow murderer" of three rich widows, whom the F.B.I. is pursuing in a nationwide manhunt.

When we first see Charles Oakley, he is lying on a bed in a darkened room in a shabby boarding house in Philadelphia. A wad of bills is strewn on the bedside stand and on the floor next to it. The proprietress of the rooming house, Mrs. Martin (Constance Purdy), a kind busybody who is nonetheless clueless about Oakley's true nature, knocks and enters to tell him about two "friends" who have been inquiring about him and will return. It turns out that these men are not in fact friends, but law enforcement officials. Seeing the pile of cash scattered about,

Mrs. Martin tells Oakley that he ought not to leave money lying around: "Everybody in the world ain't honest, you know." After Mrs. Martin leaves, Oakley lifts the blinds to see the detectives waiting for him. "What do you *know?* You're bluffing. You've nothing on me." Departing from the boardinghouse, Oakley manages to elude the detectives in a chase scene that makes Oakley appear to be far more clever than his opponents.

Desperate and on the run, Oakley decides to take refuge with his unsuspecting sister and her family in Santa Rosa, a sunny and quiet small town in Northern California. Under the pretense of longing for a family reunion, Charles wires his adoring sister, Emma Newton (Patricia Collinge), to announce his imminent visit. He commences his trip, incognito, by train to visit them. The action moves to Santa Rosa, with shots of an immaculate and orderly city square and a police officer directing traffic. We're then taken inside the Newton family's home: a beautiful, but slightly rundown, older house in a middle-class neighborhood. It's late afternoon and Oakley's teenage niece, Charlie (Teresa Wright), is upstairs in her bedroom, lying fully dressed on the bed and lost in thought in a pose that calls to mind the first glimpse we had of her uncle.

Charlie, as her uncle later tells her, is the real head of her family. Her well-meaning but inattentive father, Joseph Newton (Henry Travers), returns home from his job as a teller in a downtown bank. In the evening he escapes from the daily grind by reading pulp murder mystery fiction and debating the details of the perfect crime with his amusingly oddball neighbor, Herb Hawkins (Hume Cronyn). Charlie's mother, Emma, arrives from doing an errand downtown. Charlie worries that her mother's life as a housewife with three children and a husband to care for leaves her no time to be something else besides a mother. A bright and successful student, Charlie is nonetheless a trusting, small-town girl who is infatuated with her sophisticated and well-traveled uncle. Thinking that a visit from Uncle Charlie is just what the family needs to "shake them up" (it does and how!), she goes to wire him only to find that her uncle has, she believes, telepathically "heard her" request and will arrive soon on the train.

In this first scene introducing Charlie and her family, and in many others to come, the film makes a conspicuous connection between Oakley and Charlie, who is named after him. The two

Charlies are one of numerous pairs or doubles in the film: for example, two detectives, two murder suspects, two train scenes, the 'Til Two Bar, and two attempts on Charlie's life. Although their moral characters are diametrically opposed—Charlie is a sensitive and morally innocent young woman—she and her uncle are both dreamers who are inclined to romantic notions. Charlie idealizes her uncle in spite of the fact that she knows little about him. Charles romanticizes the past—represented in the recurring kaleidoscope image of waltzing couples—and his life growing up while, ironically, denouncing the corruption he sees in the contemporary world.

Charlie is like her uncle is another way: she is far more clever than the adults around her. With the exception of her brainy little sister, Ann, who senses that Uncle Charlie is some kind of a threat, Charlie is the only one in her family who is perceptive enough to discover the secret Oakley harbors. In an act of hubris, Charles gives his unsuspecting niece a gift—an emerald ring taken from one of his murder victims and, Charlie notices, faintly engraved with the victim's initials: " T.S. from B.M." Later, after the detectives alert Charlie regarding their suspicions, this ring will constitute crucial evidence of her uncle's guilt.

Charlie tells Oakley she *knows* him and knows that he is keeping something "secret and wonderful" about himself from them. When she vows to find it out, Oakley simply says, "It is not good to find out too much, Charlie." As events unfold, we see that Charlie's picture of her uncle, sadly, bears no relationship to reality—though Oakley is right that Charlie will suffer if she finds out about him.

This Thing Called Knowing

Charlie claims to *know* her uncle. Philosophers call this knowledge of persons *knowledge by acquaintance*. This kind of knowledge is distinguished from *knowing how*, which involves knowledge of a skill or procedure, for example, the knowledge that Emma Newton has of how to bake a cake or the knowledge of how to program a VCR to tape a Hitchcock movie (a skill that many philosophers lack!). When Oakley calls the detectives' bluff saying, "What do you *know*? You've got nothing on me," this knowledge of the facts that establish that Oakley is the merry widow murderer is what philosophers call *propositional knowledge.* This is knowledge of propositions or beliefs—representations of reality that are either true or false. Philosophers are most interested in analyzing what constitutes propositional knowledge or knowledge of facts. Philosophers usually agree that (at least) three conditions are required: belief, justification or warrant, and truth.

Belief and Justification

Going back to Plato, philosophers have proposed that knowledge is a species of belief—justified true belief. Yet some critics have challenged the belief requirement, saying that one can have knowledge of a fact without believing in its truth.

For example, when detective Jack Graham tells Charlie that her uncle is under suspicion for murder, she goes to the library to read a newspaper article she knew he hid. She thinks that by doing this she will establish that he is harboring a harmless secret. Instead Charlie discovers that the ring her Uncle Charlie gave her bears the same initials as the last murder victim of the "merry widow" strangler. What Charlie learns provides overwhelming evidence of her uncle's guilt; but the news is so devastating, she might well say to her self "I don't believe it!" Is this knowledge without belief? As philosophers have noted, belief is not something that is under our direct control. We usually form beliefs without choosing or desiring to do so. Because the proof of Uncle Charlie's guilt is so solid and Charlie is a reasonable person, she cannot help but believe he is guilty. In saying to her self, "I don't believe it," Charlie is expressing her shock at what she has learned, not her disbelief in the evidence. So this example, and others like it, does not establish that a person can have knowledge without belief.

A belief is not knowledge simply because it coincides with the truth—this might just be luck. In order for a belief to qualify as knowledge the belief must be based on solid *warrant* or evidence. Plato first discussed this insight about knowledge in his dialogue, the *Theaetetus*. Recall the 'Til Two bar where Oakley forcibly takes his niece to interrogate her on what it is she knows about him. The clock on the front of the bar reads (and is permanently stuck at) two minutes to two o'clock. Suppose an inattentive person walking by the bar looks at the clock reading two minutes of two and he forms the true belief that the time is what the clock says it is. His belief is true, by accident, but this belief is not knowledge because a broken clock does not provide the kind of reliable evidence on which knowledge is based.

Truth

Virtually all philosophers hold that knowledge requires truth. After all, knowledge involves moving beyond mere appearances to grasp how things really are. Yet philosophers disagree about what it means to say that a belief or a thought is true, and they have presented three main theories or accounts of truth: coherence, pragmatist, and correspondence accounts. According to the coherence account, espoused by G.W.F. Hegel (1770–1831) and Brand Blanshard (1892–1987), what makes a belief true is its coherence or agreement with other beliefs. A belief is true if it forms part of a system of mutually consistent beliefs that provide a complete picture of the world. At the start of the film Charlie believes that her uncle is a wonderful man and is innocent of any crimes. These beliefs are true since they agree with all the other beliefs that she accepts, for example that her uncle's presence is beneficial for her family. Charlie's belief that her uncle is a wonderful man then becomes false, according to the coherence account, because what Charlie believes has changed. But the objective *facts* about her uncle have not altered—Charlie's *beliefs* about him have changed. Because the coherence account makes truth a relation between beliefs and not a relation between a belief and the state of the world, the coherence theory falters as an account of truth.

After Charlie discovers the truth about her uncle, to spare her mother, she decides to conceal what she knows from her family and the police. Using the ring as leverage, she threatens to go to the police if her uncle does not leave town. As Oakley's train departs from the station, he detains Charlie and tries to throw her off to keep her silent about what she knows. Charlie manages to resist him and Oakley falls to his death when she pushes him away. At the end of the film, only detective Jack Graham (in whom Charlie has finally confided) and Charlie know what her uncle was really like. Emma and the townspeople believe that Charles was a wonderful man. Their belief is true, on a coherence account, because it is consistent with the other beliefs that Emma and the others accept about him. But the story is poignant precisely because we understand how deluded Emma and the townspeople are. The proponent of the coherence theory may counter that Emma and the townspeople fail to have a "complete" set of beliefs about the world, for there is evidence about Charles they are overlooking. But this reply acknowledges a flaw with the coherence account: that the truth of a belief should pertain to adequately representing the way the world actually *is*, not simply cohering with other beliefs one accepts.

The pragmatist theory of truth, endorsed by American philosophers William James (1842–1910) and John Dewey (1859–1952), holds that what makes a belief true is its usefulness or "cash value": a proposition is true provided that believing it enables the believer successfully to predict and navigate her environment. The detectives' belief in the proposition "Charles Oakley may be the merry widower" is true, for example, if believing this over the long run furthers their goal of tracking down all likely suspects.

But this pragmatist account has problems as well. Oakley was under active suspicion until the other suspect, who was tracked down in Maine, died while attempting to get away from the police. The F.B.I. then assumed the other man was guilty, and did not follow up on further evidence, including a photograph of Oakley, that could have established his guilt. It served the purposes of the F.B.I. to disregard their suspicions about Oakley and accept that the other man was guilty, for it was more expedient to call off the search. This shows that objectively false beliefs can be useful to believe. A pragmatist might reply that truth is what is useful to believe "in the long run." After Charlie tells Jack Graham about her uncle's attempt to kill her, it does not serve his interests to go on believing in Oakley's interests. So in the bigger picture of things, on a pragmatist account, a belief in Oakley's innocence is false. But we can also imagine that instead of Charlie pushing her uncle off the train, he instead killed her and Jack never learned the error of his belief in Oakley's innocence. The fact remains that no matter how convenient or useful it was to think the search was over, the other suspect was not guilty of the crimes. A belief may be useful to hold over the long run, but this utility does not amount to truth.

As *Shadow of a Doubt* illustrates, accepting the truth may, in fact, be very painful and destructive. Plato, in his famous allegory of the cave, compared human beings to prisoners who have spent their entire lives in an underground cave with a fire behind them. They are shackled so that they cannot turn around: they see only the images on the wall in front of them. These images are the shadows cast by other people who carry various objects as they traverse a walkway behind the prisoners and the fire. Under these circumstances, the prisoners mistakenly think the only reality that exists are the images on the wall in front of them. If the prisoners were released from their bonds, and looked behind them, they would be bewildered by what they see. With his allegory Plato is saying that the average person in her everyday life uncritically accepts many false beliefs— she mistakes appearance, the shadows on the wall, for reality, the higher truths that are found in the life outside the cave. Because replacing illusion with reality can be a painful and uncomfortable process, Plato believes that most people are not up for such a challenge. It would be better for all but a few exceptional individuals—those who have the souls and intellectual capacities of philosopher-rulers—to remain in the dark about the true nature of reality.

We might well question Plato's assumption that not everyone can benefit from learning the truth. But the ending of the movie, with Charlie mourning the loss of her illusions about her uncle as well as her own lost innocence, at least raises the question if Charlie is better off knowing what she has learned. It might be more useful, for the purpose of carrying on with her life as it was before her uncle arrived, if Charlie were to go on believing in her uncle's goodness. Yet the utility of this belief does not change the facts of Oakley's guilt. The pragmatist theory fails as an account of truth.

The truth of a proposition is not a matter of its agreeing with other propositions, or advancing our interests and goals. A proposition is true provided it corresponds with reality. This is the view of the *correspondence* theory of truth, an account that originated with Plato and his famous pupil Aristotle (384–322 B.C.E.), and was later defended by, among others, the Oxford philosopher J.L. Austin (1911–1960). What makes Charlie's belief that Uncle Charlie is the merry widow murder true is that he did, in fact, commit these crimes. This theory captures the view held by many philosophers and non-philosophers alike that truth is *objective*: it is mind independent. Charlie's belief when she discovers the evidence against her uncle that he is guilty is true, because it corresponds to the facts of the case.

Charlie was mistaken in her belief, early in the film, that she *knows* her uncle. Athough such personal knowledge requires more than just knowing facts about her uncle, it does require some such propositional knowledge. And her central beliefs about him—like he's a good person—were wrong. With the two attempts that Oakley makes on Charlie's life as he tries to keep her silent, we might wonder why it is that no one other than Charlie is suspicious of the two "accidents." The Platonic philosopher, Iris Murdoch (1919–1999) would say that as much we want to know the truth, we also try to shield ourselves from it because learning the truth is sometimes too much to bear.[2] Our attempt to know the truth is also made more difficult because people sometimes try to mislead or deceive us. *Shadow of a Doubt* features a lot of deception, major deceptions as well as little white lies. Are some of the lies that are told to keep people from learning the truth about Oakley morally justified?

I Kant Tell a Lie

The German philosopher Immanuel Kant (1724–1804) argued that we have a moral *duty* to tell the truth on all occasions. Moral duties are actions that we *ought* to perform. Some duties are *hypothetical*: these are actions that are required on the assumption that we desire some goal or other. If Charlie's little sister, Ann, for example wants to be a bookworm, then she ought to read two books a week, as she promised herself she would do. Other duties are *categorical*: these are actions that we are obligated to perform under all circumstances, regardless of our goals and projects. Kant believed that telling the truth was an unconditional or categorical duty that holds in all circumstances.

Kant's reasons for thinking this have to do with his ideas of how to test the moral worth of an action. The formulation of his test that has received the most attention is known as the "Categorical Imperative." According to this fundamental principle

---

[2] See her *Metaphysics as a Guide to Morals* (Harmondsworth: Penguin, 1992).

of morality, a person must determine if the reasons she has for performing an action could be universally adopted. Can you consistently want, for example, *everyone* to break a promise when doing so serves his or her interests? If you are attempting to make yourself an exception to a practice—keeping your word—that you otherwise endorse, then you ought not to break your promise.

It's obvious, Kant thinks, that an act of lying, no matter what the circumstances, does not pass the test of the Categorical Imperative. To see why, let's consider what he would say about the lies the detectives tell to get into the Newton home in order to take a picture of their suspect, Oakley. Kant would argue that no matter how well intentioned the detectives are, their action cannot be universalized. The detectives could not want their action of lying to be put in place as a universal policy. For if it were, the faith they and the rest of society place in the truthfulness of what other people say would be undermined. Their own lie wouldn't have been believed!

Kant also held that in lying, we betray the dignity of the person to whom we lie. This is because Kant thought that a central source of human worth lies in our ability to "legislate" or freely decide how we should live. In deceiving the Newton family the detectives prevent them from forming an independent response to the truth about Uncle Charlie. In doing so, the detectives deprive the Newton family of their dignity.

We can agree with Kant that telling the truth is essential for societal trust. But Kant may go too far in arguing that failing to tell the truth in an exceptional situation would bring about such a breakdown in trust. The detectives, or the rest of us, most likely, would not endorse the practice of telling a lie whenever it serves one's interests to do so. The adoption of such a policy of deception writ large *could* lead to a breakdown of trust. But the detectives could endorse a more limited policy of lying whenever there is no other way to gain necessary information. This means that the detectives' actions can be generalized, depending on the *reasons* for their action. Kant is right that we should not make ourselves an exception to a policy that we otherwise think it is good to follow, and there is more to say in Kant's defense. But we may still think that there can be legitimate exceptions to a practice that is otherwise, all things considered, good to follow.

John Stuart Mill (1806–1873) proposed a theory of morality, utilitarianism, that might enable us to see why this is so. Mill argued that the reason we think moral rules such as, "one ought to tell the truth" or "one has a duty to keep one's promises," are correct is that these rules have proven to be the ones that promote greater utility: the greatest happiness for the greatest number of people. Here utility is the sum of the pleasure and pain that would result if the action were performed. Mill argued for the principle of utility, which says that an action is morally right if it brings about the greatest amount of utility for all concerned in comparison to alternative courses of actions. Mill argued on utilitarian grounds that the practice of lying leads to the collapse of social trust. But he disagreed that lying under *all* circumstances is morally wrong. Mill argued that it was possible that an occasional lie could be justified if the consequences outweighed any harm that came from telling the lie. In contrast to Kant, a utilitarian would hold that it is morally permissible for the detectives to lie to the Newton family if doing so promotes greater utility than telling the family the real reason for their visit to Santa Rosa.

To sort out Mill's claims here, we can distinguish between two different sorts of utilitarian theory found in his writings: *Act* utilitarianism, the most common form of utilitarianism, holds that an action is morally right provided that it maximizes utility. *Rule* utilitarianism says that an action is morally right if it is an instance of a rule that would maximize utility if all were to follow it. In agreeing with Kant that lying, in general, is wrong, Mill may be reasoning as a rule utilitarian. If everyone were to tell the truth this would maximize utility in the long run since it would make for the social cohesion that is central to society. Depending on the action's consequences, the detectives' lying to the Newton family could bring about greater utility than telling them the truth. Act utilitarianism allows us to make exceptions to rules that otherwise followed over the long run would bring about beneficial results.

Full Disclosure

What about Charlie's deceptions? Charlie fails to be forthcoming with the detectives about what she knows about her uncle, in particular, the evidence of the ring as well as her uncle's virtual admission of guilt when she confronts him. She also shields her mother from the truth about her uncle. Was what Charlie did right in these cases?

First, consider Charlie's failing to tell the detectives what she knows. Arguably, what Charlie did was simply a failure to disclose what she knew and not lying. But Charlie has the evidence that establishes his guilt, and when the search is called off, she knows that the detectives mistakenly think her uncle is innocent. Even if she doesn't proclaim his innocence, in failing to divulge what she knows she misleads the detectives. Her lack of honesty also enables Oakley to continue to roam free and commit other murders. Followers of Kant who disagree with his strong stance on lying nonetheless think of our moral obligations as binding duties. One of the relevant duties that apply to Charlie's situation is the obligation to prevent harm to others. In letting her uncle go free, these Kantians would say that Charlie fails in her moral duty to act so as to, whenever possible, prevent harm to others. In contrast, act utilitarianism would say that it is morally permissible for Charlie to withhold information from the detectives if and only if doing so brings about the greatest utility for all concerned.

In spite of their differences, Kant and utilitarians agree that the application of moral principles must be impersonal and impartial. But Kant and contemporary Kantians have been criticized for thinking of morality in terms of rules and duties. Critics, especially feminist critics, argue that Kant and utilitarians ignore the special role of personal relationships and the happiness of one's loved ones in assessing what it is best to do. These criticisms have particular relevance for understanding Charlie's lack of full disclosure. For it is likely that Charlie failed to tell the detectives what she knew for fear that her mother would find out and be devastated. But was Charlie right to want to keep the truth from her mother?

A Feminist Angle

Let's consider a feminist approach to this question. Hitchcock is often accused of being a misogynist and it's not hard to see why. Hitchcock is known for the "male gaze": women are presented as they would be looked at by men, or presented in such a way as to encourage men to look at them as sex objects (sometimes with horrible results). Women in his films are frequently the victims of stranglers and psychotic slashers, and *Shadow of a Doubt* is no exception to this practice. Charles Oakley is a surprisingly sympathetic figure in spite of the dinner-table speech in which he implicitly denounces his murder victims as "faded, fat, greedy women." Men in Hitchcock films are frequently depicted as under the control of domineering mothers—think of Norman Bates in *Psycho*, for example, or Mitch Brenner in *The Birds*. In *Shadow of a Doubt*, there is the suggestion that neighbor Herb Hawkins may be languishing under the influence of a demanding mother. But the film also presents a touching and sympathetic portrayal of Charlie's mother, Emma, and of their relationship as mother and daughter. Proponents of feminist ethics would say this relationship is relevant in assessing Charlie's decision not to tell her mother the truth.

According to feminist ethics, a decision about the right thing to do should not be based on an abstract principle or duty, but instead should be supported by considerations regarding the welfare of the people about whom one cares.[3] This view has particular relevance for understanding the relationship between Charlie and her mother. Charlie believes the life that Emma has led as an unworldly housewife leaves her poorly equipped to comprehend the truth about her brother. It is out of care and concern for her mother's welfare that Charlie withholds the truth from her mother. Here we can see that the film is a coming-of-age story in which Charlie must learn how to balance the demands of impartial morality—the request from the detectives to divulge what she knows—and her own desire to pursue the truth against the special concern and love she feels for her family. It is not possible for Charlie, no matter how wise she has become, to resolve the clash between these conflicting demands in a way that does justice to everything that she values.

Plato's Cave Again

Early in the film, as noted, Hitchcock represents himself as a character who deceives others. But as the film draws to a close,

---

[3] For more on feminist ethics, and the particular version known as *the ethics of care*, see Chapter 11 in this volume.

we see another view of the relationship between an artist, such as Hitchcock, and the truth.

There are significant similarities between the cave that Plato describes and our experience of film. In a movie theater we sit in a darkened room with our eyes straight ahead, transfixed on the images that we see on the screen in front of us. In the case of fiction such as *Shadow of a Doubt* these images bear little relationship to reality. There is no Uncle Charlie on the loose going on his killing spree of unfortunate widows. But like the images the prisoners see on the walls of the cave, the uncritical observer might take what he sees on the movie screen for reality. If Plato were alive, he would be concerned about this capacity for generating illusion in the audience, a feature that, to a Platonist's dismay, draws many viewers to the cinema! Hitchcock's cameo as a deceiver would give Plato reason to worry. But we also see Hitchcock develop a position that would challenge Plato's view that an art form such as film is far removed from truth and reality.

Of the many twists and turns in the plot, none is more puzzling than the detectives' decision to call off their investigation of Oakley. Recall that the detectives manage to take a photograph of Oakley that they can use to secure an eyewitness identification of the murderer. The government does not follow through on this, and assumes Oakley is innocent, when the propellers of a plane chop the other suspect as he attempts to avoid apprehension. The camera—here a stand-in for the camera of the director—provides the evidence for the truth of Oakley's guilt, if only the detectives would make use of it. To be sure, the camera is part of the deception that the detectives perpetrate on the Newton family. It could also, however, lead the detectives to uncover the truth about Oakley, if they were to go one step further and show the picture to the eyewitness.

Hitchcock is perhaps suggesting that film and the film director stand in a dual relationship to the truth. Film has the power to take in the viewer and deceive. But movies also contain highly true-to-life images and scenarios that are relevant for our lives if we will take the time to observe and analyze them. *Shadow of a Doubt* is an illustration of the capacity of film to help us see the truth about our lives. Seemingly good people turn out to be murderers, families have dark secrets, and we struggle with our decisions to withhold the truth from our loved ones to spare them pain.

In a world where things may not be what they seem, it takes more than a sharp mind to know how things really are. We need to have the moral courage to "face the facts," as Charlie does. Although the cultivation of a questioning attitude is the antidote to deception, the film also ends with the somber implication that there is a price to be paid when we insist on pursuing the truth as Charlie does. As Socrates and his interlocutors were well aware, dispelling falsehoods can be a painful and unsettling process.[4]

---

[4] I thank Felicia Curran and Thomas Wartenberg for their very helpful comments. William Drumin's excellent *Theistic and Methodological Foundations of Alfred Hitchcock's Artistic Vision* (Lewiston: Mellen, 2004) also proved invaluable.

3

Rope: Nietzsche and the Art of Murder

SHAI BIDERMAN and ELIANA JACOBOWITZ

If it's a Hitchcock film, someone has to die, but in *Rope* (1948), death strikes right in the first scene, in which two college students strangle their former classmate, David Kentley (Dick Hogan). *Rope* is far from being a typical Hitchcock film. The movie is constructed of just eight, very lengthy takes, a technique meant to mimic "real life" interactions, which required great precision and accuracy from everyone on the set. After employing this technique for the first time in *Rope*, Hitchcock would use it, in modified form, just once more (in *Under Capricorn*, a year later).

Except for the opening titles, the movie in its entirety is shot indoors, within the closed confines of a New York City apartment. Even the murder itself seems terribly clean. No blood is spilled (unlike in *Psycho* where we see the blood spilling into the bath drain), and the murderers' clothes remain clean and their manner calm (unlike in *Torn Curtain* where the murderer's jacket is ruined and his hands are covered with blood). David, the victim, to whom we were never introduced, is neatly tucked into a chest, and though the chest remains in view during most of the movie, the first few minutes of the film are the last we see of him.

Then we see the murderers—flamboyant, rich, and spoiled Brandon (John Dall) and his fragile pianist friend Philip (Farley Granger)—prepare for a party planned for that same evening. On the chest placed in the center of the living room, refreshments are rearranged and candles are lit. The chest resembles an altar set for a kind of Black Mass and the party a sacrificial

feast. The murder weapon—the rope—with which they strangled David, is left in plain sight, hanging from the corner of the
chest. Adding to the eeriness of the scene, we soon recognize
the party guests as David's father and aunt, his fiancé, and
Brandon and Philip's old teacher. All but Brandon and Philip
expect David to show up, and they muse about his out-of-char-
acter tardiness.

The Original Junior Mint

Why was David murdered? As Brandon puts it, "Davids of this
world merely occupy space, which is why he was the perfect
victim for the perfect murder." This was no killing in self-
defense or under extenuating or mitigating circumstances, but
murder "for the sake of danger and for the sake of killing." They
murdered David just because they could, because they chose to,
and because they felt entitled to. Contemptuous of the norms of
conventional morality, convinced of their own superiority, they
aimed to accomplish the perfect crime in pursuit of their warped
aesthetic of murder. "Murder can be an art," Brandon says, "the
power to kill can be just as satisfying as the power to create."

Seinfeld fans may recall the episode in which Jerry and
Kramer inadvertently launch a (refreshing) junior mint into the
body of a patient during his operation. Concerned that their
unconfessed misdeed is going to result in the patient's early
demise, Jerry later exclaims, "We're like Leopold and Loeb!"

Rope's plot bears an uncanny resemblance to the real-life
murder of Richard Loeb and Nathan Leopold (1924), whose trial
was dubbed "the trial of the century," that early viewers of
Hitchcock's movie were undoubtedly familiar with. Leopold and
Loeb, Illinois college students, kidnapped and murdered a third
student. They conceived and carried out a deranged scheme for
a "perfect murder" as a means of establishing their superiority
over ordinary people. *Rope* was based on a 1929 play by Patrick
Hamilton, though Hamilton claimed he never heard of the Loeb-
Leopold case until after the play was produced. Still, especially
for American audiences, both the play and the film do evoke the
notorious 1924 thrill killing.

What inspired the fictional Brandon and Philip to believe in
the right of a superior few to flout conventional morality were
the iconoclastic teachings of their prep school don, Rupert

Cadell (James Stewart). An academic and intellectual, Cadell has turned to publishing books in philosophy, despite their "small print, big words, small sales." A winsomely glib man of great intellect and power of judgment, Rupert is eminently comfortable in the world of ideas. Able in polite conversation and clever repartee to defend his radical theory that murder should be made into an art for the privileged few individuals of superior intellect and imagination, Rupert is fond of using concepts and theories to provoke and shock conventional people and bolster his reputation for "dangerous thinking," all the while treating such concepts merely as abstractions on the intellectual plane.

Cocktail Party Banter

By Hollywood standards, *Rope* is an unusually philosophical film. Not only is Rupert a publisher of philosophical books who assumes "people can not only read but people can think," one well-known philosopher is even mentioned by name: German philosopher Friedrich Nietzsche (1844–1900). At the party, Rupert begins, in his playful way, pontificating on the aesthetic of murder and the prerogatives of the superior few, then Brandon chimes in, adding his vigorous defense of such ideas. Mr. Kentley is taken aback, incredulous at such suggestions.

Brandon continues, "The few are those men of such intellectual and cultural superiority that they're above the traditional moral concepts. Good and evil, right and wrong, were invented for the ordinary, average man, the inferior man, because he needs them."

Mr. Kentley responds, "So obviously you agree with Nietzsche and his theory of the superman."

"Yes I do."

"So did Hitler."

Brandon retorts, "Hitler was a paranoid savage. His supermen, all Fascist supermen, were brainless murderers. I'd hang any who are left. But then, you see, I'd hang them first for being stupid. I'd hang all incompetents and fools anyway. There are far too many in the world."

Having grown weary of the conversation, Mr. Kentley replies, "Then perhaps you should hang me, Brandon, because I'm so stupid I don't know whether you're serious or not. But in any case I'd rather not hear any more of—forgive me—your contempt for humanity and for the standards of a world I believe is civilized."

During Leopold and Loeb's trial, they said in their defense that they had been inspired by Nietzschean ideas. Are purposeless killing or Hitler's militaristic "master race" agenda legitimate applications of Nietzsche's ideas? Answering this question demands that we understand his philosophy, but it's not easy to give an executive summary of Nietzsche's philosophy. The more deeply original, iconoclastic, and countercultural voices are, the easier it is to misunderstand and fail to appreciate them, not to mention to misappropriate them for purposes poorly suited to them.

What makes it even worse is that there are tensions within Nietzsche's work itself that make certain matters of interpretation vexed questions and make workable rapprochements nearly impossible.[1] Neither easily reconciling nor casually disregarding such tensions does justice to the richness of Nietzsche's thought. If Emerson was right that consistency is the "hobgoblin of little minds," then Nietzsche's mind was expansive indeed.

What Nietzsche Can Teach Ya

Despite such challenges, and the impossibility of doing Nietzsche justice in short compass, let's begin with the notion of Nietzsche's "superman," which of course has nothing to do with Clark Kent and Lois Lane. Sometimes translated "overman," in German Nietzsche's *Übermensch* (though we'll just refer to "superman") is the culmination of his vision for a new morality. It's the experience of the "will to power" in a high and refined form and modeled in the life of an excellent creative artist who makes of his own life a work of art. The "will to power" is the innate drive in all living things to gain and express power. According to Nietzsche, we're all driven by the will to power all of the time. Our task, then, is to express the will to power in high and refined ways. A child stepping on ants just for the thrill

---

[1] Peter Berkowitz has argued persuasively, for example, that Nietzsche's immoralism and nihilism stand in uncomfortable contrast with his ethical convictions; his perspectivism and rejection of the transcendent with his metaphysical commitments; and his skeptical speculations with his desire to be understood. See his excellent *Nietzsche: The Ethics of an Immoralist* (Cambridge, Massachusetts: Harvard University Press, 1995).

of killing them is a low, brute expression of the will to power. Shakespeare writing *Hamlet* is a high, refined expression of the will to power.

Nietzsche famously claimed "God is dead." This is not so much a statement of atheism as a rejection of all transcendent values, either from a realm of Platonic truths or from a Christian heaven. Despite his Christian upbringing, Nietzsche came to think of such theology as radically wrong. Even if God exists, what he saw in his culture was that God no longer exercised control over the minds and lives of even professing believers. "God is dead" could be interpreted "God, even if he exists, is irrelevant." He thought it might take time for people to sink their teeth into the implications of their practical atheism, but that in time they would. The era of God's being central to our existential concerns and philosophizing, he thought, is past. God's dead, and we killed Him.

Nietzsche rightly saw that, if "God is dead," there are major implications. For example, so long as we are the product of a benevolent Creator who loves us all equally, endows us with inalienable rights, and invests each of us with inherent dignity and worth, we are all essentially equal. Our equality is in no way compromised or challenged by incidental differences between us in talent, ability, or intelligence. In God's eyes, such differences pale into insignificance. Without God, though, the differences become more significant. We may still honor civil agreements to uphold equal rights of protection under the law, but no longer do such agreements rest on sturdy metaphysical foundations.

When we look around, we see that people don't appear to be equal at all. Nietzsche thought that "equality" and "equal rights" are marks of cultural decline and degradation, that the distinction between higher and lower classes is essential for every strong age, and that we eliminate them to our peril. By insisting on equality, we overlook the truly virtuous characteristics that conduce to strength and power. By privileging the weak, we extol as virtues what actually are vices. Nietzsche saw Jesus's Sermon on the Mount as a paradigmatic example of this reversal of ancient virtues and vices, and saw himself in the role of returning ethics to its original form.

Nietzsche's rejection of transcendent foundations for ethics doesn't mean that he renounced ethics altogether. To the contrary, he thought that the death of God, which he considered a true account of our circumstances, invests us with new and powerful imperatives. His central task was to clarify these, which characterize the best life for humanity. Nietzsche felt that we derive the moral imperative to invent "festivals of atonement" and "sacred games" that enable the very best human beings to command the greatest things.[2]

Nietzsche's religious language demonstrates that there is something right about our transcendent impulses. But he argued that we have been told the wrong story about how to make best sense of, and how to satisfy, those impulses. To make ourselves worthy of having killed God, he said, those rare few among us who can are to make themselves gods, a crucial recurring theme in Nietzsche's philosophy.

A few select individuals are able to accomplish truly great feats. Mozart, Picasso, Napoleon, Shakespeare—these are examples of men who, if not Nietzschean supermen, at least approached his ideal. If their achievements required some neglect of conventional obligations to family or friends, a defiance of traditional systems, or personal dangers, that's perfectly alright. Such individual excellence and achievement take priority, for it's the true nature of ethics.

The famous painter Paul Gauguin (1848–1903), who shirked his familial responsibilities by leaving his wife and children to move to the South Seas and pursue his craft, might be another example of someone approximating the Nietzschean superman. The highest pursuit of his art and most passionate love trumped his conventional duties to family. Neglecting everything else, he did what he felt he had to do to achieve his highest level of personal excellence, and in the process bequeathed to the world the fruit of his art. Nietzsche viewed art as the best antidote for the human condition, the "saving sorceress, expert at healing. She alone knows how to turn these nauseous thoughts about the horror or absurdity of existence into notions with which one can live."[3]

Nietzsche wanted to spur those who are fit to the highest kind of excellence that human beings are capable of. He wouldn't want us merely to venerate him as a great thinker, or to exalt his

---

[2] *The Gay Science* (New York: Vintage Books, 1974), p. 125.
[3] *The Birth of Tragedy* (New York: Vintage, 1967), p. 7.

ideas, but to put them into practice and launch out on our own to find our own distinctive voice and make our own unique contribution to the only world we'll ever inhabit. He would encourage us to take up tasks that ennoble and inspire, that push us to our limits and give our lives meaning, even if there is no overarching ultimate meaning or purpose in life.

Nietzsche felt this insight was perhaps most important regarding philosophy. The trick to being a great philosopher, for Nietzsche, is to think and act well for yourself. It's not merely to cram your mind with the thoughts of other philosophers, endlessly critiquing and assessing them or, worse, becoming preoccupied with the biographies of philosophers while overlooking their work. The professionalization of philosophy, he thought, sadly privileges encyclopedic knowledge of the history of philosophy and exhaustive scholarship and criticism of other philosophers, rather than the noble task of seeking wisdom founded on a true understanding of reality and the human condition. If he's right, philosophy shouldn't, as it too often has, lead to ardent partisanship toward some philosophical or political school of thought, nor to self-aggrandizing displays of knowledge. It should instead conduce to original and creative work designed to uncover the true nature of the world and to manifest genuine excellence.

Having the Form of Nietzsche

Brandon, clearly the dominant player among the killers, claims to be a follower of Nietzsche, and he assumes that Rupert is as well, although he has his doubts over Rupert's willingness to practice what he preaches. So is Rupert's protégé a true student of Nietzsche?

There are, admittedly, some superficial ideological points of resonance between Brandon and Nietzsche. Consider, for example, Nietzsche's guiding motif of the "will to power." Brandon understands the murder of David as an expression of his and Philip's power, and seems to lament weakness more than anything else. Being weak, he thinks, is always a mistake, because it's ordinary, and Brandon sees himself as anything but that.

Weakness is a telltale sign of inferior men, Brandon thinks, along with some other reliable indicators like incompetence, stupidity, foolishness, low cultural status, lack of education, all of which lead to meaningless lives.[4] Standard, conventional morality is for such inferior people only, whereas the truly superior can forge a new and higher morality of their own. An ordinary man might think about the perfect murder, but the superior few actually accomplish it.[5]

This bears at least a passing resemblance to Nietzschean notions of the superior few whose talents and abilities exceed those of ordinary men. Their achievements are more valuable than conventional ethics, "slavish morality" as Nietzsche called it, and such supermen are active agents, not merely passive observers or admirers (recall that Brandon characterized Rupert as more likely to admire than to act).

Nietzschean supermen create their own moral rules, constrained by reality and the human condition rightly understood, privileging such virtues as courage, power, boldness, and daring. And they live their lives as artists. Brandon always lamented not having more artistic abilities, until he realized that murder itself could become an art form. Then he set out to act on his aesthetic of the perfect murder in defiance of traditional moral norms. He effects aesthetic touches like serving from the chest containing David's body and binding the first-edition books (reflecting the world of ideas in which Rupert is so comfortable) in the very rope used to kill David. He explicitly says that, if Rupert *were* to uncover the truth, his old mentor would be sure to understand his and Philip's artistic angle on the murder.

Not only does this aesthetic dimension of the killers' strategy accord with the primacy Nietzsche gave to the artistry of the superman, it also points to a sense of self-deification in the eyes of Brandon. He would probably consider David's murder and the ceremonial party afterwards to represent a Nietzschean festival of atonement or sacred game. Brandon's artistic touches themselves, the nervous Philip is convinced, are designed not just to heighten danger, but to risk getting caught, almost as if Brandon wants an audience to see "how brilliant"

---

[4] On what basis did Brandon consider David—a Harvard undergraduate, from a high social class, and characterized by Janet as very bright—inferior? Brandon would have been hard pressed to give a nonarbitrary reason for his selection.

[5] Recall the recurring fun conversations about the perfect murder between Charlie's father and the neighbor in *Shadow of a Doubt*.

he is. What good is a deity without worshipful subjects beholding his handiwork? Brandon's efforts to manipulate his surroundings, too, orchestrating the reunion of Kenneth (Douglas Dick) and Janet (Joan Chandler) for example, illustrate his exalted view of his own powers.

Appearances Can Be Misleading

So Brandon in particular does display features at least vaguely reminiscent of Nietzsche's superman, but how deep is the resemblance? Not very. Neither Brandon nor Philip would have passed Nietzsche's test. As a pianist, Philip was probably, of all the characters in the movie, best able to tap into the healing essence of art and use it to transform himself. Instead of using music as his major form of expression, though, he seems to play only when he has nothing to say. The piano is a secondary form of expression for him, mostly something to hide behind. Philip is a failure even as an artist, unable to transform his creativity into philosophical creativity, and he will never play that debut at the town hall.

Nietzsche's supermen live free of fear, but Philip's worry about getting caught is not his main disqualifier from being a superman. The weakness of both Philip and Brandon is that, despite faith in their strength and superiority, they are actually examples of inferior men who don't understand their true nature. Guilt shouldn't be a motivator, because we ought to be motivated by "higher" impulses than something so lowly and slavish as mere guilt. If there's such a thing as an order of rank among souls and a health proper to the soul, as Nietzsche thought, we shouldn't settle for an experience of our will to power in a lower or less refined form than we're capable of, as Brandon and Philip did. What should motivate us to do better is the recognition that in failing to reach our highest potential we're showing a kind of weakness that needs to be fixed.

The superman is the one who recognizes the chaos of life, not the one who adds to it. He doesn't seek to bully others before they bully him. That would be missing the point, for a bully forever depends on the existence of an audience. The process of becoming a superman is an internal process where one "delights the spirit so that it turns creator and esteemer and lover and benefactor of all things."[6] Had Brandon gone through such a process and emerged a superman, he would have sought to bestow goodness on others, not destruction. He would have become a giver of life, not a taker of life. Nietzsche believed the superman throws off the constraints and shackles of morality (wrongly construed) not to become immoral, but rather to combat the forces of barbarism by taking on a more demanding ethical task.

Brandon turns Nietzsche's emphasis on creativity and life as art into a monstrosity. While Nietzsche spoke of life as art, Brandon insists on crass murder on an unsuspecting and innocent victim as art. Brandon construes his post-murder exhilaration ("We're alive, truly and wonderful alive," he tells Philip) as proof that he's truly a superman. But Brandon at that moment is as far as possible from the Nietzschean ideal he's seeking to achieve. Nietzsche wrote of our creative power as a tool to transform our nihilistic existence into something beautiful and rewarding. So although Brandon's an eager student of Nietzsche, he's not a very thorough or perceptive one. Not everything done in the name of Nietzsche is Nietzschean.

Which reminds us of the one point Brandon got right. The Fascist enlistment of Nietzsche's name to the cause isn't evidence that this was a good fit, and there's good reason to think it wasn't. Nietzsche spoke about the possibility of an individual achieving a higher life, not a race or group of people (at least after he gave up his early dreams of a Wagner-inspired artistic rejuvenation of Germany). Generally he was against grouping people by race, looking rather to art and philosophy across cultures to elevate man above the beasts.[7]

Beyond that, though, Brandon is no superman or representative of Nietzsche's views. A true superman would have no need to prove himself like Brandon did or to engage in Brandon's petty act. And Brandon may have been brash and reckless, but not truly courageous.

---

[6] *Thus Spoke Zarathustra: A Book for All and None* (New York: Modern Library, 1995), p. 327.
[7] For an extended discussion of this issue, see "The Master Race" in Walter Kaufmann's *Nietzsche: Philosopher, Psychologist, Antichrist* (Princeton: Princeton University Press, 1974).

Rupert's Response and Responsibility

On the basis of evidence Rupert notices, he begins to suspect that Brandon and Philip hurt David, though he could hardly believe it. His playful and provocative cocktail conversation had been a way to reside in the world of ideas, but now he is facing the hideous prospect that his former students have committed a horrible crime. Part of the suspense of the movie is to see what his reaction will be. Brandon and Philip weren't good students of Nietzsche, but had they faithfully applied the teachings of Rupert? What would Rupert's response be?

When Rupert finally flings open the chest to discover David's body, the books resting on it are thrown off, symbolizing the clash of the world of ideas and the world of actions. Ideas have consequences. The movie teaches us that ideas are powerful and can be dangerous, but thinking for ourselves is priceless.

Rather than being pleased with or proud of Philip and Brandon, Rupert is horrified at the gruesome discovery. Brandon insists that Rupert had simply *talked*, but he and Philip had *acted*. Rupert's poignant reply is worth repeating in its entirety:

> 'Til this very moment this world and the people in it have always been dark and incomprehensible to me. And I've tried to clear my way with logic and superior intellect, and you've thrown my words right back in my face, Brandon. You were right to. If nothing else a man should stand by his words. But you've given my words a meaning I never dreamed of. And you've tried to twist them into a cold logical excuse for your ugly murder. No, they never were that, Brandon, and you can't make them that. There must have been something deep inside you from the very start that let you do this thing. But there's always been something inside me that would never let me do it, and would never let me be a party to it now. . . . tonight you've made me ashamed of every concept I ever had of superior or inferior beings. And I thank you for that shame, because now I know that we are, each of us, a separate human being, Brandon, with the right to live and work and think as individuals, but with an obligation to the society we live in. By what right do you dare say that there's a superior few to which you belong? By what right did you dare decide that that boy in there was inferior and therefore could be killed? Did you think you were God, Brandon? Is that what you thought when you choked the life out of him? Is that what you thought when you served food from

his grave? Well, I don't know what you thought or what you are. But I know what you've done. You've murdered! You've strangled the life out of a fellow human being who could live and love as you never could. And never will again.

Rupert's response is not at all what Brandon had hoped for. Rupert is mortified at Brandon's misguided effort at self-deification, his presumption that he was superior to David when he clearly wasn't. And now Rupert is ashamed of every thought he'd ever had about superior and inferior beings.

Rupert's renunciation of inequality and passionate talk of equal rights doesn't sound Nietzschean, though we've seen that Brandon misapplied Nietzsche and that even Nietzscheans can affirm societally upheld basic rights—though to what degree those rights can be sustained without a firmer foundation than Nietzscheans allow remains an open question. Mr. Kentley, perhaps more than anyone, consistently sounds like a moral realist who believes in the realm of transcendent and binding moral standards that Nietzsche denied.

Rupert says he feels shame, and that he needs to stand by his words, but then he distances himself from the crime by insisting that his words were given a meaning he never intended. But when Mr. Kentley had reacted incredulously to Rupert's provocative suggestions and their obvious literal meaning earlier and assumed Rupert couldn't be serious, Rupert had assured him he's "a very serious fellow" and there was no humorous intent. Clearly Brandon had taken him seriously. Can Rupert, Brandon and Philip's mentor and teacher, so easily disavow responsibility here?

Nietzsche said that the only true test of a philosophy is whether we can live by it. Rupert finds out that he can't live by the philosophy he has been espousing. And, presumably, Brandon wouldn't be able to live that philosophy either. Though life itself can and should be made a work of art, according to Nietzsche, it seems that murder cannot be. We must overcome the self-imposed limitations of humanity, but this does not involve murder as a creative art form. In popular fiction, perhaps Hannibal Lecter succeeds in making art of murder, but he is insane. There are some limitations that cannot be overcome. So murder wouldn't be forbidden as a violation of a command-ment or a transcendental value, Nietzsche would insist, but because we can't live with it.[8] The taboo of murder serves the pragmatic function of sustaining a valuable life-affirming illusion.

Rupert's comfort in the world of ideas made him effective at challenging people's assumptions, making them think, and shaking them from their lethargy. But a good teacher is also responsible for giving serious thought to the legacy he leaves his students, aware of the connection between ideas and actions. Reading Nietzsche, too, is bound to challenge assumptions and make us think. You can agree with him or not, but he mustn't be ignored.[9]

---

[8] Fyodor Dostoevsky raises the issue of whether one can live with a murder, both in *Crime and Punishment* and in *The Brothers Karamazov*. Woody Allen's *Crimes and Misdemeanors* is a reply to Dostoevsky. See Chapter 3, by James Lawler, in *Woody Allen and Philosophy: You Mean My Whole Fallacy Is Wrong?* (Chicago: Open Court, 2004), edited by Mark T. Conard and Aeon J. Skoble.

[9] Thanks to Rick Mayock for his most helpful insights.

II

Horrors Without End

4

Psycho: Horror, Hitchcock, and the Problem of Evil

PHILIP TALLON

> You have to remember that *Psycho* is a film made with quite a sense of amusement on my part. To me it is a fun picture. The process through which we take the audience, you see, it's rather like taking them through the haunted house at the fairground.
>
> —ALFRED HITCHCOCK, interview in *Movie 6*

Though known widely as the master of suspense, Hitchcock's cinematic weight can also be felt in the world of horror. Hitchcock's movies deal with evil in the form of human greed, violence, destructive natural occurrences and war. Most of Hitchcock's movies took the form of the thriller, but from the beginning of his career to the end (1927's *The Lodger* to 1972's *Frenzy*) he occasionally delved into darker territory. In his more chilling films, Hitchcock puts on display events that raise one of the most fundamental questions in both philosophy and theology: "Why, if God exists, would He allow evils to occur?"

The Why Question: Philosophy and the Problem of Evil

In his *Dialogues Concerning Natural Religion,* David Hume quotes Epicurus:

> Is [God] willing to prevent evil, but not able? then he is impotent. Is he able, but not willing? then is he malevolent. Is he both able and willing? whence then is evil?[1]

---

[1] David Hume, *Dialogues Concerning Natural Religion*, Book X.

Hume puts his finger precisely on the crux of the problem. A morally excellent and perfectly powerful God, it seems, could and would stop any evils, anywhere. Other philosophers join Hume in this dumbfounded feeling. J.S. Mill, J.L. Mackie, William Rowe, and others see no reason why such an allegedly loving and capable being as God would behave so poorly. If God exists he must be weak as a pussycat or extremely negligent—the ultimate deadbeat dad.

Yet some of the premier philosophers and theologians of the West have affirmed both God's goodness *and* power, resolving the tension by proposing some greater good that God would prevent if he eliminated all evil. Following the conflicted but brilliant Augustine (354–430), many thinkers have credited free will as the culprit in causing evil. Human freedom, so the train of reasoning goes, is necessary for genuine relationship, and so is a good that outweighs the evils resulting from it. Other theologians and philosophers have proposed character development as a good benefit that comes through suffering, and therefore acquitted God from the charges weighed against Him. Many have found these arguments convincing, perceiving that a moral agent might allow certain evils if and only if there were greater good to be gained.

However, some kinds of evil defy our ability to see the good that would outweigh them. These evils are often called "horrendous evils" and they often seem, on the surface at least, to resist any explanation or justification. Upon perceiving them, they thwart our ability to see how they could ever have a positive meaning.

Where do we perceive horrendous evils? Why, we see them on the news, in the history books, and, of course, in the movies. So let us turn to Hitchcock's films and see if we can discover something of the nature of horrendous evil, by examining the horror film.

Hitchcock and Horrendous Evils

Throughout his career Hitchcock had an uncanny ability to manipulate the fears of audiences. A fearful man himself, scared of the dark and unnerved by the police, he seemed eerily in tune to the public psyche.

In 1936 he shocked moviegoers by killing off an innocent little boy in *Sabotage*. The little boy was, unknowingly, carrying a bomb. Yet, though the boy was ignorant of the fact, the audience was made painfully aware of it. Through a series of delays the boy neglects to drop off the bag containing the bomb (given to him to deliver by his terrorist father), and so the boy, a puppy, the bag, and the bus he is riding on are destroyed in one quick blast. Many moviegoers felt that Hitchcock was reprobate for allowing such an injustice to happen to an innocent boy.

No doubt what disturbed audiences about the bomb exploding on the bus was not the simple loss of life, but the incredible mismatch between the cute innocence of the boy and his nasty demise. The wrongness of the thing partly derives from a sense of injustice or unnecessary suffering, but also from the *aesthetic incongruity* of the event.

These sorts of shocking juxtapositions occur elsewhere in Hitchcock's canon. In *Rear Window,* the characters are disturbed by a husband's ability to chop up his own wife in a bathtub. In *The Birds,* the seemingly innocuous nature of the threat heightens the frightening effect. Hitchcock cheekily casts against type by using crows, gulls, and sparrows as figures of *menace.*

But perhaps his most famous use of disturbing juxtapositions was in a tight little horror film shot by a TV crew and costing under a million dollars.

Horrendous Evils in *Psycho*

Psycho premiered in 1960 and, though it was an immediate hit with filmgoers, it was scorned by critics. Today it enjoys the high esteem of critics, ranking as Number 18 on AFI's Top 100 list—the highest rated of the three horror films on that list.[2]

While horror played a smaller role in many Hitchcock films, in *Psycho* it fills the whole lens. In *Psycho* we find not one or two horrendous elements, but an entire movie constructed around the horrendous. From the opening title sequences, which feature credits that appear and then become fragmented and unreadable, Hitchcock plays up disjuncture and incongruity.

---

[2] Compare, for example, Bosley Crowther's July 17th, 1960, *New York Times* review, and any of the recent reviews on www.RottenTomatoes.com. Psycho's increased esteem can also be seen in how far it outranks the two other horror films on the AFI list: *Silence of the Lambs* (#65) and *Frankenstein* (#87).

We open with a serene cityscape, and the titles rush onto the screen to give the place, date, and time (Pheonix, Arizona. Friday, December the 11th. Two forty-three PM). The effect is to establish the complete "everydayness" of things—which will create a higher contrast, of course, when things get weird.

Marion Crane is on her lunch break, having a tryst in a hotel room with a man from out of town. The two lounge on the bed, half-dressed, Marion in a white bra and slip. They are intimate, but their relationship is going badly. Marion's boyfriend, Sam, is saddled with debt left to him by his father, and he doesn't want to marry until he is financially stable. She doesn't want to keep wasting her life on a relationship heading nowhere. This could be a conversation held in any number of rooms around the world.

The movie begins to break out of "everydayness," however, when Marion Crane, in a desperate stab to make the relationship work, steals forty grand from her workplace and heads for central California, where her boyfriend lives. Hitchcock begins to introduce jarring contrast, as we see, just after the theft, that Marion's underwear has turned from white to black—signaling an abrupt shift in her character.

Marion and her theft occupy the first third of the movie. Will she get caught? Did that policeman suspect something? How long before her boss finds out? The audience is shown a number of details, most of which, it turns out, are unimportant.

Marion checks into a motel for the night, under a false name ("Marie Samuels"). While checking in, she begins a conversation with the desk clerk, Norman. Though he is young and good looking, it quickly becomes apparent that all is not right with Norman. A deeply conflicted person, he seems a whirl of contradictions. He is both charming and endearing and, at times, creepy and offensive. He sometimes makes bold, perceptive statements like, "What are you running from?" And then follows them with contradictory statements that reveal his own personality, "People never run away from anything." Norman is bullied by his mother, whom he wishes he could "curse," but who also is his "best friend."

Norman and Marion have a compelling conversation, in which Norman talks about how we are all caught "in our private traps," from which we never escape. He states that he was born in his trap and that he "doesn't mind it anymore" or, at least, he "pretends" not to mind it. This conversation deeply affects Marion.

At this point Marion decides to return home and give back the money—in order to keep from stepping into her own trap "deliberately." As she leaves to go back to her room, Norman asks her name. She answers "Marion Crane" instead of giving her assumed name, an indication that she wants to move away from fragmentation and toward wholeness again. Marion returns to the room, calculates how much she owes, takes a shower, and is promptly stabbed to death with a butcher knife by someone who seems to be "Mother."

Hitchcock plays up the horror of the scene—which made many people scared to shower for years afterward—in several ways. He misleads the audience by constructing a story which is derailed by the murder. In Hitchcock's words, "the first part of the story was a red herring . . . to distract the viewer's attention in order to heighten the murder."[3]

To mislead the audience, Hitchcock also cast a very famous actress, Janet Leigh, in the role of the victim. As he says, "It's rather unusual to kill the star in the first third of the film. I purposely killed the star so as to make the killing even more unexpected" (p. 269).

Finally, Hitchcock uses jarringly quick edits, with stabbing music and sound effects that simulate the brutal murder, all without showing a single knife entry. The effect is jarring and disturbing, causing even the most hardened of horror fans to wince as they are forced to *imagine* naked flesh punctured by cold steel.

The rest of the movie is taken up with the investigation of the disappearance of Marion Crane. Marion's sister, boyfriend, and a private detective all join together. The detective (Arbogast) tracks Marion to the Bates Motel but is quickly killed by "Mother." Marion's sister and boyfriend follow in Arbogast's footsteps, checking out the Bates Motel, and when they do, discover the partially embalmed corpse of Mother in the basement. Norman, dressed as Mother, tries to kill Marion's sister but is stopped by Marion's boyfriend Sam.

---

[3] Francois Truffaut, *Hitchcock*, revised edition (New York: Simon and Schuster, 1985) p. 269.

The movie concludes with a police psychologist's explanation of Norman's shattered mental state, how he murdered his own mother and now, in order to erase the crime, has begun to impersonate his mother. The mother side of his psyche takes over, and "Mother" has told the police about Norman's crimes. The movie ends with a shot of Norman, sitting quietly in his cell, thinking to himself as "Mother."

The events of *Psycho* paint a picture of radical injustice. Marion Crane's theft is probably deserving of *some* kind of punishment, but she scarcely deserves the fate she suffers. Moreover, all the characters in the film seem to be punished out of proportion to what they deserve. The eager detective Arbogast, investigating the disappearance of Marion Crane, gets nothing but a knife in the face for his troubles. And Norman Bates, the perpetrator of these horrendous actions, seems the most unfortunate of all, a deeply fragmented and tormented person, born into his own trap.

Aesthetics of the Horrendous

Events like those in *Psycho* strike us at a gut level as deeply disturbing. It's not inappropriate that *Psycho* horrifies us; rather it is fitting that it has this effect on us. *Psycho,* without the shower scene, or the revelation of "Mother's" withered corpse, would not deal effectively with the subject matter.

In aesthetics (the philosophy of art), some recent attention has been given to what defines horror. Noël Carroll, in *The Philosophy of Horror,* writes:

> In horror fictions, the emotions of the audience are supposed to mirror those of the positive human characters . . . the characters' responses counsel us that the appropriate reactions to the monsters in question comprise shuddering, nausea, shrinking, paralysis, screaming, and revulsion.[4]

This certainly rings true for the viewers of *Psycho.* When the characters scream, excitable people in the audience are likely to scream as well.

---

[4] From *The Philosophy of Horror,* reprinted in *Aesthetics: The Big Questions,* edited by Carolyn Korsmeyer (Oxford: Blackwell, 1998), p. 276.

Returning to the Hitchcock quote at the beginning, it seems difficult, at first, to see how he could construe Psycho as a "fun" picture. Robin Wood, in his book *Hitchcock's Films*, claims that Hitchcock "has not really faced up to what he was doing when he made the film."[5] Certainly, I think, the Hitchcock quote de-emphasizes the fear the movie evoked in audiences. A widely reported anecdote tells of a man who wrote to Hitchcock saying that after seeing 1955's *Diabolique*, his wife refused to go in the bath, and after *Psycho*, his wife refused to shower. Hitchcock sent the man back a short note saying, "Send her to the cleaners."

Amusing as it is, this story attests to the power of horror movies to deeply trouble us, even long after the credits have rolled. Why then do we go see them? And how can they possibly be construed as "fun"?

Noël Carroll is again helpful here, as he notes that horror movies, like haunted houses, arouse in us a deep curiosity. We take pleasure in the revelation of horrors, and "the disgust that such beings evince might be seen as part of the price to be paid for the pleasure of their disclosure."[6] In this sense, and maybe this sense only, Hitchcock is correct about the "fun" of *Psycho*—we desire to see, to know, just how horrible monsters can get.

What defines a monster, though? Carroll defines monsters as "(physically, though generally not logically) impossible beings" (p. 281). This definition is problematic. First off, defining monsters as impossible beings would exclude Norman Bates as a proper subject of horror since, not only is he a *possible* being, but is actually based on the serial killer, Ed Gein.

Secondly, Carroll's definition does not explain why it is that impossible beings engender the feeling of horror. Given what I know about the universe, it's not possible that a being could derive superpowers from earth's yellow sun. And yet Superman, though technically an impossible being, does not fill me with horror.

If, however, we replace Carroll's definition of a monster with this definition: "A monster is a being that displays severe disorder or disproportion in fundamental ways," we will have an

---

[5] Robin Wood, *Hitchcock's Films* (Cranbury: Barnes, 1977), p. 114.
[6] *The Philosophy of Horror,* reprinted in *Aesthetics: The Big Questions,* edited by Carolyn Korsmeyer (Oxford: Blackwell, 1998), p. 282.

account that fits much better. Under this definition, Dracula, Frankenstein's monster, King Kong, Hitler, and Norman Bates may all be defined as monsters—despite the varying degrees of sympathy they engender—since they display severe disordered-ness or disproportion.

Frankenstein's monster is almost like a human, but not quite, giving him a grotesque quality. King Kong is like a normal ape, but too large. Dracula possesses incredible life and vitality, but only at the expense of other lives. Hitler possessed skill and intelligence—good traits in and of themselves—but directed at bad ends. Norman's psyche is divided in two, making him both a charming, vulnerable young man, and that young man's own dangerous and destructive protector.

In all these cases there is some deep incongruity at the cen-ter of the monster's being. It is this disorder and disproportion which lie at the root of horror. *Psycho*, then, we can see, dis-plays a perfect fit between the nature of the subject matter and the way it is presented. While dealing with the subject of dis-proportion and disorder, the movie itself is strategically frac-tured, shocking the audience with jarring transitions, and evincing proper revulsion.

Psycho, however, like a haunted house at a fairground, remains a mere artifice—unable to penetrate the fourth wall and do physical harm to the viewer. We can conceivably understand that some people may desire to experience horror as part of the price paid for satisfying their curiosity. The question that remains, however, is "Why would a good God allow such hor-rors to occur *in the real world*?"

Horrendous Evils in Philosophy

"Horrendous evils" (of the kind we see in *Psycho*) have received little attention in the history of the discussion of the problem of evil. Recent work in the area, however, has begun to take account of them and the unique problem they create for the those who believe in God. Marilyn McCord Adams's book, *Horrendous Evils and the Goodness of God*, shows how these evils add force to the logical problem of evil.

The logical problem of evil goes for the jugular, as it were, stating that God's existence is *incompatible* with some or all evils. Depending on the argument, either certain kinds of evils or any evils whatsoever rule out the existence of a good and powerful God. Adams frames the argument like this: In order for God to be good, He must be good to every single person. Horrendous evils, on the surface, destroy the possibility that a person's life may have positive meaning. So horrendous evils make us doubt that God is good, or even exists at all.[7]

What is perhaps most striking about the way Adams defines horrendous evils is that they are not determined primarily by *moral* categories. The positive meaning of lives of both victim and perpetrator may be ruined by participation in horrendous evils. Furthermore, they may occur even when there is no deliberate evil choice. We see a paradigm case of horror, I think, in the person of Norman Bates, a man who ruins the lives of others, and who is also ruined. Morality does not help us to see what is most salient in these situations, as both the violator and violated suffer much the same fate. The primary criteria for horrendous evils, as we have briefly discussed, is *aesthetic* in nature—since the punishment so grotesquely outweighs any possible crime.

Classical aesthetics appeals to concepts like proportion, fittingness, and unity to define what makes something beautiful. In the case of horrendous evils, there is a deep disunity and unfittingness. Some have spoken of poetic justice, but what Marion Crane and Norman Bates suffer is a very un-poetic, grotesque parody of justice. So the events of *Psycho*, and events like the ones in *Psycho,* cast doubt on traditional justifications of God in the face of evil.

As Marilyn Adams suggests, horrendous evils are so destructive because they have the ability to destroy any possible positive meaning for a person's life. Why do they have this power? Not merely because of the loss and pain involved, but because of the *kind* of loss—so senseless and cruel. They destroy meaning because of the disproportion between the amount of moral evil involved and the horrifying results.

Adams advances the idea that it is *this kind* of horror which gives such strength to the logical problem of evil. If horrors, by definition, rest upon the idea of radical disproportion and disorder, why would God allow them? In this way, we can see that

---

[7] For more on this see Marilyn McCord Adams, *Horrendous Evils and the Goodness of God* (Ithaca: Cornell University Press, 1999), p. 148.

Psycho, in helping us to perceive the grotesque nature of certain events, actually plays a part in raising the question about God's goodness, power, or existence.

Horror and the Free Will Defense

There have been any number of responses to the problem of evil in the history of philosophy and theology. We will now look at just three attempts to make sense of evil, and see whether they can incorporate the kind of events depicted in *Psycho.*

First, there is the Free Will Defense, recently developed by Alvin Plantinga, and classically stated by Augustine of Hippo. According to this argument, all evil has its source in the free will. So morally bad choices by humans or non-human persons (fallen angels) are to blame for all the evil that occurs. We can see how a great deal of the evil in the world is caused by wrong choices. Many wars, rapes, murders, deaths from starvation, deaths from disease, and car accidents could have been avoided if certain persons had made good choices instead of bad ones.

When pushed to explain natural disasters, Plantinga cites evil spirits.[8] Augustine places the blame on Adam and Eve, the original progenitors of the human race (according to the book of Genesis), who, in choosing to eat the forbidden fruit, brought suffering on all humanity.

In any case, according to the basic Free Will Defense, all the evil in the world stems from the gift of free will. And, according to this line of thought, God gave us free will because it is necessary for a genuine relationship with Him and other humans, and is therefore a good massive enough to outweigh any resulting evils. So, because of free will, God is justified in allowing us to make bad choices.

Yet, when we apply this theory to the events in *Psycho,* we do not find a neat correspondence between the evils that occur and the goods which justify them. Perhaps the most obvious example of moral evil, the theft of the forty thousand dollars, is

---

[8] Though Plantinga's response to the problem of evil may sound strange to modern readers, it is worth noting that his "Free Will Defense" is not an attempt to give God's actual reasons for allowing evil, merely logically possible reasons, in order to deflect the formal argument that theism is inconsistent. For more on this see his short book, *God, Freedom, and Evil.*

nearly irrelevant to the events of the second half of the movie. It has next to nothing to do with what ultimately happens to Marion; rather, it is merely by chance that Marion winds up in the Bates Motel. Marion's fate is not punishment for her actions, just bad luck.

As for Norman, his disturbed psychological condition is best understood as the result of both bad choices *and* natural causes. Because of the death of his father, Norman grew up as the only child of a clinging, demanding mother. According to the psychologist in the movie, the two lived together in isolation. When his mother found another man, Norman's stunted development prevented him from taking it in stride. He murdered both of them. This sent him into an even deeper psychosis, with his mind split between Norman and "Mother."

The main moral evil operating here is probably to be blamed on Norman's mother, for her poor job at raising Norman. Secondarily, Norman is probably at least partly responsible for his crimes, though much of this would depend on how mentally ill he is, and it seems that he is *very* mentally ill.

The point that emerges is that, at least in this case, the evils that occur far outweigh the positive benefit of free choice, which sends us on a search for other responses to the problem of evil.

Horror and Soul-Making Theodicies

One alternative response, used by contemporary philosopher John Hick and derived largely from Irenaeus in the third century, is the idea that suffering is beneficial for developing our characters. This seems promising at first, as it explains why God might allow a lot of evil in the world, even evil not resulting from free choices. Perhaps God wants to help us "grow up"— allowing us to strengthen morally as we deal with hardships and trials.

This will not work when applied to the problem of evil in *Psycho*. Certainly it may in some situations—often people talk about how overcoming some obstacle helped them to grow personally—but in *Psycho*, we see lives completely *destroyed* by evil. Norman's matricide and subsequent homicides only shatter his character, and simply end the lives of those who get too close to him.

Seeing the insufficiency of responses like this to horrendous evils, Marilyn Adams concludes that no sufficient "reasons why" can be given in order to explain the occurrence of horrendous evils. Instead, she proposes that God has no moral obligations to His creation, but does love us and so ultimately restores everyone from their shattered conditions. This may be a successful maneuver in defending God's existence, but it seems to sacrifice the traditional understanding of God's goodness. The question remains, is it possible to hold on to the idea that God is morally good and yet allows horrendous evils?

Horror and the Principle of Honesty

The closest attempt so far has come from philosopher Richard Swinburne, who proposes a wide variety of goods that would be eliminated if God stopped all evils. Among the goods he proposes are the ones already discussed: free will, character development, and responsibility. But Swinburne admits that there may be situations where these goods are not present, yet evils still occur. These are normally what are known as *gratuitous evils*—evils that are not justified by any directly corresponding good.

What could justify gratuitous evils—including horrendous evils? Swinburne suggests that while a specific good may not be operating every time an evil occurs, if God systematically stopped all evils that had no corresponding good, this would consist in his systematically deceiving us.

Calling this the Principle of Honesty, Swinburne states that such a systematic deception would itself be an evil, and so at times, it may be that evils occur which outweigh the specific goods that, by necessity, must make possible the occurrence of evils.[9]

What this amounts to, it seems, is a very high premium placed on the truth. God, according to Swinburne, will not deceive us, and so allows us to see the full consequences of our evil choices. Faced with this evil, we feel shock, revulsion, and horror—and these feelings are entirely fitting, as well as being, in a sense, beneficial.

---

[9] Richard Swinburne, *Providence and the Problem of Evil* (Oxford: Oxford University Press, 1998), p. 140.

A Proper Answer?

Is this a sufficient response to the problem of evil? In a way, it hearkens back to the Hitchcock quote from the beginning. Hitchcock construes *Psycho* as a fun picture. Why? Because, as I have suggested, it allows audiences to satisfy their curiosity, while exacting the price of revulsion. Perhaps, in an analogous way, the occurrence of horrendous evil is a part of bringing home the truth about evil.

The Christian tradition has often, following Augustine, defined evil as a privation (or lack) of proper order.[10] According to this line of thought, the sinful person exists in a state of disordered goals and disproportionate desires. Throughout his writings, Augustine construes beauty and goodness in much the same terms—as the presence of proper order.[11] To choose evil is to move way from proper order—to introduce chaos at the center of the human person. In other words, when we make evil decisions we become more and more like monsters.

So the fact that evil gravitates toward the grotesque, disordered, incongruous, is not *foreign* to the nature of sin but *inherent* in it. *Psycho*, in all its shockingness and horror, paints a true picture of the destructive deformity of sin. If, as Noël Carroll indicates in *The Philosophy of Horror*, our revulsion at horrors is "part of the price to be paid for the pleasure of their disclosure," then perhaps also the existence of horrors is part of the "price to be paid" for knowing the truth about evil (p. 282).

Is this an adequate response to the problem of evil? Certainly, at best, it is an incomplete beginning. If believers are to be justified in affirming God's goodness and power we would need to know more than *why* God allows horrors, but also *how* He will repair the lives of those who suffer. But this would take us beyond the scope of this chapter, and would require looking further than the movies, even insightful movies such as *Psycho*.

---

[10] Augustine of Hippo, *Enchiridion* (see Chapters 10, 11, and 12).

[11] For examples of this connection between the proper ordering of both goodness and beauty, see Augustine's *On Free Will* and *Of True Religion*, both contained in *Augustine: Earlier Writings* (London: SCM:, 1953).

5

The Birds: Plato and Romantic Love

RAJA HALWANI and STEVEN JONES

> It all goes to show that with a little effort even the word 'love' can be made to sound ominous.
>
> —ALFRED HITCHCOCK[1]

At the time of its release, Alfred Hitchcock said of *The Birds*: "It could be the most terrifying motion picture I have ever made."[2] To say this about a movie released after *Psycho* is surely to create quite a flap! Exposing the ugly side of what many consider to be warm and fuzzy *is* terrifying. As suggested in this chapter's title, we refer not only to birds, but also to romantic love.

Philosophers distinguish between different kinds of love: the love between friends or siblings, and between parents and their children; the love for all humanity; and romantic or personal love. Romantic love is the kind that blossoms between Melanie and Mitch during *The Birds* and that might have existed at some point between Mitch and Annie, the schoolteacher.

Love's Turbulent Flight

Romantic love obviously has wonderful aspects. Experiencing its passion is usually intensely pleasurable. Love can spur lovers to become morally better people in general. And love makes people's lives meaningful. We don't deny any of these claims.

---

[1] François Truffaut, *Hitchcock*, revised edition (New York: Simon and Schuster, 1985), p. 288.

[2] Publicity quotation from the film's poster and trailer.

However, romantic love also has its drawbacks. We focus on certain facts about love that people tend to neglect, allowing them to ignore questions about its place in their lives and what attitudes they should have towards it. Our claim about love's ugly side is not confined to cases of "false" or failed loves, but also, crucially, to cases of "true" love.

Because of the very natures of autonomy and romantic love, the issue of the rationality of love primarily arises due to the conflict between the two.[3] Lovers must often compromise on certain decisions and actions (because such decisions are, or should be, taken jointly). Sometimes a lover even sacrifices these for the sake of the beloved's desires.[4] Compromise and sacrifice also play a role in how romantic love affects one's life. Say Mitch meets Melanie, falls in love, and the relationship takes a serious turn. Mitch's life changes to Mitch's-life-with-Melanie, and he uses the pronoun 'we' to refer to his future.[5] If Mitch remains passive as his life changes, romantic love undermines his autonomy. This remains true even when—as usually happens—lovers *retroactively* consent to love's presence.

Romantic love also erodes autonomy because lovers are emotionally dependent on each other. This dependency often leads them to experience unpleasant emotions such as jealousy, anger, and bitterness, even though these feelings are not justified or rational on every occasion. It also often leads lovers to *act* irrationally, as when the jealous lover snoops through his beloved's belongings. Love can also make lovers impatient and curious. It induces Melanie, a busy socialite, to abandon her normal weekly schedule, purchase lovebirds, drive for two hours, commandeer a boat across a bay, and sneak the birds into a stranger's house, though she could have waited until the week-

---

[3] Many philosophers have noted the tension between autonomy and love. Foremost is perhaps Jean-Jacques Rousseau, whose views on this issue are scattered among his many works. But see especially *Second Discourse*, *Émile*, and *New Heloise*.

[4] On joint decision making when in love, see Robert Nozick, "Love's Bond," in *The Examined Life: Philosophical Meditations* (New York: Simon and Schuster, 1989), reprinted in *The Philosophy of (Erotic) Love*, edited by Robert Solomon and Kathleen Higgins (Lawrence: University Press of Kansas, 1991).

[5] On the use of 'we', see Nozick, "Love's Bond." The use of 'we' is a weak version of the union theory of love, perhaps originally found in the speech of Aristophanes in Plato's *Symposium*, according to which the lovers desire to meld together to form one entity. The union theory is criticized by Alan Soble in "Union, Autonomy, and Concern," in *Love Analyzed*, edited by Roger Lamb (Boulder: Westview, 1997).

end was over and surprised Mitch in San Francisco. Not all lovers act in such ways, but when they do, they act against their typical proper judgment.

Most importantly, emotional dependency opens lovers up to undesirable potential contingencies *because* love ties their individual fortunes together. Being in love means facing the contingencies of having one's lover cheat, of dealing with his sicknesses, unhappiness and depression (when they occur), or even his death, should he die first. To love another is to invite into one's life happiness and joy; but it is also to invite misery and pain. Because these contingencies are undesirable and painful and because one cannot control their occurrence, romantic love endangers one's autonomy.

So romantic love pecks away at—though it doesn't completely undermine—autonomy. Indeed, the emotions of romantic love tend to be much more intense, and the dependency more thoroughgoing, than those of friendships or sibling relationships. Since we value both autonomy and love, and since autonomy is necessary for people to be the authors of their own lives, we need to question love's rationality.[6]

Is it rational to have romantic love in one's life? This serious question can and should be raised by the lover him or herself and by third parties, such as the lover's friends and family members. Whether being in love is overall a bad or a good thing is precisely what this question seeks to determine. However, even if being in love is overall a good thing, it always comes at some price, namely, some detraction from autonomy. There is always *some* cost to love. Signaling this idea during the opening scene of *The Birds* at the pet store, Mitch coyly reveals to Melanie his knowledge that she is not a saleswoman by saying to the captured canary, "Back to your gilded cage, Melanie Daniels!" The implication is that the only cost-free type of love—perhaps the view of love initially adopted by Melanie and Mitch—is the idealized love that exists in a fully controlled—a gilded—environment. In the real world, such love does not exist.

Both Plato's *Symposium*—a seminal work on love—and Hitchcock's *The Birds* move us to confront the seriousness of

---

[6] Many philosophers consider autonomy to be of supreme value. Immanuel Kant made it, along with rationality, the foundational concept of his moral theory.

love, the former by pressing the issue of its place in our lives, and the latter by pressing the more basic issue of what attitude we should have towards it.

Socrates Flips Romantic Love the Bird

Plato (428–347 B.C.E.) wrote all his philosophical works in dialogue form. In the majority of them, the principal character—and Plato's usual mouthpiece—is Socrates (470–399 B.C.E.), Plato's teacher. The *Symposium* consists of a number of characters giving speeches praising love.[7] Socrates's speech instructs us to abandon the usual view of romantic love in favor of a life of contemplation of the Form of Beauty, a non-spatial, non-temporal entity embodying the essence of what beauty is and functioning as the ideal of what temporal beauty should be. All Platonic Forms are the non-spatial, non-temporal, uncreated, and eternal essences of what they are Forms of. For example, the Form "Birdness" is the essence of what birds are—of what makes any bird a bird.

Plato's Socrates assumes that all beauty is uniform—that the beauty of a face is the same *type* of beauty as that of a mind or of an idea. If so, he reasons, to pursue *true* love, we ought to fall in love with *true* beauty. And what truer beauty is there to love other than its ideal Platonic Form? To Plato's Socrates, the lover *starts* with loving a young, beautiful boy (as was the custom at the time),[8] but eventually, and by climbing the "ladder of love," arrives at the Form of Beauty and Goodness, his final destination and object of his true love:

> This is what it is to go aright . . . into the mystery of Love: one goes always upwards for the sake of this Beauty, starting out from beautiful things and using them like rising stairs: from one body to two and from two to all beautiful bodies, then from beautiful bodies to beautiful customs, and from customs to learning beautiful things, and from these lessons he arrives in the end at this lesson,

---

[7] *Symposium* (Indianapolis: Hackett, 1989—Plato's other major work on love is the *Phaedrus*). Our understanding of the *Symposium* partly relies on Martha Nussbaum's interpretation. See "The Speech of Alcibiades," in *The Fragility of Goodness: Luck and Ethics in Greek Tragedy and Philosophy* (New York: Cambridge University Press, 1986), reprinted in *The Philosophy of (Erotic) Love*.

[8] See Kenneth Dover, *Greek Homosexuality* (Cambridge, Massachusetts: Harvard University Press, 1989).

which is learning of this very Beauty, so that in the end he comes to know just what it is to be beautiful.[9]

One interesting aspect to Socrates's speech is the claim that true love is the love of the Form of Beauty and Goodness. Those listening to the speech at the banquet would have been surprised by such a claim, for people (then and now) usually believe that true love is the love of another person, not some higher philosophical form. Nonetheless, the Socratic claim is familiar; it is a variation of a more general one, namely, the idea of devoting one's life to the love of a non-human entity, such as justice and bird watching. We shall also see that Socrates's claim is quite alluring.

Another Fox in Socrates's Henhouse

Socrates's speech does not conclude the *Symposium*, indicating that Plato might not be fully convinced by it. Instead, Alcibiades (450–404 B.C.E.), a young, beautiful, Athenian general, crashes the party and gives the final speech. Perhaps reflecting Plato's desire to undermine the readers' confidence in the truth of Socrates's speech, Alcibiades proclaims, "I hope you didn't believe a single word Socrates said: the truth is just the opposite!" (*Symposium*, p. 64). He continues with an honest account of his unrequited love for Socrates and shows us how it humiliates him and makes him suffer. Going against the prevalent norms, Alcibiades, the younger man, ends up pursuing Socrates, the older one: "Socrates is the only man in the world who has made me feel shame—ah, you didn't think I had it in me, did you?" (*Symposium*, p. 67). Alcibiades might have been a shady character, but he was clearly in love with Socrates, and his concluding speech wonderfully illustrates the contingencies of love, its ups and downs, and its tendency to compromise one's autonomy.

The two speeches by Socrates and Alcibiades fly in opposite directions. While Socrates asks us to love the Form of Beauty, Alcibiades directs us to retain the usual type of love: for an individual, unique person. Through these two speeches, Plato reveals the pros and cons of each view. The Socratic option is tempting

---

[9] *Symposium*, p. 59. Strictly, these are the words of Diotima, a wise woman from Mantinea, who instructs Socrates in the art of love and whose views constitute Socrates's speech.

because it allows us to abandon the messiness and the contingency of love in favor of an entity, the Platonic Form of Beauty and Goodness, which is eternal and fully reliable. But it requires us to relinquish the experience and joy of person-to-person romantic love. On the other hand, Alcibiades's option is the one we are accustomed to—it promises us the euphoria, the beauty, and the attendant sexual and emotional pleasures of romantic love. But this love, as we have seen, erodes our autonomy.

One may wonder whether we have to choose between the two options. Clearly, one can be in love with the Form and also have a companion. One can also be in love with another while pursuing, say, a career in medicine. In these respects, the two options are not mutually exclusive. But then again, these options do not illustrate the views in the speeches of Socrates and Alcibiades. Keep in mind that when Socrates counsels that we love the Form Beauty, he is talking about *romantic* love, that the Form be the object of this love (*Symposium*, p. 51). And when Alcibiades talks about Socrates, it is Socrates who is the object of his romantic love.

Insofar as romantic love is exclusive, we can only truly love one object at a time. In this respect, we either romantically love the Form or another person. The options would not be between, say, Mitch pursuing a law career and loving Melanie, but between loving the law and loving Melanie.[10] As Martha Nussbaum puts it, the story of Alcibiades "shows us clearly that we simply cannot add the love of Alcibiades to the ascent of Diotima . . . Socrates was serious when he spoke of two mutually exclusive varieties of vision" ("The Speech of Alcibiades," pp. 197–98).

By showing us the allure of each vision, Plato pushes his readers to address the question of the rationality of love. He does not answer the question but is content to show us the importance of raising and thinking about it.

Caw of the Wild: *The Birds* and Love

Since, as we have seen, romantic love is serious business, the calamitous nature of *The Birds* becomes understandable. While

---

[10] It's a popular belief that exclusivity is an essential feature of romantic love. While it is clearly logically possible to simultaneously romantically love more than one person, it is practically and even psychologically difficult to do so. See Soble, *The Structure of Love*, Chapter 9, and *The Philosophy of Sex and Love*, Chapter 6.

not denying that the film can and does have multiple meanings,[11] we view it as Hitchcock's warning about romantic love: love has some ugly feathers in its cap and its place in one's life needs to be considered and taken seriously.

The bird attacks dramatically display these ugly feathers. Indeed, the typically opposed themes of romance and horror work well together because Hitchcock draws a parallel between characters who do not have a proper regard for romantic love and people who do not have a serious appreciation for the power of birds. Hitchcock said that the screenplay appealed to him precisely because it involved "ordinary, everyday birds" (Truffaut, *Hitchcock*, p. 285). If one thinks of love as being simply a nice, cuddly thing, one will have a distorted understanding of it. So we have a film showing the ominous aspects of love.

The movie begins with a foreboding title sequence and opening scene of birds circling above Union Square, San Francisco, but quickly dissolves into flirtatious banter between the film's main characters, Melanie Daniels (played by Tippi Hedren) and Mitch Brenner (played by Rod Taylor) about—of all things—lovebirds. The contrasting elements of the opening scenes indicate that the movie will not simply scare us, but will also make us think about romantic love. The pet store scene begins to establish the idea that both Melanie and Mitch take love lightly, which Hitchcock reinforces in the playful way Melanie pursues Mitch: purchasing lovebirds and stealthily taking them to the Brenners' house in Bodega Bay.[12] As the story progresses, the bird attacks occur whenever the characters treat romantic love lightly, irresponsibly, or wrongly.

For example, a seagull attacks Melanie as she glides through the bay from Mitch's family house. Melanie's attitude towards love, culminating in the boat scene, is to take it lightly, treating it as a game of hide and seek. She changes her mind at the last minute and gives the lovebirds to Mitch's sister Cathy (played by

---

[11] Donald Spoto, for example, interprets the movie as being about human relationships in general in *The Art of Alfred Hitchcock* (New York: Anchor, 1992). Camille Paglia approaches the film from a gender-based perspective in *The Birds* (London: British Film Institute, 2002).

[12] We rely here also on cinematic conventions to know early on in the film that the flirtation between Melanie and Mitch is not for its own sake but the beginning of love between them.

Veronica Cartwright), indicating her fickle and possibly manipulative attitude towards love. This attitude is rewarded, so to speak, with a bird attack. Later, the discussion between Melanie and Annie Hayworth (played by Suzanne Pleshette), in which the two women exhibit some jealousy and possessiveness regarding Mitch's affections also ends with a bird attack, albeit a failed one (the bird merely flies into Annie's door).

The bird attack on the children during Cathy's party occurs after Melanie divulges to Mitch the selfish attitude of her own mother towards her family. Although Melanie's complaint concerns a lack of parental love, such love is often a product of romantic love. An irresponsible attitude towards the former indicates a generally irresponsible attitude towards intimate relationships.[13] The birds swoop down the Brenners' chimney and, later, go after the school children, after Mitch's mother Lydia (played by Jessica Tandy) expresses a selfish and potentially obstructionist attitude towards the blossoming love between Melanie and Mitch. In all these scenes, characters approach romantic love without proper concern.

After the attack at the school, the film's centerpiece unfolds. Having escaped to the restaurant, Melanie describes her ordeal. At first, no one believes Melanie's story. In fact, the "learned amateur ornithologist" Mrs. Bundy (played by Ethel Griffies) dismisses Melanie's tale and claims, "Birds bring beauty into the world. It is mankind who insists on making it difficult for life to exist on this planet." Mrs. Bundy clearly underestimates the power of the birds. The subsequent explosive attack on the town proves Mrs. Bundy wrong, and it also draws the audience back to the film's other theme: the place of love in one's life. The accusations of the hysterical mother in the diner—underscored by their direct delivery to the camera—are not senseless ravings. Perhaps unwittingly, she makes the connection: it is only when Melanie (love) enters into Bodega Bay (Mitch's life) that the disasters begin to occur. Love is not an undiluted good; it has its dark side, a side not usually talked about and symbolized, perhaps, by the mother's plea to the restaurant patrons to lower their voices while discussing the bird attacks, so as to shield her children from such talk.

---

[13] In this scene, the birds attack only the children, perhaps reminding us that a child often pays for her parents' lack of love.

   Like Plato, the way Hitchcock positions the scenes of the bird attacks and the way he represents the attitudes of the film's characters towards romantic love are designed to raise the question of the place of love in our lives by warning us of treating it lightly. But while Plato pushes us to consider whether to have love in our lives, Hitchcock addresses the proper attitude to adopt towards love.

The Wind Beneath Love's Wings

The caged lovebirds provide one crucial recurring motif in the film. Interestingly, they are the only peaceful creatures in the movie. While Melanie carts these birds from the city to the country by automobile and boat, they calmly perch next to one another. While the Brenners' house literally falls apart around them, they merely utter a few chirps. They seem content to wait for their next adventure in Melanie's car. Indeed, the final line of *The Birds* has Cathy begging Mitch to bring the lovebirds along for the family's flight from Bodega Bay. "They haven't harmed anyone," she says. But how is it that *this* pair escapes the horrors around them? One clue is the cage, a familiar, confined, and controlled environment. For to avoid the vulnerability and contingencies of love, the love must be "conducted" in complete isolation from the world, in the safety of a cage. This ideal situation is not generally possible for human beings—not unless the object of our love is something non-human, such as Plato's Forms. To think that one can escape love's contingencies is to manifest an improper understanding of it.

   But the question remains: If romantic love has its ugly side, how *should* we approach it? The answer is: wisely and maturely. Individuals need to reflect on the place of romantic love in their lives—hence Plato's contribution. Once love is accepted, lovers need to be courageous and wise to face up to its contingencies: that a beloved might not be worthy of her love, that he may cheat on her, that he may die, and so on. They need to understand and accept that the pleasure of love comes at the price of the loss of some autonomy, and that there are no safe loves in this world.[14] To treat romantic love as a trifle, as Melanie and

---

[14] Raja Halwani defends a similar, Aristotelian view of love in his *Virtuous Liaisons: Care, Love, Sex, and Virtue Ethics* (Chicago: Open Court, 2003), Chapter 2.

Mitch initially do, is to reveal an incomplete understanding of and an improper attitude towards it.

Reminding us of the positive aspects of love, Hitchcock's characters mature as the film progresses. In the opening scene, Melanie doesn't know the difference between a canary and a lovebird. The first attack by the gull catches Melanie—and the audience—completely by surprise, as do the knock on Annie's door and the assault at Cathy's party. Yet Melanie does learn something. Perhaps seeing a pattern, she gives warning signals and orders for the next battles: a furtive "Mitch" before the sparrows funnel down the Brenners' chimney, stern directions to Annie to keep the children out of the playground, and then frantic warnings to anyone outside the restaurant. By the end of the movie, she's capable of identifying a finch, a crow, a sparrow, and a seagull. Her wisdom is passed along to Mitch as well, and they prepare for the next attack by successfully boarding up the openings to the Brenners' house.

They don't bargain on the birds' ability to break through the roof. Up to that point, the birds had only aimed for easy targets, such as unguarded hairdos, windows, and doors. What the birds—and love—are capable of can never be fully predicted. So it's wise to remember that wisdom itself is not omniscience. Melanie can be forgiven for her final excruciating, terrifying, and even dumb ascent to the attic to seek out the source of whatever could possibly be making that eerie, bird-like noise!

That Melanie makes this mistake on her own and that both Mitch and Lydia rescue her, certainly indicate hope for the family's future, now including Melanie. Together, they all survive. In fact, together (with the lovebirds in tow) they all drive off into the golden rays of the rising sun. The omnipresence of the birds and the simultaneous rise of their calls may allude to the idea that the road is not completely clear for the relationship between Melanie and Mitch. But no romantic couple matures so as to conquer all the contingencies of love. Indeed, the best they can do is to face them courageously, maturely, and wisely.

As in the film, we never see "The End." The scene inside the car ends with the accepting embrace between Melanie and Lydia, the Brenner matriarch. Whereas almost every other scene in the film ends with the characters looking fearfully to the sky, this one ends with the two women reassuringly looking to each other. Hope springs from the growing wisdom and responsibility of all those connected to the love and the lovers.

To Nest or Not to Nest

Hitchcock very loosely based *The Birds* on the short story of the same title by Daphne Du Maurier.[15] In the short story, as the bird attacks increase in ferocity and frequency, the main character, Nat Hocken, infers that among the aggressors are hawks that "ignored the windows" and "concentrated their attacks upon the door" (Du Maurier, "The Birds," p. 123).

Hitchcock explicitly rejected the use of birds of prey in his film. It is the focus on "normal, everyday" birds that makes the film especially eerie and that enables the parallel with the normal phenomenon of romantic love. Like your everyday bird, love is warm, fuzzy, and can bring much joy and happiness. However, we must be cautious: love also diminishes the autonomy of the lovers and renders them vulnerable to more of life's contingencies. We must treat it wisely and responsibly, and one crucial way is to reflect on its place in our lives.

Like *The Birds*, we have focused on the negative aspects of love to highlight them, with no intention of downplaying its positive aspects. Plato noticed the complexities of love, and, to his credit, brought them to his readers' attention in the *Symposium*. But so did *The Birds*: to understand romantic love—to escape in Melanie's car in the ominous yet hopeful last scene—we must treat love wisely, virtuously, with the *gravitas* that it deserves. It is *The Birds'* ability to yield meanings such as this one that makes it a true work of art rather than simply a scary yet entertaining movie.

---

[15] Daphne Du Maurier, "The Birds," in *The Treasury of Du Maurier Short Stories* (London: Gollancz, 1960).

6

Featherless Bipeds: The Concept of Humanity in *The Birds*

SCOTT CALEF

Man is a featherless biped.

—Plato

Behold, Plato's man!

—Diogenes, displaying a plucked rooster

Man is a featherless biped *with flat fingernails.*

—Plato

The isolated assaults are intensifying into a full-blown, aerial blitzkrieg. Bodega Bay is under attack. Diving and crashing like kamikazes, birds are launching themselves into phone boxes, swerving automobiles, and people's faces. The calm streets of this once quiet oceanside hamlet are now a whirlpool of mayhem, blood, and broken glass.

Struggling to reach the relative safety of the nearby Tides Restaurant through a chaos of beating wings and fallen bodies, Melanie Daniels and Mitch Brenner finally stumble inside. The tumult outside heightens the dining room's eerie stillness. Only moments before, a busy lunchtime crowd had been debating the possibility of such a massed avian offensive. Now the people are all gone. As Mitch and Melanie tread cautiously further into the interior, they realize that everyone is huddled in a side hallway. And then a hysterical mother steps forward, confronts Melanie, and blames her for the plague, crying out, "Who are you? What are you? Where did you come from?" A slap from

Melanie silences her, but not the questions; they hang in the air, demanding an answer.

The overwrought mother raises the central questions of the film. Who are we indeed? When the mother, Doreen Lang, accuses Melanie, she is looking directly into the camera, and thus, subjectively, at us, the viewers. The question seems not to be directed solely at Melanie, but at us all.

What is the relationship between Melanie and the birds, and by extension, between humans and non-humans? Are humans unique? If so, how? How do we differ from non-human animals? How are we the same? Are humans "above" the other species?

These questions—about human nature, how we define ourselves, what it is to be human, and our place in the grand scheme of things—concern the philosophy of personhood. Hitchcock was a master psychologist of suspense. His insight into human nature and his uncanny ability to manipulate and play upon its expectations place him in the highest ranks of cinematic genius. So *The Birds* can be viewed as a highly entertaining (and shocking) meditation on human identity by one of Hollywood's most observant directors.

Issues of identity constitute a recurring motif in *The Birds*, especially early on when the themes of the film are being laid out. Consider the various confusions about "who's who." When Miss Daniels (Tippi Hedren) first encounters Mitch Brenner (Rod Taylor) in the pet store, she assumes a false identity. Pretending to be a salesperson, she tries to remove a bird from its cage only to have it escape. As Mitch captures and then re-confines the feathered fugitive he says, "Back in your gilded cage, Melanie Daniels." When Melanie asks, "What did you say?" Mitch replies, "I was only drawing a parallel, Miss Daniels." This immediately introduces a parallel between humans and birds. In the context of that parallel the identities of humans and birds are both in question. Melanie confuses canaries with lovebirds, strawberry finches she calls simply "red birds" and molting birds are identified by their "hangdog expressions!" Raymond Durgnat insightfully notes that the film is "as much about whatever is manlike in birds as whatever is birdlike in man."[1]

---

[1] *The Strange Case of Alfred Hitchcock* (Cambridge, Massachusetts: MIT Press, 1974), p. 344.

Melanie marvels that Mitch knows her when she's been pretending to be someone else and doesn't recognize him. When they part company she has an employee at her father's paper identify him through his license plate number. Tracking down his apartment, a neighbor refers her to Bodega Bay, where Mitch spends weekends. Arriving there to deliver love birds, she's momentarily stymied when the post office staff can't decide whether Mitch's sister Cathy (Veronica Cartwright) is named Alice or Lois. When the clerk points out the Brenner home across the Bay, Melanie, confused about who "the Brenners" are and obviously wondering whether Mitch is married, asks, "Mr. and Mrs. Brenner?" She's told the Brenners are Mrs. Brenner and the two kids. Confused again about who the kids are, she's informed they're Mitch and the little girl. When Melanie arrives at school teacher Annie Hayworth's house to discover the actual name of the little Brenner girl, Annie (Suzanne Pleshette) calls from her garden, "Who is it?" "Me," answers Miss Daniels (a rather odd answer from a total stranger to someone who can't see her), to which Annie replies, "Who's 'me'?" Although Annie was directing her remark at Melanie, the question is an ungrammatical way of asking, "Who am I?" Hitchcock shifts the thematic focus from Cathy's identity to Melanie's, and then, through the general nature of Annie's ungrammatical question, to the identity of Annie and each of us.[2] Annie claims to be an open book, but then immediately corrects herself: "Or rather, a closed one."

After being struck by the gull, Melanie dissembles again by pretending to be an old college friend of Annie's. At the Brenner home for dinner, Melanie asks whether a portrait is of Mitch's father. Meanwhile Lydia (Jessica Tandy), on the phone to Brinkmeyer, asks "Who? . . . Well, what's he got to do with it?" And of course, there's the pivotal scene in the Tides when Doreen Lang demands to know what Melanie is. Note Melanie's mysterious identity in the scene at the car as she prepares to leave the Brenner residence after dinner. Melanie says to Mitch, "I thought you could read my character," indicating that he doesn't know her.

---

[2] Concerning Hitchcock's playful use of grammar, many have remarked on the film's supposedly "ungrammatical" advertising campaign, which announced: "The Birds Is Coming".

In the quotations introducing this chapter, Diogenes reduces Plato's account of humanity to absurdity by showing graphically that birds without feathers aren't human. The attempt to escape this logic by modifying the definition to include *flat nails* surely misses the point (and not *only* because Diogenes could have pounded his rooster's claws with a hammer). Whatever it is that makes us human, it isn't our fingernails! But then, in what *does* our humanity consist? And what does *The Birds* have to say about it?

Highbrows, Owls, Eggheads, and Ostriches

Aristotle, Plato's pupil for twenty years, argued in *De Anima* that humans are to be defined by their capacity for reason and the quality of their souls. Plants have a "nutritive soul"; they absorb nutrition, grow, and multiply. Non-human animals like birds possess in addition a "sensitive soul"; they feel and perceive. To this extent, they have ideas of a sort. But only humans have a rational soul. We think, draw conclusions, contemplate abstract ideas, weigh and assess evidence, and so on. According to Aristotle we are to be defined, not by our featherless, naked bodies, but by the potency of our minds. Intelligence distinguishes us from the other animals, makes us unique, and places us at the pinnacle of the natural world.

Or does it? Mrs. Bundy (Ethel Griffies), the ornithologist, supports Aristotle by arguing that neither crows nor blackbirds would "have sufficient intelligence to launch a mass attack. Their brain pans are not big enough." And yet, surely birds can make inferences and connect ideas. Pigeons, for example, can learn to peck targets to receive food pellets. They know that if they want food, they should peck the target, and when they do want food, they peck. Why not count this as reasoning? They don't peck the target *instinctively*; they must *figure out* that's how to get fed. The thought process may not be conscious, but many of our thought processes are unconscious or pre-conscious. I know that if I want a sip of coffee I should lift my cup, but I don't bother to tell myself this every time I take a drink. Differences of intelligence between humans and non-humans are arguably differences of degree, not of kind.[3] Moreover, some

---

[3] Not all philosophers would agree. Even if both humans and birds reason, we may still

humans are incapable of reasoning. Fetuses, infants, the severely mentally handicapped, the comatose, the grossly intoxicated, the sleeping—all these are human, but not "intelligent" or rational. A pigeon might very well be more adept at problem-solving than any of these humans. But beyond this, the Latin-spouting Mrs. Bundy, probably the most educated and intelligent person in the room, is simply dead wrong. She has drawn the wrong conclusions. For all her education, she's a "bird-brain"!

Mrs. Bundy says, "Let's be logical." In logic there's a basic argument form known as "modus tollens." Modus tollens arguments start with an "if . . . then" statement, and then deny the truth of the "then" clause (the consequent). This allows us to validly infer the denial of the "if" clause (the antecedent). Mrs. Bundy's argument is a modus tollens argument. She claims that *if* the birds were to launch a mass attack, *then* they would have to be intelligent. But they are not intelligent—their brain pans are too small. (This is the denial of the "consequent".) Therefore, the birds are not attacking (denial of the antecedent). Miss Daniels, she rationally concludes, must be mistaken.

While various townsmen debate endlessly what it all means or what should be done about it, plain facts are ignored.[4] They can't act because they can't accommodate events into their preconceptions of what's possible; rationality is of no use in understanding the inexplicable and uncanny.[5] Hitchcock very cleverly leaves any indication of why the birds might be attacking unanswered. Reason is impotent against the irrational, and perhaps the sphere of irrationality is much wider than we care to think.[6] Why then should reason be thought to make us superior?[7]

---

be capable of reasoning of a qualitatively different sort. Perhaps only humans can reason about historical events or abstract subjects like mathematics, for instance.

[4] As the Doreen Lang character exclaims in exasperation, "If that young lady saw an attack on the school, why won't you believe her?"

[5] Susan Smith maintains that the film's overall epistemological concern is "with using the birds to challenge theoretical, abstract forms of knowledge." *Hitchcock: Suspense, Humour, and Tone* (London: British Film Institute, 2000), p.140. Epistemology is the branch of philosophy concerned with the nature of knowledge.

[6] Love and the other emotions hardly seem susceptible to rationality and are often as mysterious and unknown as the bird attacks themselves. Lydia, for example, admits she doesn't know how she feels about Mitch's fondness for Melanie, or even whether she likes Melanie. She confesses too that her departed husband really knew and understood the children, but she doesn't.

[7] We might think that reason confers a survival advantage and is therefore selected for, evolutionarily. This isn't obvious, however. It might not be "rational" for an egret to think

Donald Spoto observes that "seeing" and "not seeing" are recurring motifs in the film (Mitch spies Melanie with binoculars and foils her attempt to escape from her prank unnoticed; Fawcett's eyes are plucked out; Cathy is attacked while playing "blind man's bluff"; a girl's glasses are stepped on and broken as the students race to relative safety in town). In the movie, "I see" has the sense "I understand" (as when Annie says "Oh, I see" after Melanie tells her the birds in her car are love birds, or when Lydia, echoing Annie, says "I see" on learning from Mitch that Melanie has driven to Bodega Bay to deliver the birds for Cathy's birthday). Spoto points out that the expressions "I see" or "You see" are used over two dozen times in the film and that "every sequence concludes with a character staring out into space. . . . Unseeing gazes and faulty vision needing correction—the point is impossible to ignore in *The Birds*."[8] But notice: Since birds have keener vision than humans, if "seeing" means "understanding," the implication is that birds may understand more than we do. Just because *we* don't know why they're attacking doesn't mean *they* don't know!

Humans are frequently depicted as stupid, rash, and ignorant in the film, sometimes confessing themselves to be such. (In keeping with Hitchcock's lifelong suspicion of police, the Bodega Bay sheriff is particularly clueless.) When Mitch cross-examines Melanie as to why she tore up her letter to him, she says the message "seemed stupid and foolish." "Like jumping into a fountain in Rome," he teases.[9] Elsewhere, responding to Mitch's question by saying that she would be staying with Annie, he remarks, "How stupid of me." After finding Annie dead in front of her house, Mitch's bright idea? Pick up a rock and throw it at the death-dealing flock! Almost as smart as the irascible salesman in the Tides whose brilliant suggestion is for

that every movement in the swamp water is a crocodile; the belief would be false. But egrets might survive longer if they "irrationally" clung to these typically false beliefs than if they didn't!

[8] *The Art of Alfred Hitchcock: Fifty Years of His Motion Pictures*, second edition (New York: Doubleday, 1992), pp. 336–37.

[9] The gossip column in a newspaper owned by one of Melanie's father's competitors reported that while in Rome she had jumped into a fountain naked. The clear parallel is of a bird in a bird bath. ("Bird" was common slang for women in the 1960s.) Mitch's remark displayed an astonishing lack of intelligence if his goal was indeed to win a second date.

humanity to grab their guns and "wipe them off the face of the earth." Mitch says "I don't know" or "we don't know" at least half a dozen times in response to avian attacks. Susan Smith notes that Mitch's "smug, complacent display of superior knowledge ('Ah, but *I know you'* [to Miss Daniels in the pet store]) is increasingly eroded by the birds, a process which culminates in Lydia's relentless questioning of him just prior to the penultimate attack on their home"[10]:

> **LYDIA:** Where will we go?
> **MITCH:** *I don't know.* I think we're safe here for the time being. Let's get the wood in now.
> **LYDIA:** What happens if we run out of wood?
> **MITCH:** *I don't know!* We'll break up the furniture.
> **LYDIA:** *You don't know! You don't know! When will you know?* When we're all dead?

On the other hand, near the movie's close as the Brenner family is preparing to leave the house, Hitchcock deliberately creates the impression that the birds are thinking.

A Little Birdie Told Me

Perhaps, then, it isn't knowledge, intelligence, or rationality that distinguishes us from our feathered "friends," but the capacity to use language. René Descartes thought so.[11] Because linguistic utterances are too complicated, varied, and infinitely adaptable to be generated by purely mechanical (or neurological) means, they must be due to the workings of the soul. Only humans use language and only humans have souls, so Descartes argued.

This argument overlaps the rationality argument. Many philosophers insist that when we believe anything, what we believe is *that some proposition is true.* If I think the love birds are harmless, what I believe is that the sentence "the love birds are harmless" is a true sentence. But then, all beliefs concern language. Consequently, philosophers have often concluded that

---

[10] Susan Smith, *Hitchcock: Suspense, Humour, and Tone,* (London: British Film Institute, 2000), pp. 129–130

[11] Descartes (1596–1650) is usually regarded as the father of modern philosophy, though he made important contributions to numerous other fields as well.

beings without language lack beliefs too. And if birds cannot believe anything, they cannot know or be rational either, since knowledge seems to be just an especially secure kind of true belief and rationality has to do with arriving at beliefs sensibly rather than foolishly.

We should remember, however, that many counter-arguments from our discussion of rationality apply here too. Not all humans can speak or understand language, and arguably some non-humans (apes like Wasoe, for example) can use language. In the context of the film, birds are certainly *said* to talk; Hitchcock conspicuously raises the issue. When Melanie arrives at the menagerie to pick up the myna bird for her aunt the flustered and "flighty" Mrs. MacGruder is asked, "And he'll talk?" She replies, "Why, yes, of course he'll talk. Well, no, you'll have to teach him to talk." But he *can* be taught to talk, and so has the *capacity* for speech, even if it's not at first apparent.[12] When Mitch unmasks Melanie's pretense to be an assistant in the shop by saying "Back in your gilded cage, Melanie Daniels," she asks, "How did you know my name?" Mitch's answer? "A little birdie told me." The myna bird is reintroduced when Melanie mentions her general semantics course at Berkeley; she plans to learn new obscenities to teach the myna and so shock her aunt. People, on the other hand, are represented as mute. Upon witnessing the gruesome scene at the Fawcett farm, Lydia rushes out, mouth gaping, reduced to silence by the horror she's just seen. Even after driving all the way home, she can't utter an articulate sound. Melanie, trapped in Cathy's bedroom and reduced to a bloody, catatonic mess, can neither escape nor cry out for help. If our humanity is tied to our capacity to use language, are we then only intermittently human? That doesn't seem right, and so something's wrong with the language theory.

Freeeeebird!!!!!

Other philosophers have argued that humans alone possess free will. Jean-Jacques Rousseau (1712–1778), for example, claims that only humans are free, and that animals operate solely on

---

[12] There's a great difference between *imitating* speech and *understanding* it. Perhaps what is crucial is not the capacity to speak but to comprehend. However, animals arguably can do this, at least to an extent, and hence this difference between humans

the basis of instinct. Humans and animals, he argues, experience the same natural impulses, but humans can either acquiesce to or resist the promptings of nature; animals can only yield. Thus, he says, "a pigeon would die of hunger near a basin filled with the best meats" though it could "very well nourish itself on the food it disdains if it made up its mind to try some."[13] Because animals cannot deviate from the courses prescribed by their natures they have no capacity for self-improvement. Human nature, on the other hand, allows us to oppose our natural inclinations. Hence, we can rise above them (or, significantly for Rousseau, degenerate through failing to heed them). It's in part the human capacity to behave unnaturally which makes us unpredictable and spontaneous. It also allows us to exhibit, for example, moral virtues like courage, which requires us to calm or overcome our instinctive fears and act contrary to them. (An example would be Mitch leaving the Brenner house and wading though a virtual sea of gulls and murderous crows to fetch the car in the closing scene.) Non-humans, according to Rousseau, lack this talent, but must forever follow the rule prescribed by their natures; one bird is pretty much like the others of its species since all operate on the basis of the same in-born dispositions.

Hitchcock, however, makes these claims seem too simple. His birds behave unpredictably and unnaturally. No explanation for their dangerous and aberrant behavior is ever offered in the film, and the Brenner chickens, at least, have the capacity to resist their natural appetites. They won't eat, even though nothing's wrong with their feed and they don't seem sick. The same is true of Fawcett's poultry. Moreover, if self-preservation is a paradigm of instinctual behavior, the film's birds are less "instinctual" than the humans. A gull with a "natural" survival mechanism wouldn't break its neck on Annie's front door (or smash into windows, phone boxes, cars . . .). Hitchcock depicts humans, on the other hand, as mostly exhibiting herd behavior.

---

and animals may also be a difference of degree, not of kind. Fido can fetch my paper or slippers when I ask for them, and when I say "Beg!" he doesn't roll over, and when I way "Roll over!" he doesn't beg (usually!). Hitch repeatedly draws our attention to the philosophically debatable topic of animal communication.

[13] *Second Discourse on the Origin of Inequality Among Men* (New York: St. Martin's Press, 1964), pp. 113–14.

So far from controlling their terror and rising above it, they generally succumb when provoked to blind panic and reflexive fight or flight responses.

Consider: When the first gull strikes Melanie in the dingy, Mitch says that it almost seemed to do so "deliberately." The townsfolk marvel that the birds seem to be *planning* a mass attack. But planning and deliberating require freedom and the power to choose among alternatives. On Melanie's first visit, Annie Hathaway asks of the birds, "Don't they ever stop migrating?" Migration is another clear-cut case of instinctive behavior. But Mitch also "migrates" as he commutes from San Francisco to Bodega Bay every weekend. A parallel is thus suggested between the patterns of humans and birds. Annie further mentions to Melanie that she'd wanted a cigarette for twenty minutes but couldn't stop working in the garden because "tilling the soil becomes compulsive." If humans have addictions, habits, and compulsions, how do these differ from instincts? Are we really freer than the birds? (Indeed, in their power of flight, birds symbolize freedom, as in the expression "free as a bird.") The film repeatedly depicts humans as trapped, locked up, caged, or behind fences (for example, the helpful clerk at the post office appears initially behind a wire enclosure; Melanie gets trapped in a phone booth; the family and Melanie are later hunkered down in the boarded-up Brenner house where Melanie is once again trapped in the upstairs room).[14] Unlike these jailbirds, Hitchcock depicts nearly all of the birds outside.

Philosophical discussions of freedom typically focus on either the question of "free will" or on broader political questions concerning social liberty. Let's see how the question of human uniqueness might be addressed in a more societal context.

---

[14] John Locke uses the example of being locked in a room to argue that freedom is not merely doing as we please. *An Essay Concerning Human Understanding,* Book II, Chapter 21, Section 10. Suppose Melanie was trapped in the room but was a masochist or deviant who found large, intimidating birds (especially cocks) erotic or exciting. That fact that she *loved* being in the room and didn't want to leave wouldn't mean she stayed freely. Although she would be doing what she wanted, she couldn't do otherwise. The difference between the turned-on Melanie and the terrified Melanie is not that one is free and one isn't, but that the one is lucky and the other unlucky. The fortunate Melanie *wants* to do the very thing she *must* do.

Birds of a Feather Flock Together

Aristotle maintains that man is by nature a political animal. He argues that a cityless man is on his own, like a solitary piece in a game. The checker that has been jumped and removed from play no longer has any significance; its meaning is wholly defined by its relationship to the other pieces and the board position at any given time. Politically detached humans are similar. We are defined by our roles and the place we occupy in others' lives. Thomas Hobbes, a seventeenth-century British philosopher, argued that only humans can enter genuine political communities. Prior to society humans exist in a "state of nature" without law, religion, or morality, and consequently, in a condition of perpetual war. To escape this inhospitable scene where life is "solitary, poor, nasty, brutish, and short" humans create a social contract. Under this covenant they surrender some of their freedom and agree neither to do, nor suffer, injury from one another. A sovereign is installed and authorized to use force to preserve the peace and enforce the agreement. In short, the government acquires, from the people and through their consent, a monopoly on the right to use violence. Though life in society requires us to forsake certain selfish tendencies, the liberty of average citizens is enhanced since they can now pursue happiness and prosperity under conditions of stability, peace, and security.

There's something to this view. An entirely lawless individual might be thought an inhuman or subhuman savage. Perhaps what makes us different from most animals—what makes them so utterly *other*—is that they're *wild* and we're not. In the early 1960s when *The Birds* was produced, however, racial strife and the struggle for equal rights were in full force. The Cold War had led to the Cuban missile crisis and Berlin Wall. In a time of great national divisions and confrontations, the possibility of obtaining reconciliation and security through a social contract seemed remote. Do we retain vestiges of barbarism that even society can't eradicate? *Is* it our nature to seek our own good through co-operation, renunciation and civility? Mrs. Bundy resists rumors of a mass bird attack partly because different species never flock together. The birds, however—both black and white—demonstrate in the film far more capacity for unity and integration than people. Although some might think humans unique in their capacity for social coordination, Mitch likens San Francisco to "an anthill at the foot of a bridge."

Hitchcock goes out of his way to show humans either breaking the law in the film or expressing little concern for it and ordinary standards of decency. For example, when Lydia's chickens won't eat she assumes Brinkmeyer sold her bad feed. Mitch, a lawyer, cites the principle: "*Caveat emptor,* mother." Lydia dismisses this with the comment, "Never mind the law." She further disparages the authorities when told that the Santa Rosa police had been summoned to investigate the Fawcett incident: "What good will they do?" At Davidson's pet store Mitch claims Melanie should have been put behind bars for a practical joke that caused a plate glass window to be broken. Yet another parallel between Melanie and the birds, who smash glass in various scenes.

Melanie several times faults Mitch's manners, even stooping to call him a louse (an epithet he accepts). Following the attack on Melanie in her rented skiff, Deke, afraid that she'd been hurt on his property, worries that he might be frivolously sued. Both Melanie and Lydia trespass, entering other's homes without the slightest qualms. In the film there are drunks, intruders, loudmouths, liars. During Melanie's visit to the Brenner home for dinner, Cathy, talking about Mitch's legal practice, states matter-of-factly that most of his clients are hoods. When Lydia defends him by saying that in a democracy, everyone is entitled to a fair trial, Cathy replies, "I know all about that democracy jazz; they're still hoods." She goes on to regale Melanie with the fact that one of her big brother's clients shot his wife in the head six times (for changing the channel during a ball game, Mitch adds with a laugh). In what sense then are we entitled to claim commitment to law as a defining and distinguishing characteristic of humanity? Is humanity a matter of degrees, with the virtuous and obedient having a greater share? Is obedience to law even always a good thing? When it isn't, is it better to be "inhuman" than human?

"Your Heavenly Father Feeds Them"

Some argue that humans are unique because of their special relationship with God, or by virtue of being made in God's image. We're distinct because God favors us over the rest of creation. After all, Jesus said we're worth more than many sparrows (Luke 12:7). While perhaps not strictly speaking a philosophical position, the view is worth commenting on since Hitchcock raises the issue so poignantly. Unfortunately, although we're partial to thinking we're like God and God loves us best, the film contradicts this comforting and romantic view.

The drunk in the Tides quotes the scripture: "the birds of the air neither sow nor reap, yet your heavenly father feeds them." God cares for all creatures. And what are the birds of the air being fed by God? People! Dan Fawcett's eyes! How then can we claim to be God's favorites? Because we go to church (or wherever) and pray? The drunk calls it "the end of the world." Revelation 19:17–18 describes Armageddon in part:

> And I saw an angel standing in the sun; and he cried out with a loud voice, saying to all the birds which fly in midheaven, "Come, assemble for the great supper of God; in order that you may eat the flesh . . . of all men, both free men and slaves, and small and great."

The gulls in Santa Cruz were said to be "drawn to the light." This is also the sheriff's explanation for the bizarre incident where hundreds of birds fly down the chimney of the Brenner home: Birds are attracted to the light. But Jesus, in the Gospels, is "the light of the world." So perhaps the birds also honor their creator in their own way. In the Gospels, the Holy Spirit descends as a dove at the moment of Jesus's baptism. This avian metaphor for the Holy Spirit has been retained in Christian iconography through the ages. And is it an accident that angels have wings? "But these foul fowl are evil!" I can almost hear you say. Well, the only thing *called* evil in the film is Melanie, after the mother blames her for the outbreak (though as I pointed out earlier, the mother is staring us, the viewers, straight in the eye, as if to say, "I think *you* are evil!")[15]

After the gas station explodes, there's a fascinating aerial view of the city, as gulls begin to gather for attack. Although one

---

[15] Durgnat suggests that "An emphasis on Hitchcock's moral severity might suggest that the birds are a metaphor for something evil in man, or an incarnation of his latent cruelty. . . . In their attack on the town they act mainly as catalysts. Human disunity, hatred and panic do most of the actual damage" (p. 339).

might regard the perspective as a "bird's eye" view, Hitchcock stated it was *God's* view—a perfectly objective shot.[16] But then, from God's point of view, the birds are in the sky—in Heaven—and the humans, down below and engulfed in flames—in Hell. True, in the end Melanie and the Brenners find salvation (or so we dare hope). The birds, however, are also saved.

Ultimately, Hitchcock doesn't refute the theories discussed in this chapter—all of which have merit and able defenders—so much as raise questions and suspense through challenging our preconceptions—about nature, what's possible, and ourselves. Reflection on *The Birds*—like philosophy itself—prompts self-reflection. Hitchcock said *The Birds* "could be the most terrifying motion picture I have ever made!"[17] Is anything more terrifying than really looking at oneself?

---

[16] From the DVD bonus material commentary, *About the Birds*, at 49:30.
[17] From the liner notes to the the Collector's Edition DVD.

7

Hitchcock's Existentialism: Anguish, Despair, and Redemption in *Breakdown*

SANDER LEE

The nightmare experience of being fully conscious yet taken for dead, and unable to communicate with those who are about to dispose of your body, is the climactic situation in *Breakdown*.

Breakdown was the seventh episode of Hitchcock's popular TV series, *Alfred Hitchcock Presents* (1955–65), and the first episode to be directed by Hitchcock himself.[1] The shows in this series echo some of the themes, both positive and negative, of Hitchcock's theatrical movies of the 1950s and early 1960s. All these works clearly articulate darker existential themes of dread, anguish, and despair. At times they also display more optimistic possibilities, like authenticity and freedom, inherent in the views of philosophers such as Martin Heidegger, Martin Buber, and Jean-Paul Sartre.

As in two of Hitchcock's films of the same period, *Rear Window* (1954) and *Vertigo* (1958), the protagonist in *Breakdown* experiences a near-fatal encounter that triggers anguish so profound it compels him to re-examine his life. He's initially afraid to confront his true feelings, but a sudden and terrifying life-threatening challenge acts as a catalyst to bring him face to face with his deepest fears.

---

[1] According to Donald Spoto, production for *Breakdown* took place on 7th–10th September, 1955. It was actually broadcast on 13th November, 1955. It's available on the DVD *Alfred Hitchcock Presents: Season One* (1955).

Strike First and Ask Questions Later

In his introduction to *Breakdown*, Hitchcock is seated at a table
reading a paperback book. He begins by observing that paperbacks will never replace hardbacks because, although they are
fine for reading, they make poor doorstops. By joking that the
primary advantage of hardback books over paperbacks lies in
their trivial ability to serve as doorstops, Hitchcock is able to
suggest both that his short television "plays" are no replacements for his feature films, yet, ultimately, the differences
between them are relatively trivial.

After praising Louis Pollack, the author of the short story on
which *Breakdown* is based, Hitchcock goes on to say that "like
the other plays of our series, it is more than mere entertainment.
In each of our stories we strive to teach a little lesson or point
a little moral, advice like mother used to give, you know, 'walk
softly but carry a big stick', 'strike first and ask questions later',
that sort of thing." He further instructs us that the play's message
is particularly relevant for those of us in the audience who have
ever "given an employee the sack," or who plan to do so. He
concludes with his usual joke at the expense of the sponsor,
telling us that we will see the play "after the sponsor's story
which, like ours, also strives to teach a little lesson or point a little moral."

Despite his jokes, Hitchcock has told us that *Breakdown*
resembles his feature films in all but trivial ways, and especially
in its ability "to teach a little lesson or point a little moral."
Furthermore, while humorously suggesting that its "lesson" is no
more significant than clichés justifying violence or commercials
urging unnecessary purchases, he nonetheless directs the audience's attention to the serious implications of the story we are
about to see.

Breakdown begins with overhead shots of Miami Beach,
eventually focusing on the scene of two men in robes reclining
in lounge chairs while a woman dressed in business attire takes
dictation from one of the men (Joseph Cotten). The phone rings
and the woman answers and gives the phone to Cotten telling
him that it's a call from the New York office.

The caller turns out to be an employee named Humka who
is responding to a note from his boss firing him. He begs his
boss, whom he calls "Mr. Callou" (Cotten), to reconsider.

Impatiently, Callou tells Humka that the reasons for firing him were clearly explained in the note. A corporate executive named Mr. Merlin had recommended his termination not because of any fault on his part, but in conformity with the implementation of a new sales policy. Humka argues that his work in accounting should not be dependent on policies in sales and, when Callou rejects this claim, Humka becomes openly emotional. He can't believe he is being fired after so many years in the same job and he demands that Callou tell him what he is to do. Callou retorts angrily, "Good Lord man, you're not being sent to Siberia." He explains that Humka will receive six months severance and tells him that there are other jobs. Humka responds by saying:

> Oh no, no Mr. Callou, there aren't for me. Don't you see? After all these years, the company is, well it's just like our own business. My whole family, my children feel they belong to it and it to them. I just can't go home and face them if this is true. . . . Don't you see, it's the upset, it's the suddenness. If a thing like this can happen, then I can't be sure of anything. . .anything! This is the last thing I thought could happen!

When he received the shocking note informing him of his termination, Humka assumed that it was the result of a foul plot carried out by an evil Merlin acting without the knowledge of his benign employer. So he instinctively reached out to his "Mr. Callou," the ultimate source of all authority, meaning, and justice in his world. Humka has based his life, and that of his family, on this belief in the fundamental fairness of the company. His call is like a prayer that he desperately needs to be answered.

I-Thou versus I-It

The Jewish theologian Martin Buber (1878–1965) has suggested that God only enters the lives of those who wish it. If one chooses to live one's life without God, then no evidence of his existence will appear. But once one chooses to open oneself up to the possibility of God, by initiating a genuine dialogue with Him, Buber claims that a true "I-Thou" relationship is possible. Buber contends that only by allowing oneself to be completely vulnerable before God can one construct an authentic and loving relationship with another person.

In Buber's terms, Humka calls to initiate an "I-Thou" dialogue with his god and is stunned when the all-powerful "Mr. Callou" treats him as a thing rather than a person. This rejection triggers a profound despair in Humka, a despair so great that we can't help worrying that he may be driven to suicide. What Humka doesn't realize is that Callou, far from being a god, is instead a self-obsessed man who has chosen to maintain an "I-It" relationship with the other people in his life, talking at them about his concerns as though they were inanimate listening posts. Rather than working to obtain a genuine discourse with others, he engages in what Buber calls "pseudo-listening."

As Humka becomes more emotional in his outburst, Callou holds the phone further and further from his ear as if to escape the intrusion of Humka's anguish. Because of this, Callou is slow to respond, leading Humka to conclude that something has gone wrong with the phone connection. Callou uses this as an excuse to hang up on him, to avoid his responsibility for Humka's anguished despair by shifting the blame onto a mere technological "breakdown."

After hanging up the phone, Callou and his nameless business colleague have the following exchange:

CALLOU: Imagine that, he was crying.

COLLEAGUE: I heard him.

CALLOU: I hate that kind of weakness.

COLLEAGUE: What do you expect, three cheers? After all, the bottom has just dropped out of the man's whole world.

CALLOU: He didn't have to weep about it. He should show some control of his emotions.

COLLEAGUE: Well, I suppose so, within reason. It's not a good idea to try to control them beyond a certain point. He may have saved himself from something worse by breaking down now.

CALLOU: Saved himself from something worse? Like what?

COLLEAGUE: Oh, I don't know, maybe from killing himself, maybe from hating you, maybe even from trying to kill you.

CALLOU: (*changing the subject*) Well, should we try for marlin this afternoon?

COLLEAGUE: I guess so.

CALLOU: If they're running, I may stay until tomorrow.

COLLEAGUE: You just can't sit on the beach and relax, can you?

CALLOU: I'd go nuts trying to do nothing but nothing.

Angst and Authenticity

Our first exposure to Callou reveals him to be just the sort of person whom the German philosopher Martin Heidegger (1889–1976) would describe as indifferent or inauthentic. Heidegger urges us to view our lives as inseparable from all that is around us, and, through the experience of dread or *angst* (a realization of one's genuine mortality), he describes how we are faced with the choice of either becoming authentic or inauthentic. The authentic person chooses to fulfill her true caring nature, even though this means exposing the vulnerable parts of herself to a world of others who can sometimes treat her harshly. The inauthentic person, by contrast, chooses to hide her real nature behind a mask designed to superficially avoid the demands of others without exposing her true self to the inspection of the world.

One senses that Callou has lived his whole life in this way. He cuts himself off from the rest of the world and classifies everyone (including himself) in terms that deny the genuine, ongoing connections between them. He hides his true feelings behind a mask of normalcy. His impatient characterization of Humka's despair as hateful "weakness" typifies his concealment of his own true feelings and the derivative nature of his smug philosophy of life. Thus, Callou's choice to live his life as an unfeeling person is epitomized by his reaction to Humka's "weakness." Rather than becoming emotional, he retains his composure, removing the source of the demands being made upon him by simply hanging up the phone, a response wholly inadequate to deal with Humka's desperate appeal for human understanding. When his colleague strikes too close to home in his analysis of the dangers of repressing one's emotions, Callou immediately changes the subject to fishing.

Bad Faith

We can also describe Callou using the work of the French philosopher Jean-Paul Sartre (1905–1980). Callou behaves in a manner that Sartre describes as 'bad faith'. Bad faith occurs when a person lies to himself and thereby refuses to accept his freedom and the responsibility that goes with it. One common form of bad faith discussed by Sartre derives from our desire to become simultaneously conscious (that is, free) and complete. We want to control everything, especially the reactions of others to ourselves, while maintaining the fiction that they choose to be with us, and admire us, of their own free will. In acting as though this desire is realizable, and in punishing others, such as Humka, when they fail to participate in this fantasy, Callou chooses to engage in self-deception. He must know that his goal of being godlike is unattainable, yet he pretends to himself that his egocentric actions are somehow justifiable.

We next see Callou sitting behind the wheel of his car driving back to New York on Route 1 (the fastest route available in 1955, and perhaps also significant because Callou is all about "number one"). Forced by a detour onto a narrow back road, Callou sees a guard up ahead urging members of a prison work detail to get into the back of a truck. As he tries to pass, a bulldozer unexpectedly emerges from a dirt road to his left, slamming into the driver's side of his car. The screen goes black. Images return initially through a foggy haze and we immediately become aware that the point of view of the film has shifted. Where before we watch Callou from the traditionally neutral third-person perspective, we now shift to the first-person. From this point on, we move back and forth from Callou's perspective to that of the third-person. Hitchcock makes the audience experience the confined nature of Callou's character.

Callou is initially alone and we hear his internal thoughts as a voice-over. Trapped behind the wheel of his car, Callou comes to realize that he is paralyzed, unable even to close his eyes.[2] Fighting the natural tendency to become hysterical in such circumstances, Callou struggles to evaluate his condition objectively, looking for practical strategies by which he can ensure his rescue to a hospital where trained professionals can analyze his body's breakdown and repair it. He systematically moves down a checklist to determine his exact condition (he can feel slight pressure on his chest, he can still hear, it's just quiet, and so on).

Callou ponders the fact that he appears to others as a dead body. This thought leads him to panic as he contemplates the possibility that he could be buried alive like a character from a

---

[2] A condition similar to that of the characters trapped in Hell in Sartre's famous play *No Exit*.

horror tale by Edgar Allen Poe. We hear him struggle to regain control as he reduces the problem to its most rational elements. This isn't a problem that can be solved by emotional outbursts; he must calmly think of a strategy to alert others that he is still alive. When he discovers that he can move the little finger on his left hand, he plans to tap it as loudly as possible to get his rescuers' attention. His opportunity comes when men from the sheriff's office finally arrive. The noise from the rescue vehicles, unfortunately, obscures his tapping and no one notices his moving finger when he is taken to the city morgue. Lying on a stretcher overnight with a sheet over his face, he is determined to get the coroner's attention with his finger in the morning. It may be his last chance to avoid the terrifying prospect of premature burial. "It's all right, I'm not going to break down . . . . It's just so long, so dark, very long, heavy." The shot of Callou's frozen face underneath the coroner's shroud is one of Hitchcock's most haunting images.

But Callou's practical strategy breaks down when, in the morning, he is unable to move his finger as the coroner and his assistant discuss his cause of death. As Callou realizes that he is lying on his hand and, therefore, his last hope for rescue is destroyed, he finally gives in to all the pent-up anguish that he has within him. This final breakdown is so massive that he uncontrollably begins to weep. Just as they are about to cover his face for the last time, the doctor notices a single tear streaming from one of Callou's eyes. Realizing that he is alive, the doctor moves off to get his instruments. His assistant, Jessie, reassures Callou by speaking directly to him for the first time since his accident. Looking into his eyes and smiling he says, "It's all right. Don't worry fellah, we know. You'll be all right. We'll take care of you." We see a first-person shot of the assistant's face with the tearstain running down the screen. "Thank God! Thank God!" Callou tells himself. With this, the screen goes black and the story ends.

This last scene gives us perhaps the best visual representation possible of the differences between Buber's "I-It" and "I-Thou" relationships. When they thought he was only a corpse, an inanimate object, the Doctor and Jessie examined him objectively, speculating on the reasons for his body's breakdown, much as mechanics might discuss a car that has stopped working. Once they discover that he is alive, Jessie immediately

moves into the personal mode, speaks directly and even intimately to Callou. Indeed, Jessie's words are the most compas-
sionate of the entire episode, the kind of words that Callou
should have spoken to Humka earlier.

The lesson of this story is clear. It is only when Callou has
given up all attempts to rationally control his fate that his salvation is possible. In Heidegger's terms, the accident triggers
Callou's experience of existential *Angst,* and with it the "call to
conscience." While Callou refuses to answer the call by inau-
thenically clinging to his mask of rationality, he is doomed to
the horrific prospect of premature burial. It's only at the end,
when he reveals his "caring," that he shows himself to others as
an authentic self, one deserving of concern.

And, as Buber suggests, once one chooses to be completely
vulnerable, he opens himself up to the possibility of initiating a
genuine dialogue with God. This is why Callou is able at the end
to thank God. By finally allowing himself to be emotionally
naked before God, he may now be able to construct authentic
and loving relationships with other people. Although the story
ends with this revelation, one cannot help but think that Callou
has undergone a Scrooge-like transformation after which he will
be a more humane boss. One imagines that his first act after
regaining the use of his voice will be to call Humka, apologize
for his earlier insensitivity, and re-hire him. Callou will also,
however, be forced to endure a painful process of re-adjustment
to his broken physical condition.

While one could argue that Callou's "callous" treatment of
Humka has no causal connection to the horrible fate that befalls
him in the auto accident, Hitchcock has made it very clear in his
introduction that the two are meant to be connected so that the
story might "teach a little lesson or point a little moral."
Hitchcock has even told us "that the play's message is particularly relevant for those of us in the audience who have ever
'given an employee the sack', or who plan to do so." In this
way, he unmistakably asserts that Callou's misfortunes are the
direct result of his behavior towards Humka. Such immediate
and deserved divine punishment may not be evident in the real
world. But in Hitchcock's "company," like that of Mr. Callou, he
is the deity, the ultimate source of all authority, meaning, and
justice in his aesthetic realm. While Humka's faith in Callou was
misplaced, our faith in Hitchcock, as moral *auteur,* is not.

In his final remarks, Hitchcock humorously compares his own situation to that of Callou. Trapped inside the television set, Hitchcock tells us that his survival depends on our willingness to avoid the impulse to literally turn him off. Hitchcock thereby jokingly implies that he too is filled with Heideggerean dread at the prospect of death (non-being). As a TV image, he has had the added misfortune of actually experiencing nothingness and returning to tell the tale. His pretend terror at the prospect of the television being turned off, a fate which we know befalls him after the show every week, humorously reinforces our genuine fears that even a momentary end of being is a horror beyond our collective imagination.[3]

Existential themes permeate much of Hitchcock's work of the 1950s both in television and film. In *Breakdown,* as in the films *Rear Window* and *Vertigo,* a man experiences an accident that eventually forces him to confront his fears, resulting in an honest acceptance of the vital role played by our feelings in the creation of a meaningful life. A Stoical disciplining of emotions must not stifle authentic living or the capacity for human sympathy.[4]

---

[3] In *The Purple Rose of Cairo* (1985), Woody Allen makes use of the same joke when he has a character in a film beg the manager of the movie theater not to turn off the projector: "No, no! Don't turn the projector off! No, no, it gets black and we disappear. . . . But you don't understand what it's like to disappear, to be nothing, to be annihilated!" Even fictional characters are plagued by the same sorts of existential ghosts that haunt "real" contemporary artists such as Allen and Hitchcock. For a fuller discussion of Allen's films, see my *Eighteen Woody Allen Films Analyzed: Anguish, God and Existentialism* (2002).

[4] While *Breakdown* and *Rear Window* agree on this point, *Vertigo* presents a more complex picture. In that film the quest to uncover and experience one's inner feelings and desires may in fact open the door to unimagined horrors and leave us permanently stranded, like the film's protagonist Scotty, on the precipice of an abyss. For a fuller discussion of these issues, see my essays: *Alfred Hitchcock: Misogynist or Feminist?* In *Post Script: Essays in Film and the Humanities* 9:3 (Summer 1990); *Existential Themes in the Films of Alfred Hitchcock* (Philosophy Research Archives, Volume XI, 1985).

III

The Reeling Mind

8

Vertigo and the Pathologies of Romantic Love

NOËL CARROLL

Vertigo by Alfred Hitchcock appears to be one of those films that could not sustain a second look. Once one has had the opportunity to reflect upon its plot machinations—once one gets free of the emotional undertow of the hot-wired ending—you would think that all of its incredible improbabilities would leap out, making a second viewing, if not impossible, then, at least, risible.

Isn't the plot within the plot just too absurd, practically speaking? Gavin Elster's scheme is so clever it's dumb. So many things could have gone wrong (and, if it wasn't a film, they would have).

For example, if John 'Scottie' Ferguson is such a good detective, what's the likelihood that he would not, sooner or later, have discovered the real Mrs. Elster in her home away from town? Wouldn't a smart investigator—and the film assures us that Scottie is smart—do enough background sleuthing and interviewing to realize that there are one too many Madeleine Elsters? And how can Elster be so sure that Scottie will flee the scene of the crime, thereby allowing him and Judy Barton to slip away? Would a murderer really rest the entire success of his plot on the likelihood that Scottie would be overtaken by vertigo on the stairway? What if Scottie didn't look down? And, in any event, recall that Scottie almost makes it to the very top. One more flight and the jig would have been up for Elster and Judy. Surely Elster's plan is implausibly risky; it is way too baroque.

Nor are there only problems with the crime plot. Almost as soon as the film ends, inquiring minds want to know how

Scottie ever got off that rooftop after his first bout of vertigo. And, with respect to the second story, one wonders, if Scottie and "Madeleine" were intimate in the first part of the film, how then does he fail to recognize that Judy feels the same, has the same beauty marks, freckles, and blemishes, kisses the same, smells the same, and so on, the second time around? *The New Yorker* called the film "far-fetched."[1]

Perhaps on an initial viewing of *Vertigo*, the amazing serendipity of it all is masked by the affective velocity of the narrative. But surely upon a second encounter with *Vertigo*, most viewers should be emotionally sober enough to find almost laughable the frictionless clicking into place of the various parts of this Rube Goldberg plot. And yet we don't. Many keep coming back for more, regarding *Vertigo* as among Hitchcock's greatest accomplishments, if not his greatest. It cannot be the rickety thriller plot that accounts for this acclaim. What does?

My suggestion is that what viewers find so compelling about *Vertigo* is not the mystery story, which is so patently contrived, but the love story. For the love story—or, more accurately, the love stories—provide the audience with the opportunity to engage in a carefully structured meditation on the nature of romantic love. Specifically, *Vertigo* enables the viewer to discover certain of the pathologies to which romantic love is *naturally prone*, given the sort of process romantic love is. *Vertigo* deserves its reputation less as a masterpiece of suspense and more as a contribution to the philosophy of love.

Aristotle, Philosophy, and Drama

In his *Poetics*, Aristotle observes that "poetry [drama] is something more philosophic and graver than history, since its statements are rather of the nature of universals, whereas those of history are singulars. By a universal statement I mean one as to what such and such a kind of man will probably or necessarily say or do, which is the aim of poetry."[2] In other words, accord-

---

[1] See the liner notes to *Vertigo: The Collector's Edition* from *The Alfred Hitchcock DVD Collection* (Universal City: Universal, 1996).

[2] Aristotle, "Dramatic Imitation: from the *Poetics*," in *Aesthetics: A Critical Anthology*, edited by George Dickie and Richard Sclafani (New York: St. Martins Press, 1977), p. 214.

ing to Aristotle, drama (including literature and, for us, the motion picture) is not constrained to portray precisely what actually happens in all its detail; drama streamlines events (or event-types), pruning them of distracting clutter, in a way that makes their recurring patterns salient. Just as an overhead map provides us with a more legible picture of the way to our destination than is evident on the ground, drama may provide us with a clearer view into the dynamics of human affairs than that available first-hand from messy reality.

Of course, drama is more concrete than philosophy. Undoubtedly, this is one of the reasons why it is more accessible than philosophy; it engages emotion and judgment with vivid particulars (which is exactly what our pragmatic human mentality is most suited to deal with). But a drama is, at the same time, a concrete *universal.* For, it still trades in abstractions—character-types, for example, like Iago, who clarify certain human personality tendencies by being designed in such a way that any features are omitted from the portrayal of the character that might deter us from seeing him squarely as the *kind* of person who revels in evil for its own sake. Such characters are the epitome or paradigm of the human potentials they exemplify. They are ideal types.

But poetry not only supplies us with an inventory of possible human personality types and the schematics of their underlying syndromes; it also sketches the kinds of behavioral scenarios that are likely to evolve when certain character-types interact—when, for instance, two headstrong people, like Antigone and Creon, each convinced of their own rectitude, find themselves on opposite sides of an issue. (It's not pretty.)

Aristotle thought that drama could help us understand potential or probable courses of human events by illustrating (as ideal types) the kinds of people there are or can be, as well as the patterns of behavior that are likely to take shape when those kinds of people interact. Scottie and Judy are types of the sort Aristotle had in mind. And *Vertigo* is an exploration of how things are likely to go when these two types attempt to negotiate a relationship.

Obviously, *Vertigo* is primarily a love story. Effectively, the crime provides a pretext for the courtships. The amount of screen time that is lavished on the two love affairs is far greater than that allotted to the murder and its solution. Though *Vertigo* is typically classified as a suspense film, it is more accurately thought of as a romance. But it is not just the time spent on the two affairs that marks *Vertigo* as a love story. It is also the peculiar intensity of the passions involved, especially as they are annotated by the lush, often sentimentally charged musical score by Bernard Hermann. Though Hitchcock is typically acknowledged to be the master of suspense, his range is much greater. He is also an astute observer of amorous obsession, as many of his other films, including *Notorious, The Paradine Case,* and *Marnie,* attest. *Vertigo,* quite simply, is his most impressive treatment of the subject of the darker side of love.

Earlier it was alleged that *Vertigo* is a contribution to the philosophy of love. But how, it might be asked (in a skeptical tone of voice), can a narrative movie like this one contribute to the philosophy of anything? No generalizations are propounded and, in any event, even had they been uttered, without accompanying argumentation, some would maintain that they would scarcely count as genuine philosophy. And yet, in virtue of its structure, *Vertigo* is able to engage its audiences in thinking about love and to guide them forcefully to certain insights regarding its nature, including, most significantly, its inherent fault lines.

Vertigo does not stage this meditation outright after the fashion of a René Descartes. Rather, it presents the audience with a structure that elegantly prompts the viewer to think about love in both its brighter and its darker aspects. That structure, of course, is the "double" romance: the first putatively between Scottie and Madeleine, and then the ostensibly different one between Scottie and Judy Barton. By juxtaposing these two affairs sequentially, the film invites—even nudges—viewers to compare and contrast them. Though, perhaps needless to say, our assessment in this matter must be revisited by the conclusion of the film, nevertheless, as the film begins to unfold, we are introduced to something that at least initially appears to us as akin to a normal love relationship, which then we can later use to locate what is going horribly awry when Scottie meets Judy.

That is, by means of the parallel romances, *Vertigo* enlists the viewer as a co-creator in an analysis of love and its predictable malaises. The analysis of romantic love is not articulated in the film by a character nor announced from on high by a voice-over narrator. Rather the film presents us with two love stories whose convergences and divergences are so entwined that it is hard to imagine a thoughtful viewer who does not take up the invitation to compare and contrast the two scenarios for the purpose of making note of what is healthy and unwholesome about them.

The analysis of love and its pathologies available from *Vertigo* is worked out in the mind of the viewer. *Vertigo* neither performs the analysis itself nor does it offer any evidence for its conception of love. Rather, *Vertigo* maieutically draws the evidence and reasoning that supports its philosophy of love from the viewers, as Socrates educes geometry from the slave in the *Meno*. (The word "maieutic" comes from the Greek and pertains to the action of a midwife drawing an infant from the mother's body during birth. The word is also traditionally used to refer metaphorically to the process by which Socrates prompts insights from his interlocutors, such as Meno, who, by using their own resources, answer the questions and problems Socrates poses for them to solve.)

In *Vertigo,* the parallel-romance structure functions in a way comparable to a rhetorical or leading question. It elicits conclusions by recruiting the ratiocination and the standing beliefs of the audience to do the pertinent work of reasoning and analysis.

Love and Fantasy

What is perhaps most striking to us about these parallel cases is that what is pathological in the second affair is also something that is present as a natural ingredient in the first affair, namely, fantasy. What *Vertigo* succeeds in illustrating so compellingly is that a natural, facilitating component of romantic love can also be the very thing that derails it. Fantasy can be the glue that cements lovers together or that which destroys the very possibility of genuine love.

Although it may strike you as fairly obvious that fantasy— such as Scottie's projection of his memory of Madeleine onto Judy—is a recipe for romantic disaster, it may seem bizarre to claim that fantasy has a rightful place in normal love. And yet it does in several different registers.[3] Most obviously, sexual fan-

---

[3] For an account of the role of fantasy in romantic love, see Robert Solomon, *About Love: Reinventing Romance for Our Times* (Lanham: Rowman and Littlefield, 1994), pp. 153–160.

tasies energize the onset of infatuation and keep it going. Indeed, sexual fantasizing persists throughout most enduring love relationships.

But romantic love involves more than sexual fantasy. In the early stages of infatuation, whenever apart, the lovers dream of being back together again. Falling in love is essentially future-orientated; it involves the counterfactual anticipation of spending more time with the beloved and eventually of imagining a life together. So, romantic love is born in fantasy.

And once love blossoms, each lover must mobilize the imagination in order to picture what it is that will win the heart of the beloved and then he or she proceeds to act in accordance with that image. Courtship typically requires role playing from both parties. They must envision what will count as their "best behavior" in the eyes of their partner and then enact it. It is a matter of mutually reinforcing seduction in which both lovers imaginatively transform themselves—generally by expanding upon qualities they already presently possess or that are potentially readily within their reach. It is rare that a successful romantic relationship flourishes where the participants do not try—at least to some degree—to stoke the fantasies of each other.

Moreover, romantic love requires as a condition for its very existence a certain feat of imagination—that the lovers transcend their conception of themselves as absolutely discrete individuals and imagine themselves as one; that each of the lovers takes the interest of the beloved's to be his or her own. This involves an essential transformation of one's conception of oneself, a transformation that in large part requires going beyond what is factually given. The lovers must imagine that they are literally two parts of a larger whole.

But this is not the end of it. For, fantasy is also what enables the lovers to grow, both as a couple and as individuals. A feature of love, identified by writers like Stendhal, is the tendency of lovers to idealize the beloved.[4] Within bounds, this sort of fantasy is a very good thing. For, it encourages the beloved to live up to the idealization of the significant other. This is what the ancient Greeks, like Aristotle, thought was a virtue of certain forms of male-to-male love. The love of a virtuous partner pro-

---

[4] Stendhal, *Love* (London: Penguin, 1975).

vides an incentive to improve—to make oneself as attractive in every way as the beloved imagines one can be. Thus, if everything goes right in this process of mutual idealization, not only is each member of the couple enhanced, but the couple itself becomes something larger and greater.

Falling in Love

As we first start following the budding relationship between Scottie and the woman we suppose to be Madeleine Elster, we are led to believe that, though "Madeleine" is troubled, the ensuing romance is a normal one—at least by Hollywood standards. Fantasy, of what initially appears to be the benign sort, seems clearly at work. It is undoubtedly a mark of Hitchcock's genius that he is in large measure able to communicate this cinematically.

Idealization comes into play when Scottie first encounters "Madeleine" at Ernie's restaurant. Hitchcock has the actress Kim Novak, in profile, freeze in a portrait-like pose for Scottie's first close-up glimpse of her. Remember that this is Scottie's subjective point of view. To him, she appears to have the perfection of a work of art. Throughout the portion of the film where he is following her, he observes her sitting still, composed as if a statue (his Galatea). And she is expressly compared to a painting, namely the one of Carlotta Valdes. Seen from Scottie's perspective, "Madeleine" strikes us visually as a human artwork. This is one way that Hitchcock conveys that Scottie is coming to idealize her.

In one of the most famous moments early in the film, Scottie follows "Madeleine" into the somewhat drab, rear entrance of a building. When he peeks through the door that she has just closed behind her, there is a wondrous burst of color. She is in a florist's shop and there are bright flowers everywhere. The contrast with the muted palette in previous shots is striking. One feels that one has just been introduced to a new realm. What has been saliently marked is the exfoliation of Scottie's fantasy. The pronounced color, like that of the land of the Wizard of Oz, in the film of the same name, suggests that we are within Scottie's mind, privy to his subjectivity.

Hitchcock also conveys the feeling of fantasy by the way in which he orchestrates the sequences of Scottie tailing the fake Madeleine. The very activity of trailing someone is itself virtually obsessional. But, in addition, the gliding camera, the gliding cars, the absence of street noise, the rhythmic music, punctuated by silence, and the regular alternation of Scottie's point-of-view shots with long shots of "Madeleine's" car are mesmerizing, almost hypnotic. It is as if we are inside a trance. Indeed, the use of lighting, including mist, and color throughout give the film a dreamlike texture, where the trance and the dream, of course, belong, first and foremost, to Scottie.

After "Madeleine's" "attempted" suicide, the two speak and they begin to weave what seems to be a lovers' web of mutual fantasy. Scottie comes to regard "Madeleine's" welfare as his own. He begins to play the role of her "knight in shining armor."[5] He reaches beyond himself and becomes her designated "rescuer."[6] And "Madeleine's" mysteriously phrased, parting words to Scottie rehearse a lover's counterfactual wish for a future together; she says "I loved you and I wanted to go on loving you."

If fantasy appears to be a natural and even healthy part of romance as *Vertigo's* first love story unfolds, it is precisely what wrecks the second love affair. After Scottie is released from the hospital where he was treated for a mental breakdown following the death of Madeleine Elster, Scottie begins revisiting the places where he first encountered her. Standing outside the florist shop mentioned earlier, he chances to see Judy, a woman who despite her dark hair and somewhat vulgar demeanor bears a resemblance to the very blonde, regal "Mrs. Elster." At this point in the film, neither Scottie nor the audience is aware that the reason for the similarity is that this *is* the woman Scottie fell in love with earlier. She was hired by the husband of the real

---

[5] Minus Jung's commitment to archetypical men and women (the animus and the anima), the following quotation could serve as a partial summary of *Vertigo*: "Just as the animus projection of a woman can often pick on a man of real significance who is not recognized by the mass, and can actually help him to achieve his true destiny with her moral support, so a man can create for himself a *femme inspiratrice* by his anima projection. But more often it turns out to be an illusion with destructive consequences. . . ." See Carl Jung, "Marriage as a Psychological Relationship," in *The Philosophy of (Erotic) Love,"* edited by Robert Solomon and Kathleen Higgins (Lawrence: University of Kansas Press, 1994), p. 187.

[6] In the first half of the film, Scottie is led to believe that "Madeleine" is confused, often lost, helpless, and virtually without agency. He must take over. In a way, though with opposite effect, he acts in the same manner with the same beliefs with respect to Judy. He treats her as though she were without agency.

Madeleine Elster to impersonate his wife in the elaborate murder plot alluded to previously.

Scottie follows Judy to her apartment and begins to woo her. He invites her to dinner. Despite the risk of being discovered as an accomplice to murder, Judy agrees to go out with Scottie. As she confesses in a letter she never gives to him, "I made the mistake of falling in love with you" and "I want you so to love me . . . as I am myself." They have dinner—at Ernie's, of course. We know, as does Judy, that Scottie is still obsessed with "Madeleine," since we observe the way that his attention fastens upon a blonde woman in a grey suit who, from afar, vaguely resembles the alleged Mrs. Elster.

Scottie wants to see Judy again. "I want to be with you as much as I can, Judy," he says to her as she sits in her apartment—a darkened silhouette (recalling his first close-up glimpse of "Madeleine"). At first, their love affair goes smoothly. They appear very happy simply being with each other—sightseeing, strolling along a canal, and dancing together. He buys her flowers on the street.

But Scottie insists on buying Judy clothes. He describes with utter precision the kind of gray suit he is looking for to the manager at a fashionable women's clothing store. Needless to say, it is the kind of suit that "Madeleine" wore. Scottie's voice quavers with mounting frustration as he rejects outfit after outfit, until the one he wants is finally identified. It is an emotionally harrowing scene. Scottie's obsession is tangible. He reduces Judy to tears. She pleads "Couldn't you like me just the way I am?" but caves in to his will: "Well I'll wear the darn clothes, if you want me to, if you'll just like me." He also orders an evening dress, just like "Madeleine's," and wants it altered immediately.

His fixation does not abate with clothing; he wants Judy's hair dyed and coiffed like "Madeleine's," as well. Judy agrees conditionally: "If I let you change me, will it do it, if I do what you tell me, will you love me?"[7] In a final attempt at resistance, Judy does not pin her hair up as Madeleine did, but Scottie won't stop pleading. Judy relents and when she steps out of the bathroom, she looks exactly as she did when she feigned being Madeleine Elster. Hitchcock illuminates her in such a way that

---

[7] See Charles Barr, *Vertigo* (London: British Film Institute, 2002), p. 71.

as she walks out of an overexposed patch of the image into an evenly lit portion she looks like a ghost being incarnated in flesh—an illusion coming to life.

At this point and in short order, the crime plot takes over again. Scottie figures out that Judy was the woman he thought was Mrs. Elster and that she conspired with Mr. Elster, who may have been Judy's lover, in the phony suicide. Scottie drags Judy to the scene of the crime—a bell tower in an old mission— where he wraps up the whodunit part of the story. The truth ruins their relationship, and, to make matters worse, Judy, "spooked" by a curious nun she appears to take to be Mrs. Elster's ghost, falls to her death from the campanella.[8]

The second love story is far more compelling and even scarier than the crime story. As Scottie seeks to remake Judy in Madeleine's image, one can virtually sense that what he is doing is deeply wrong. It is antithetical to true love, because it involves a denial of the uniqueness and particularity of the beloved. A lover is not a type. That is why one's lover is always strictly irreplaceable. In refusing to see Judy in terms of who she actually is, Scottie turns their relationship into a perversion of love, in spite of the fact that Judy repeatedly and pointedly begs him to love her as she is.

Earlier, it was asserted that healthy love involves a degree of fantasy in the form of idealization. So the question here is: what is the difference between the sort of legitimate romantic fantasy we've called idealization and what Scottie is doing? Idealization, when it is healthy and productive, has a basis in reality—a basis in the real potential of the beloved. It acknowledges who the beloved is and values that, rather than treating the beloved as an instrument in the service of one's own needs. Scottie, in projecting his image of Madeleine on Judy, is blind to who Judy really is.

Though there is a fine line between these operations of fantasy, idealization in the good sense builds upon what can already be found either actually or potentially in the beloved. It enhances—but in a way that remains tied to reality—our view of our significant other. But the sort of fantasy that drives Scottie is blinding. He refuses to see Judy for who she is, despite her

---

[8] Their relationship has been destroyed by the "ghost of Madeleine Elster."

repeated appeals. Such a relationship is doomed. Perhaps we can interpret the violent ending of the film allegorically as the objective correlative of the destructive violence Scottie's fantasy has wreaked upon their love affair.

When Henry Higgins transforms Liza Doolittle in *My Fair Lady*, one has the feeling that he is bringing out the best in her.[9] But Scottie is imposing something on Judy that she is not. He is more of a tyrant than a lover, and the palpable cruelty of what he is doing is constantly underscored by her recurring pleas that he love her as she is.[10] Unfortunately, Judy, though she understands too well that there is something profoundly flawed in her relationship with Scottie, cannot resist him. She becomes an enabler, facilitating the projective fantasy with which Scottie burdens her. She is thus participating in her own spiritual death as an individual with a claim to be loved for herself—a plight perhaps symbolized by her literal fall from the tower. Whereas "Madeleine Elster" was reputedly possessed by Carlotta in the first part of the film, Judy Barton is possessed by Scottie in the second part.[11]

Of course, the revelation of the murder plot impels us to reconsider the meaning of the first love story. Seen in retrospect, the theme of fantasy is even more evident, since Scottie is literally caught in an illusion fabricated by Gavin Elster and enacted by Judy. Ironically, Judy becomes her own worst rival by seducing Scottie so magnificently in the guise of Madeleine; her imaginative performance as Madeleine abets Scottie's creation of the distorting idealization that will foreclose the possibility of any lasting amorous relationship between them. For, the combination of an enabler like Madeleine/Judy and a projective fantasist like Scottie is as toxic as the relationship between an Antigone and a Creon—in both cases, catastrophe seems unavoidable when personality types like these come in contact.

---

[9] Henry Higgins is working on behalf of Liza's interests, if rather roughly, and Liza knows it. Scottie, in a way that is inimical to genuine love does not incorporate Judy's interests as his own (nor does he even seem to acknowledge that she has autonomous interests) and she, moreover, is in denial regarding Scottie's behavior.

[10] In *The Second Sex* (New York: Knopf, 1952), Simone de Beauvoir discusses the ways in which the idealization of the husband by the wife can turn into a form of persecution for the former. In *Vertigo*, the man's idealization of the woman leads to her persecution.

[11] One might argue that it is Gavin Elster who really "possesses" Judy in the first part of the film. For, not only is she probably a kept woman, but he takes/makes over her identity as well.

Scottie seems to represent an especially unstable personality type. Through Midge, we derive the impression that he is wary of commitment. When he tells her that he is "still available," the look on Midge's face indicates disbelief, as though she thinks that he is deceiving himself. Scottie's vertigo, symbolically, may be a literalization of the notion that he is afraid of *falling in love*. And this anxiety, in turn, may help explain why he is prone to the kind of pathological projection that he inflicts upon Judy. It is his fear of engaging with another individual that prompts him to confect a surrogate fantasy in her stead. His "Pygmalion-complex" is a defense mechanism, a syndrome fending off romantic vertigo.[12]

If Scottie's behavior grows out of a resistance to love, Judy's self-destructive complicity with his fantasy arises from her need to be loved. But this is no way for her to realize her own hopes and desires, for it will not result in Scottie's loving *her*. So, to a certain extent, she is as delusional as he is.

Vertigo presents us with two recognizable character types. Let us call them the projector (the projective fantasist) and the enabler. And the film goes on to sketch with great clarity the predictable scenario that is apt to evolve when these two types come together and fuel each other's worst tendencies. Admittedly, the pathologies Scottie and Judy exemplify are pitched larger than life. They are far more perspicuous than the instances of these syndromes that one is likely to experience in the daily run of events. But it is a major function of drama to magnify and thereby clarify the patterns that shape human affairs, in order that we may be prepared to discern such regularities when they appear less diagrammatically in the flesh.

Knots

Drama, including ciné-drama, has the power to reveal the probable patterns of human affairs that eventuate when certain char-

---

[12] The expression "falling in love" suggests a loss of control. Scottie's romantic vertigo impels him to re-exert utter control over Judy by transforming her in accordance with his fantasy. See: Garrett Soden, *Falling: How Our Greatest Fear Became Our Greatest Thrill* (New York: Norton, 2003), p. 15. There is some evidence that those who literally fear falling are often averse to risks in other domains of life, including, perhaps, love. Fear of falling and fear of falling in love, that is, may in some cases be actually connected.

acter-types interact. Such drama is a kind of chemistry of the human heart that discloses which combinations of personalities are likely to be stable patterns and which are apt to be unstable patterns. Some of these patterns may take, among other things, the form of what the psychiatrist R.D. Laing called "knots"— situations where motives become so tangled that acting on them brings, through an almost inexorable albeit "crazy" logic, exactly the opposite result than the one you had hoped for.[13] That is precisely the sort of trap in which the enabler Judy has enmeshed herself by loving a projective fantasist such as Scottie. Moreover, it is a large part of the achievement of *Vertigo* that it is able to show us how this kind of knot—with its inevitably self-defeating "logic"—can be tied so neatly.

Undoubtedly there are readers who may argue that I have exaggerated *Vertigo's* contribution to the theory of love. Surely, some philosophers will say, the ill-suitedness of an enabler to a projector is no great discovery at all. Isn't it common knowledge?

Three things need to be said in response to this. First, when *Vertigo* premiered, we—especially the *we* of the general public—were far less sophisticated about the nature of love than we think we are now. Perhaps some or even many of us possess the understanding of certain aspects of love that *Vertigo* proffers because we have seen *Vertigo*. Second: philosophizing-through-the-movies is for the general public and not for the graduate seminar room of the research university. So *Vertigo* may in fact still be philosophically revelatory for its target audience. For, lastly, *Vertigo* may assist them in clarifying an insight into the ways of romantic love of which they were only dimly aware, if at all. That is, by means of *Vertigo*, Hitchcock lucidly demonstrates how fantasy, a natural part of romantic love, can become pathologically distorted by certain personality types to the point that love is destroyed.[14]

---

[13] R.D. Laing, *Knots* (New York: Vintage, 1970).

[14] I am not the only commentator to recognize *Vertigo* as an exploration of the ways in which the mechanisms of romantic idealization can lead to the denial of the otherness, the interests, and the autonomy of the putative love object. For a related, though more psychoanalytically inclined account, see: Robin Wood, *Hitchcock's Films Revisited* (New York: Columbia University Press, 1989), p. 385 and also Barr, p. 78.

9

Vertigo: Scientific Method, Obsession, and Human Minds

DAN FLORY

What does a pathological fear of heights have to do with how well we know a person's mind? According to one way of understanding Alfred Hitchcock's *Vertigo*, a great deal. Because it operates as a character study as well as a suspense thriller, this 1958 film enables us to examine the complicated interrelations between phobia, obsession, and rational thinking. The film presents a character who reveals in devastating detail the unacceptable costs of one seemingly practical, straightforward approach that people often presume to be helpful in tackling how we know others, yet crucially fails because it cannot detect the role that turbulent emotions may have in guiding our lives. In this manner *Vertigo* may be examined for the ways it exposes defects of comprehending the intricate mental activity of ordinary human beings according to a way of thinking that is oblivious to much of the human mind's actual workings. By virtue of its focus on these matters, the film serves as a vivid illustration of what *not* to do when seeking to know certain crucial aspects of a person's mind.

Philosophers and Zombies

Philosophers have long speculated about the proper conditions for knowing the human mind, that traditionally nonphysical entity which—for most people, anyway—typically guides their behavior. At times thinkers have derived startling insights even while exploring seemingly bizarre and unlikely dimensions of this puzzle. For example, what philosophers call "the problem

of other minds" took on much greater seriousness after the sev-
enteenth century, once the famous French philosopher René
Descartes skeptically speculated that the people outside his window might be mere automata wearing "hats and cloaks."[1] More
recently, philosophers have hypothesized about the possibility
of "philosophical zombies," which according to David Chalmers
need to be carefully distinguished from other kinds, such as
those of the Hollywood and Haitian variety. Philosophical zombies are creatures that appear physically identical to humans and
act just like them, but are utterly dead inside. Rather than being
motivated by thought, desire, or feeling, philosophical zombies
act without any sort of mental phenomena occurring. Some
philosophers have even proposed that each of us carries our
own "zombie within" in order to account for motor responses.[2]
Thinking about the human mind and its complexities, especially
over the last few decades, has taken philosophers places most
of us would never have imagined.

Yet philosophy is by no means the only place where questions of how we understand human minds have been
addressed. In particular, *Vertigo* reflects ideas about this matter
carefully enough that even philosophical zombie theorists
would do well to ponder its narrative. As a film about a character who works desperately to understand not only the convo-
luted workings of others' minds but those of his own as well,
Vertigo may be interpreted "epistemologically," by which I mean
it may be understood as exploring different possibilities of what
knowledge might be and how we acquire it. Epistemology is the
study of knowledge at its most general level, focusing on questions of how we might best characterize secure human beliefs
and what we must do to obtain them. Also called theory of
knowledge, epistemology has been a crucial part of Western
philosophy at least since Socrates in the fifth century B.C.E.,
whose concerns often focused around what knowledge is and
how we acquire it.

While a seemingly straightforward area outlined by simple
questions, epistemology has developed into a field of startling

---

[1] René Descartes, "Second Meditation," in *Meditations on First Philosophy* (Indianapolis:
Bobbs-Merrill, 1960 [1641]), p. 31.
[2] See "Zombies on the Web," compiled by David Chalmers, at http://consc.net/zom-
bies.html.

depth and complexity, particularly in the era following Descartes's skeptical speculations in his *Meditations*. One area of special interest to modern philosophers is how we know human minds, what they do, and why. What indicates that other minds besides our own exist? Why don't we generally believe that what seem to be other human beings aren't really automata wearing hats and cloaks, as Descartes proposed? How do we know that we ourselves exist, or can think and feel? Exploring these questions has at times compelled thinkers to reflect on such science-fiction-like possibilities as brains in vats or the zombies described previously, since their hypothetical status holds out the promise of telling us something revealing about what counts as a human mind and how it operates.

These questions are not matters that concern only dreamy, head-in-the-clouds philosophers. On the contrary, the accuracy and effectiveness of responses we provide to such questions have major implications for our day-to-day lives, something that *Vertigo* compellingly illustrates. How we relate and respond to others depend crucially on the ways in which we perceive them as human beings—whether we recognize them as having minds like our own, with thoughts, feelings, and desires just like we have, or even whether we consider their mental activity to deserve the same consideration and respect that we wish for ourselves. Such presumptions are easily seen at work in gender and racial relations of the recent past. When some people did not perceive women or people of color as having mental lives equivalent to their own, they typically presumed this alleged inferiority as legitimate grounds for treating these other individuals as less than fully equal.

The ways in which we presume our own minds work may also have profound influences on how we treat humanity in our own case. For example, I may think of myself as weak or soft because I regard emotions as debilitating flaws to be overcome in my efforts to become a better person. Instead, what I aspire to be—a manly individual firmly in control of his feelings, who lurks deep beneath layers of sentimentality, flab, and sagging muscle—has no need for sensitivity to such frivolous responses. Yet because I see myself as often yielding to my emotions, I lack self-respect and consider myself as less than I should be. Such an understanding of how my mind works and what is of value in it would have a profound impact on my overall self-regard.

The Hardheaded Scot

These matters of understanding how human minds operate and what counts as valuable in them may be seen at work in *Vertigo*'s narrative. The film's protagonist, John "Scottie" Ferguson (James Stewart), thinks that all one need know about someone are observable facts, details that one might glean from watching a person or looking at something written in a file. To obtain a proper understanding of that person, one organizes these details "scientifically" into an explanation deduced from "the facts." To borrow from the old TV series *Dragnet*, such an answer to the problem of knowing human minds might be called "the Joe Friday method" of discerning human mental operations. Another character who knew Scottie during his college days, Gavin Elster (Tom Helmore), describes him as "the hardheaded Scot," a portrayal that connotes stubborn resistance to unnecessary speculation and reliance on the most common-sensical, straightforward explanations possible, based on experience and observation. It even suggests the archetypal British empiricist David Hume and other like-minded members of the eighteenth-century "Scottish Enlightenment."[3] Yet interestingly, Hume also described human reason as "slave of the passions,"[4] showing that at least one hardheaded Scot saw deep limitations to Joe Friday methodologies when applied to the human mind. Such an insight into his own method's shortcomings is precisely what Scottie lacks.

Still, this old ethnic stereotype suits him and symbolizes his stance toward the world in general—an impression that is reinforced by his being a former police detective. These narrative details provide viewers insight into how Scottie understands human beings. His strictly observation-based outlook concerning what is important to know about ourselves or others severely limits his ability to understand overall human mental functioning. The film illustrates this flaw by thematizing Scottie's naively scientific approach through the metaphorical use of steps. As we'll see shortly, narrative sequences such as Scottie's encounters with Midge's (Barbara Bel Geddes) kitchen step

---

[3] See Alexander Broadie, ed., *The Cambridge Companion to the Scottish Enlightenment* (New York: Cambridge University Press, 2003).

[4] David Hume, *A Treatise of Human Nature*, Second Edition (Oxford: Clarendon, 1978 [1739–40]), p. 415.

stool and the stairs to the bell tower at the San Juan Bautista Mission may be interpreted as exemplifying as well as criticizing his limited procedure for understanding human minds. In this manner Scottie's vertigo typifies an epistemological fear of going beyond what his method allows him to know.

By way of contrast, the film provides the example of a character who utilizes a different approach to knowing human beings. Specifically, Midge's technique of appreciating others emotionally as well as factually appears much more effective when juxtaposed with Scottie's. While not infallible, her method gets to the core of who someone is much more accurately and sensitively than her old fiancé's *Dragnet* procedure. As *Vertigo's* screenwriter Samuel Taylor has pointed out, he invented Midge's character in order to humanize the rest of the story and give it a sense of reality that would otherwise be lacking.[5] The contrast, then, that she offers regarding how to think about others provides viewers with the distance needed for a more critical perspective on Scottie. The different ways these two characters seek to know others thereby suggest what amount to different representative perspectives regarding how we might understand others as well as ourselves. If viewers reflect carefully on this contrast, it can provide them with a vivid illustration of one method's failure while at the same time giving them clues concerning how they might better approach the comprehension of human minds and why they work as they do.

Vertigo and the Vienna Circle

Through its focus on Scottie's misguided way of thinking about himself and others, *Vertigo* essentially challenges a philosophical position that bears striking resemblance to that advocated by the logical positivist movement of the 1920s and 1930s focused around the Vienna Circle, a group of philosophers interested in advocating science as the only proper model for philosophy and completely eliminating the non-experiential, metaphysical claims that they felt had plagued philosophy—as well as human beings more generally—for centuries. *Vertigo* is not usually

---

[5] See "A Talk by Samuel Taylor, Screenwriter of *Vertigo*," in *Hitchcock's Rereleased Films: From* Rope *to* Vertigo, edited by Walter Raubicheck and Walter Srebnick (Detroit: Wayne State University Press, 1991), p. 288.

regarded as a trenchant criticism of the Vienna Circle, but by
thinking about how it offers viewers a protagonist who stub-
bornly seeks fact and observation oriented forms of truth, the
film provides an implicit criticism of the positivistic thinking
found in the theories advocated by Rudolf Carnap, A.J. Ayer, and
other thinkers associated with this influential movement.[6] From
the outset of the film, Scottie may be seen as consistently devoting himself to a distinctly similar method of gathering data, then
narrowly applying hypothesis construction and deduction in
order to explain the phenomena, while at the same time ignor-
ing how his actions are guided by violent emotions that his
method is unable to detect. By looking at his story in this way,
we may interpret *Vertigo* as focusing on the tragedy that accom-
panies using such a method for understanding human motivation and action, as Scottie seeks to resolve problems concerning
the intricate emotional workings of human psychology by
means of an approach that lacks any sort of sensitivity for them.

When viewed from this perspective, we may see that Scottie
repeatedly seeks to abolish human fears and emotional traumas
by working to eliminate them according to a dangerously
restricted method. By formulating comprehensive principles
about phobias and traumas based narrowly on the evidence he
gathers, this dogged follower of "the facts" works to obliterate
psychological difficulties according to inferences logically
deduced from his theoretical rules. Scottie attempts this scientific, emotional extermination early in the film in an effort to do
away with his own acrophobia. When Midge tells him there is
no cure for his fear of heights, he replies, "I think I can lick it .
. . I have a theory . . . I think if I can get used to heights just a
little bit at a time . . . progressively . . ." By carefully familiariz-
ing himself with gradually increased heights, Scottie believes he
can cure his acrophobia. Standing on a small wooden stool he
tells Midge, "Watch . . . I look up; I look down. I look up; I look
down. There's nothing to it." Progressing to a slightly higher
level on her kitchen step stool, Scottie feels so confident about
the effectiveness of his newfound form of psychotherapy that he
announces his intention to go out and buy a nice tall steplad-

[6] See Rudolf Carnap, *The Logical Structure of the World* (Berkeley: University of
California Press, 1967 [1928]); A.J. Ayer, *Language, Truth, and Logic* (New York: Dover,
1952 [1936]); and Ayer, ed., *Logical Positivism* (New York: Free Press, 1959).

der. On the stool's third step, he exclaims, "This is a cinch," showing his rising confidence in the theory he has devised and the steps deduced from it. Yet after a brief glimpse out Midge's apartment window, he swoons and falls from the chair's top step.

Scottie's attempt to apply his theory about curing acrophobia through gradual acclimation fails; his fear of heights does not admit to such rationalistic, step-by-step treatment. Here, as elsewhere in the film, Scottie grossly underestimates the power of human emotions, even as he approaches them by means of a deeply rationalistic procedure. To help us grasp the point, we might think of the film's preoccupation with steps as literalizing Scottie's reasoning method. His use of Midge's furniture corresponds to inferences from his naive principle about progressively curing a fear of heights; for example, "at step1 through gradual acclimation I will not suffer from acrophobia," "at step2 through gradual acclimation I will not suffer from acrophobia," and so on. By thinking of the film's use of steps as literalizations of Scottie's approach, we may see them as visual metaphors for the inadequate methodology that Scottie implements again and again over the course of the narrative.

Scottie as Psychotherapist

Just as Scottie attempts to eliminate his own phobia, so he seeks to do away with those of others. Later in the film, as he works to help Madeleine Elster (Kim Novak) out of her evident fear of possession by the ghost of Carlotta Valdes, he tells her, "There's an answer for everything!"—an exclamation that unintentionally echoes an article of faith from the positivist creed.[7] Prior to Scottie's enthusiastic expression of this presumption, Madeleine had told Scottie that when she was last at the San Juan Bautista Mission, horses lived in the carriage house and nuns would scold her for playing there, apparently indicating that she was previously at the mission when it actively operated more than a century before. Just then Scottie notices the statue of a gray horse. He confidently points to it and argues that it readily explains her memory. "It would have a little trouble getting in and out of a stall," he admits, but nonetheless asserts that the

---

[7] See, for example, Carnap, *The Logical Structure of the World*, especially pp. 290–92.

statue must be one of the horses she remembers—never mind that there are several other horses and memories for which he must still account, let alone that a more obvious explanation would be that the woman with whom he has fallen in love requires the attention of someone with far greater insights into the human psyche than Scottie is capable of mustering.

Scottie's obstinate conviction that every mental problem has its straightforward, commonsensical answer based on the available facts of the case, expresses his dedication to a paradigm involving data collection, hypothesis formulation, and deduction. His conviction also reveals how completely he overlooks the elaborate, and at times murky, role that emotions play in human mental lives.

Finding the Key

According to this stubborn devotee of the empirical, the trick to understanding the secret of the phenomena is to find the key, the principle that unlocks the mystery of the data. So in order to unlock the data contributing to Madeleine's fear of possession, Scottie believes one has to discover the beginning and proceed from there. At one point Scottie expresses his frustration about Madeleine's emotional disturbance, saying, "If I could just find the key, the beginning . . . and put it together," to which Madeleine adds: "And explain it away."

For Scottie, explaining the human mind's workings consists of collecting the facts, gathering details through normal observation, and then mastering them by devising a comprehensive principle that organizes the data. Even emotions like acrophobia or other mental disturbances may be understood and dealt with in this manner. They are merely an aggregate of one's life experiences that must be carefully marshaled so that their "key" may be discerned—their organization formulated according to that universal rule which allows one to explain them away. The theory that one devises to explain phenomena, then, functions like an invisible lacquer one applies over the surface of the facts as already established, but in no way alters them. Yet this outlook flies in the face of much recent philosophy of science, which after decades of reflection on the logical positivist program came to the realization that theories deeply affect what we think of as "the facts." In other words, the empirical details we gather take shape significantly according to whatever theory by means of which they are viewed. Rather than being autonomous entities that quietly await our discovery, facts are "theory-laden." The classical statement of this argument is Thomas Kuhn's 1962 book *The Structure of Scientific Revolutions*, the influence of which has spread throughout philosophy.[8]

In order to see even more emphatically the ineffectiveness of Scottie's method, we might consider his other misguided attempts to eliminate human phobias through data collection, hypothesis, and deduction. Scottie fails to solve the riddle of Madeleine's possession, for example, and his failure is literalized through an inability to climb to the top of the bell tower steps. He experiences once more that dizziness due to heights—and far worse. After a harsh and agonizing inquest into Madeleine's death, Scottie suffers a nervous breakdown and spends months institutionalized with what his doctor terms "acute melancholia," emerging, it seems, little changed from the condition in which he entered.

Despite his method's abject failure both in his own case and Madeleine's, Scottie remains committed to it, devising a way of organizing the facts so that they might fit together according to a principle that would properly explain Madeleine's suicide. As viewers, of course, we discover long before Scottie that Madeleine's insanity and subsequent suicide were hoaxes staged to make him an unwitting participant in her murder by her husband Gavin, Scottie's old school chum, and the former police detective's reputation as an emotionally naïve, hardheaded Scot with a fear of heights made him the ideal patsy for this crime. But for most of the narrative Scottie remains unaware of this deception. On the other hand, he implements his approach one last time after he meets his new girlfriend and Madeleine-looka-like Judy (Kim Novak again).

Scottie's Last Therapy Session

In his final attempt to apply the Joe Friday method and elimi-nate his emotional trauma due to Madeleine's death, Scottie

---

[8] Thomas Kuhn, *The Structure of Scientific Revolutions* (Chicago: University of Chicago Press, 1975 [1962]); N.R. Hanson, *Pattern of Discovery* (Cambridge: Cambridge University Press, 1958), pp. 1–49; and others. The quoted term is Hanson's (see p. 19).

once more goes back to the beginning and works step by step to confirm his theory about "the facts" regarding his own case. "There's one final thing I have to do," he cryptically tells Judy as they take a long drive, "and then I'll be free of the past." Having seen this young woman wearing Carlotta's necklace, Scottie now realizes he had previously worked from an incorrect hypothesis and presumed the wrong motivations behind Madeleine's death, so he acts to verify his new theory about the case by testing it at the bell tower of the San Juan Bautista mission. Angered by Judy's earlier betrayal of him, he cruelly forces her up the steps to obtain the requisite confirmation from her. In doing so, Scottie strives to achieve verification of his new theory about the case, even to the point of destroying his twisted relationship with Judy, who still loves him, in spite of the danger of being discovered as Madeleine's impostor in reality as well as in Scottie's perverse fantasies. The burden of explanation, however, weighs too heavily on Scottie for him to take her affections into account. His myopic determination to put human actions in proper explanatory order, to find the key that explains the motivations behind what occurred, propels him far beyond the point of caring about the subtleties of human relationship, even beyond the point of caring about the possibility of losing his Madeleine-substitute Judy, because he simply cannot leave these matters unresolved. His obsession for explanation, if you will, outstrips his yearning desire for love, as well as any consideration for Judy's feelings. His neurotic devotion to explanatory resolution, of course, also contributes to Judy's death and his loss of her for a second time.

Scottie's Tragic Flaw in Understanding Human Minds

Scottie's inability to fully appreciate or understand the motivations behind human events shows the tragic results of treating how we know human minds too closely according to a naive, scientific paradigm. Methods like Scottie's attempt to ground human action and motivation strictly according to comprehensive, universalistic principles. Scottie's theories about why people act in one way or another depend on a simplistic understanding of their reasons for action as absolute rules that compel them to act mechanically in narrowly determined ways.

Their reasons for acting in specific instances, then, may be easily inferred from those rules. Consequently, Scottie rationalistically attributes his own acrophobia to not being accustomed to high places and works to eliminate it through gradual, step-by-step acclimation. He further attributes Madeleine's mental disturbances to a combination of forgotten past experience and needless worries, so he works diligently to bring them to light. He apparently even believes his own romantic obsession and guilt may be resolved through a proper account of the facts, after which he will be free of those mental afflictions.

Scottie's investigations fail to adequately explain the workings of the human mind because they lack an appreciation of the noncodifiability of certain human behaviors. By "noncodifiability" I mean the imperviousness of some human actions to being explained strictly according to universal principles or rules that admit of no exceptions—their unsuitability to being captured accurately by means of comprehensive and absolute, lawlike statements. As Aristotle observed in the fourth century B.C.E., sometimes reasons for action may not be so strictly formulated. While we may legitimately seek *general* characterizations of many human behaviors, we need to realize from the outset that such formulations will be at best approximate. Exceptions to our theoretical principles must be expected.[9] This unsuitability of some human behaviors and more subtle aspects of the human mind—especially those involving our emotions—to be captured by absolute principles is precisely what Scottie fails to grasp.[10] Or, as his fellow hard-headed Scot David Hume observed, at times we may choose our "total ruin" and find nothing unreasonable in bringing it about because the commands of passion are so strong,[11] a description that seems to aptly fit Scottie, particularly in the film's final sequence.

Vertigo's focus on Scottie's method and its ineffectiveness, then, implies a critical analysis of such reasoning that narrowly employs this naïvely scientific approach to understanding

---

[9] Aristotle, *Nicomachean Ethics* [ca. 330 B.C.E.] (Indianapolis: Hackett, 1999), pp. 2, 19–20.

[10] The classic statement of arguments regarding noncodifiability and the misleading desire for universal rules derive from Ludwig Wittgenstein's later work. See *The Blue and Brown Books* (New York: Harper, 1975), pp. 17ff.; and *Philosophical Investigations* (New York: Macmillan, 1974[1953]).

[11] Hume, *Treatise*, p. 416.

human minds. Because such a perspective focuses so narrowly on rules that admit of no exceptions, it devalues emotions in favor of reason. It leaves no room for the *general* efficacy of emotion, their ability to guide us frequently to the proper conclusion without at the same time being infallible. In this manner the film implies that Scottie's epistemological stance toward human minds tremendously underestimates the role and power that emotions may play in our lives. Passions do not necessarily admit to being accurately captured by strict, law-like formulations that may then be used mechanically to comprehend every instance of them. These kinds of human mental functions are typically far more complicated than that sort of outlook can properly capture.

Vertigo and Epistemological Vertigo

Like Scottie, some philosophers fear epistemological vertigo. They fear the loss of theoretical buttresses that allow them to believe that their knowledge is secure, so they embrace outmoded, universalistic formulations of knowledge because such conceptions give them the illusion that certainty may be achieved. Rather than admitting indeterminacy or uncertainty, they anxiously embrace the idea that absolute, universal principles will always guide them in their efforts to understand the phenomena around them.[12] But in the last half-century many philosophers have moved away from reliance on these epistemological props and found that a more accurate way of understanding the world in general and human minds in particular is based in the observation made by Aristotle so long ago, namely that universalistic formulations may not always accurately capture the phenomena, particularly when it comes to the workings of the human mind.[13]

Hitchcock's film serves as a parable about knowledge of human minds that some philosophers would do well to observe. If they could come to appreciate the world without props, free

---

[12] See, for example, G.E. Moore, "A Defense of Common Sense" (1925) and "Proof of the External World" (1939), reprinted in *Philosophical Papers* (London: Allen and Unwin, 1959), pp. 32–59, 127–150; and R.M. Hare, *Freedom and Reason* (Oxford: Oxford University Press, 1963), pp. 10–34.

[13] See also John McDowell, "Virtue and Reason," *The Monist* 62 (1979), pp. 331–350.

of their desperate desires for certainty and universality as well as fear of their absence, they would be better off, epistemologically speaking. So, too, I think, would a lot of other people. The film implies that operating with a wide range of explanatory methods for understanding the human mind would greatly benefit us in our efforts to comprehend the mind's intricacies. Scottie's character suggests by negative example that we should let go of our epistemological fears and realize that what we do and think often isn't strictly codifiable—that it may not be accurately captured by means of straightforward, universal principles. More modest and supple formulations, especially concerning our emotions, might well better account for common human behavior.

This insight is the lesson that Midge's character holds out for us, and amounts to why she is so important to the believability of the narrative. Her stance toward others is both more human and more real than Scottie's. If we can achieve an awareness that attains the level of Midge's attitude toward other human beings, we might see in addition that, freed of the epistemological training wheels that some have argued must guide us, the vertigo we initially feel due to their absence will eventually go away.[14]

---

[14] This chapter borrows bits and pieces from my "Hitchcock and Deductive Reasoning: Moving Step by Step in *Vertigo*," *Film and Philosophy* 3 (1996), pp. 38–52. I would like to thank the editor of that journal, Dan Shaw, for kind permission to reproduce those parts of my earlier essay.

10

On Being Mr. Kaplan: Personal Identity in *North by Northwest*

STEVEN W. PATTERSON

North by Northwest is one of Hitchcock's most interesting and appealing films. From its stylish opening shots of busy New York streets to its climactic finale on Mount Rushmore, every moment of the film has the capacity to draw the viewer into its world, no matter how many times one has seen it. Fundamentally, *North by Northwest* is a story about mistaken identity. We are drawn in by it because on some level we realize that however improbable it may be, we too could be mistaken for someone else, be swept away from our ordinary routines, and have the course of our lives radically altered by the experience.

We may like to see our identities as something over which we have control. But no matter how sure we are that our identities are the products of our own choices, our identities may have just as much to do with the choices of others as they do with our own. In this chapter we will use *North by Northwest* to look at some of the ways philosophers have tried to understand the balance of factors that make us who we are.

What Makes Us Who We Are?

Most of us are not likely to suffer too much discomfort at the thought of someone else's being mistaken about who we are. The idea of being mistaken for a spy and being sucked into a world of espionage and adventure even has romantic appeal. We sometimes daydream about having such an adventurous life. Nevertheless, for most of us the day would come when we tired of trading coolly defiant one-liners with a powerful nemesis and of seductive overtures in train cars from the likes of Eva Marie Saint, and we would long to return to our lives of insurance payments and grocery shopping.

Well, those are probably bad examples—but the point is that most of us believe that we have a *self,* an identity that is *unique to us.* While we might find the idea of a holiday away from our *routines* appealing, very few of us would likely savor the loss of our *self.* Yet this is just what Thornhill is faced with. His immersion into the web of deception woven by Vandamm and the Professor threatens to push him so far into the role of the fictional George Kaplan that he will be unable to return to his life as Thornhill. No one wants to lose his identity, no matter how much fun he might have doing it. What is it, though, that we don't want to lose? What is it that makes us who we are?

When we first ask ourselves this question, we may find it difficult to answer—as indeed Thornhill finds it difficult to prove to Vandamm that he's *not* Kaplan. Over the centuries philosophers have had a fair number of ideas about how to answer it. Let's begin our survey of the ways in which philosophers have thought about personal identity by considering the possibility that personal identity depends upon having the same body.

License and Registration, Please

Thornhill's first reaction to being mistaken for Kaplan during his interrogation at Glen Cove is based on the body. Upon hearing Vandamm address him as Kaplan he says, "I don't suppose it would do any good to show you a wallet full of identification cards, a driver's license, things like that?" Leonard, Vandamm's chief henchman, responds sarcastically, "They provide you with such *good* ones." The point that Leonard is making, of course, is that the usual sorts of identification can be faked, and so are not reliable indicators of who a person really is. Clearly those who believe that the body or brain is what makes us who we are don't believe anything quite so simple.

Those who believe that our body or brain make us who we are will defer to much more than just a picture on an ID card. They might hold that our identity lies in our having the same DNA, or the same particular physical configuration of our brains over time. That seems a bit better than appealing to a driver's license, but it still won't tell us the whole story about who we are and how we came to be that person. We can see this readily enough if we use a philosophical tool called a "thought experiment." A thought experiment is just an imaginary case made up to test a theory. They are particularly useful when the theory one wants to test isn't accessible to normal procedures of experimentation—for instance, theories about notoriously hard-to-pin-down subjects like the self.

Imagine that unbeknownst to Thornhill, every night for the past year the CIA has crept into his bedroom when he's been asleep and painlessly replaced a few thousand of the cells in his body (let us call these originals O-cells). The replacements are duplicate cells of the exact same type and disposition that they've manufactured in their lab (call these R-cells). Thus, with each successive day, Thornhill has woken up with fewer O-cells and with more R-cells. Because the changes have occurred at the microbiological level at a very gradual pace, Thornhill hasn't noticed anything different about himself. Indeed, why should he? His body is continuing to function in the way it always has. The end result of this process, however, is that every cell in his body has gradually been replaced, effectively leaving him with an *entirely different body* than the one with which he began the year. Now this isn't so impressive. It's what happens naturally, albeit on a slightly different timeline. Even though Thornhill has a new body, no one would, at this point, wish to say that his identity is changed.

But now suppose that the CIA, instead of merely replacing O-cells with R-cells, took all the O-cells they removed from Thornhill, and bit by bit, used them along with some very sophisticated technology (let's not forget that this is an *imaginary* case) to build a new person who, physically and psychologically, is exactly like Thornhill.[1] To keep matters from getting too complicated they call this Thornhill-double "George Kaplan". The question that now arises is: which one, Kaplan or Thornhill, is the same as the Thornhill who began the year with all of his own cells? Kaplan is made up of Thornhill's cells and looks, acts, and thinks just like him. Since on the Body Theory there's nothing more to being the particular person one is

---

[1] This is a variation on the ancient "Ship of Theseus" example.

except a physical arrangement of bodily components, there is no problem with allowing psychological traits to follow physical structures in the way imagined. Thornhill himself hasn't changed in his essentials either, since the only thing that's happened to him is replacement of cells of the appropriate types. So which man, at the end of the year, is the real Thornhill?

The question is hard to answer, and there really isn't a settled-upon solution to the kind of problem it raises. What can be agreed upon is that it presents serious difficulties for the Body Theory, especially if one is inclined to believe that the Thornhill who undergoes cell replacement remains the original Thornhill even though Kaplan is walking around with a body made of cells that were originally his. The safe bet seems to be to say that we can't fully explain to others who we are simply by reference to our bodies. Though no one would deny that having the same body over time is an important *part* of our being who we are, the kinds of considerations just mentioned show that there must be more to the story. If this is right then physical evidence couldn't help Thornhill convince Vandamm. What about evidence of a different sort? Perhaps there are features of the mind to which he could appeal that could get the job done?

The Persistence of Memory (or Lack Thereof)

A few hundred years ago the English philosopher John Locke suggested that it's our collected set of *memories* that makes us who we are.[2] Since our memories are uniquely ours in a way that very little else is, and because it seems very unlikely that someone else could plausibly claim to have *our* memories, it seems very likely that our memories make us who we are.

Thornhill's protests that he doesn't know anything about Kaplan's movements or contacts can be seen as an appeal to memory. When Vandamm tells him that they know his contact in Pittsburgh is dead, he replies "What contact? I've never even been in Pittsburgh!" This is as far as Thornhill gets with his appeal to memory in the movie, but to give the memory theory a bit more of a test, we can return to our earlier thought exper-

---

[2] John Locke, *Of Identity and Memory*, as reprinted in John Perry, ed., *Personal Identity* (Berkeley: University of California Press, 1975), pp. 33–52. Perry's introduction to this volume contains a clear explanation of the finer points of this view.

iment and imagine Thornhill making the case a little more explicitly. He might say to Vandamm, "Kaplan, whoever he is, might
have memories of being in Pittsburgh, but I do not. I only have
memories of being me, Roger Thornhill. Only Kaplan could have
Kaplan's memories, and since I don't have any of Kaplan's memories, I can't be him." Would Vandamm be convinced?

Probably not. There are at least two problems here that
would stand in the way. The first is that even if we *could* have
direct access to a person's memories (which we can't), we still
wouldn't necessarily get an *accurate* picture of who he is. This
is because memory is notoriously unreliable and subject to
decay over time. Couldn't Vandamm say the following about
Thornhill's appeal to memory (and this will be more fun if you
actually imagine James Mason saying it): "Memory, you say, Mr.
Kaplan? Unfortunately for you that doesn't prove that you are
this Thornhill person. For you see, being the sort of fellow you
are, you could have purposefully had your friends at the CIA
use their chemical techniques to induce a state of temporary
amnesia, followed by a brief period of psychological conditioning to convince you that you really are Thornhill. But you're not
Thornhill, Mr. Kaplan, you're Mr. Kaplan with amnesia, and it
doesn't matter *whose* memories you *think* you have."

Thornhill would, upon hearing this objection, very likely sit
nonplussed for a moment, seriously pondering whether death
by bourbon really would be such a bad thing compared to this
conversation. Nevertheless, Vandamm would have a point. If
who we are is based on our memory, then our knowledge of
who we are is only as accurate as our memories are. Cases of
amnesia demonstrate that a person's memory can be so inaccu-
rate as to completely erase his own knowledge of the person he
was prior to the event that caused the amnesia.

Even if this weren't enough, there is another problem that
really knocks memory out of the running. The idea is that a person has a unique self if and only if he has a more or less continuous set of memories of his own experiences. A bit of reflection
on this condition will show that the memory theory is afflicted
with a nasty case of circularity. After all, it requires that for a person to have a self, he has to have memories of that self. But he
can't have the memories that are supposed to make him who he
is unless he already is that person. The problem is that one can't
have memories of his experiences unless one *already has a self*

to have memories of. So, to say that a person only has a self if he has a more or less continuous set of memories of that self is like saying that a person only has a self if he has a self—which is true, but not all that informative. It certainly doesn't tell us what we want to know, which is what makes a person who he is.

The Importance of Having Toothaches

It shouldn't be surprising, really, that memory comes up short. There are moments in *North by Northwest* itself that suggest the limitations of memory. Recall Vandamm's attempt to murder Thornhill by having him drive down the treacherous sea-coast highway leading to Glen Cove in a drunken state. Thornhill has an accident and survives, and then spends the night in jail. It is his state of drunkenness at this time that leads nearly everyone, including his mother, to distrust his memory of the assassination attempt. In a memorable sequence in the film, Thornhill returns to Glen Cove to confront Vandamm, and finds everyone there playing to the obvious distrust in his memory.

So if memory isn't reliable enough, then what is? Modern-day philosopher Derek Parfit suggests that it is *psychological continuity* that does the trick. The basic idea is that even if the continuity of a person's *memories* is broken, it can still be the case that his *other* psychological states (of which there will be many) remain connected to one another. It's those connections, Parfit says, that really are the source of identity. Even if Thornhill were just Kaplan with amnesia, there would be a good many of his mental states that would survive the loss of his memories. So Thornhill and Kaplan would be the same person regardless of the amnesia. For example, if Thornhill had a toothache prior to the amnesia, the psychological state of pain would carry over through the change, as likely would the desire to alleviate the pain. The continuity would be quite strong at more basic levels. All of Thornhill's visual perceptions would occur from the same point of view both before and after the change, his ability to speak English, drive a car, and so on, would be unaffected. On this view, all that really matters is that at least *some* connections of the right sort hold.[3]

---

[3] A connection's being of the right sort here includes its being caused in the appropriate way. With this addition, the position described is essentially that of Derek Parfit in

The downside to this view is that it significantly "waters down" our usual conception of the self. After all, when we think of what makes us who we are, we seldom think of things like toothaches and knowledge of English. Such appeals would seem pretty feeble in a case like Thornhill's, and would almost certainly hasten him to his drunken encounter with the coastal highway. But maybe that's not such a big deal.

We might think of the case of change that Thornhill undergoes as a member of what Parfit calls the "Psychological Spectrum" of cases. In this sort of case we imagine a timeline. At the near end of the timeline we have Thornhill as he is at the beginning of the movie—Thornhill at "one hundred percent Thornhill," let us say. At the far end of the timeline we have Thornhill as he would be if completely transformed into Kaplan—Thornhill as "one hundred percent Kaplan." Now at the far end we would clearly be dealing with a different person, with different memories and a different psychological life altogether than the person with whom we began. One way to think about what happens to Thornhill as the movie progresses is to think of him as moving forward on this timeline in the direction of one hundred percent Kaplan. He doesn't get there of course—let's say he winds up somewhere around forty-five percent Kaplan—but it is true that he changes along just such a continuum.

Consider how Thornhill deals with being mistaken for George Kaplan throughout *North by Northwest.* He begins, as we've seen, by denying that he has anything at all to do with Kaplan. Before too long, however, he begins playing the role, becoming more and more like a spy—more "Kaplan-like," if you will—as the movie progresses. Thornhill assumes Kaplan's identity to check out the hotel room allegedly occupied by Kaplan, he then tracks down the real Townsend at the United Nations. When he has Townsend paged he identifies himself as Kaplan. After being framed for Townsend's murder, he cleverly evades the authorities and sneaks onto the train where he meets Eve Kendall. Kendall helps him escape the authorities again, this time disguised as a porter, but eventually sends him to his

---

Reasons and Persons (Oxford: Oxford University Press, 1984). Parfit spends Part 3 of this work developing his version of the psychological continuity theory.

famous rendezvous with the crop duster. He then tracks her
down in Chicago, and confronts Vandamm at the auction. After
confronting Vandamm, he frustrates Leonard's attempt to assas-
sinate him by disturbing the auction to the point where the
police are called in to arrest him. In the back of the cruiser he
jokingly says to one of the officers: "Know who I am? . . . You've
hit the jackpot, sergeant. 'Chicago police capture United Nations
slayer.'"

All of this shows that although Thornhill begins the film as
someone who, it would seem, could not possibly be mistaken
for a spy, he develops into a spy-like role quite nicely. The
actions described above certainly do not seem like the actions
of a boozing advertising executive, and Thornhill's wry declara-
tion of himself as the "United Nations slayer" punctuates the
evolution of his character to this point. This gradual transformation fits into the Psychological Spectrum of cases. By the time
Thornhill begins his attempt to rescue Eve from Vandamm, it's
become quite clear that Thornhill has stepped firmly into the
non-existent Kaplan's shoes. He is, in a very real sense, a different man. He's much more like the man Kaplan would be, if
Kaplan were real. The question we want to consider is, does his
change along this continuum make him a different person? Does
it change his identity?

Identities, Selves, and Others

How one answers the question posed at the end of the last section depends in large part on how one thinks not about what
makes us who we are, but on how one thinks about the question itself. Philosophers like Parfit are committed to a method
that involves close conceptual analysis. For them the question is
just one of whether the criteria of identity are properly applied.[4]
Other philosophers reject this approach as too narrow. Charles
Taylor, for example, writes:

---

[4] Parfit and others like him are not at all blind to the moral implications of their views.
The difference I mean to underline in this section is a difference in how those who follow Parfit's method and those who follow methods closer to Taylor's see the questions
involved. Parfit's camp sees the question of what we are as prior to the question of who
we are and why who we are matters to us. Those in Taylor's camp find these questions
inextricably linked such that they aren't separable in this way.

To ask what a person is, in abstraction from his or her self-inter-
pretations, is to ask a fundamentally misguided question; one to
which there couldn't in principle be an answer. . . . We are not
selves in the way that we are organisms, or we don't have selves
the way we have hearts and livers.[5]

What Taylor suggests here is that the question of *what* we
are cannot be divorced from the question of *who* we are. He's
not alone in seeing it this way. The famous French philosopher,
Jean-Paul Sartre (1905–1980), certainly would have agreed.
Sartre thought that the immediate problem for human beings
was not figuring out what we are in some abstract sense, but of
forging a self-identity of our own through genuine free choice
and action. Because we have no essential nature to discover, we
are radically free to establish our own selves according to our
own freely chosen ideals and perceptions of the kind of person
we wish to be. Sartre thought that we do not *discover* our nature
through analysis, but that we *create* it through free choice.

There are serious moral implications to this way of thinking
about ourselves, for if Sartre is right, then we are responsible for
ourselves in a way that goes beyond simple responsibility for the
acts we do. On such a view we are, over and above this, responsible for the human persons we become through our choices and
actions. We are *totally responsible*, in other words, for our own
moral character. There's no appealing to prior causes in any
defense of one's actions or character. Because there is no such
appeal, our responsibility for ourselves is total and inescapable.[6]

One finds a somewhat similar idea in the works of the
ancient Greek philosopher Aristotle, who thought that our
becoming virtuous or vicious was principally a matter of acquiring virtuous or vicious tendencies through our everyday acts—
especially as they give rise to habits over time. Unlike Sartre,
however, Aristotle believed that our character depends in large
part on how well our parents and societies do at educating us
in virtuous conduct.[7] Despite this difference, we can see that

---

[5] Charles Taylor, *Sources of the Self* (Cambridge, Massachusetts: Harvard University Press,
1989), p. 34.
[6] For a succinct elaboration of the view described here see Jean-Paul Sartre, *Existentialism
and Human Emotions* (New York: Citadel, 1984).
[7] See Aristotle, *Nicomachean Ethics*, Book I, Chapter 9 and Book II, Chapter 1. Aristotle
would have disagreed with the idea of fusing the questions what we are and who we are.

both Aristotle and Sartre thought that in large part we are morally responsible for the kind of person we become, and that we are required to choose the acts that lead to that personality in way that gives due respect to their moral importance.

This is a sobering thought, as we seldom go though each day considering the impact that such mundane things as how we do our jobs or the way in which we treat our significant others in small exchanges is revelatory of our moral personality. If we follow the development of Roger Thornhill's character in *North by Northwest*, however, we can see quite clearly that it is precisely these sorts of acts that are most revelatory of the persons we are. In the opening moments of the film, to his secretary, we see Thornhill dictate an insincere note to what is obviously a girlfriend. He also "steals" a cab on the false premise that his secretary, Maggie, is sick. His line to Maggie in the cab after she protests about his taking it with a lie sums up his character nicely: "In the world of advertising there is no such thing as a lie, Maggie. There is only the Expedient Exaggeration." All of this marks Thornhill as a relatively shallow and self-interested man—a far cry from the sort of man who fakes his own death and races across Mount Rushmore to save the woman he loves.

If we are responsible for our own character development, might we not be responsible for the impact we have on the character development of others as well? Might they have a reciprocal role in the formation of *our* selves too? Recall Charles Taylor. As he sees it, we only understand what we are by understanding who we are, and we can only understand who we are in the context of a community of others. As he puts it, "one cannot be a self on one's own."[8] This is because our own understanding, not only of who we are but of what we are, is the product of an ongoing series of discussions and interactions between ourselves and others that involve ideas—such as the idea of the self—that come from shared ways of thinking and talking. If Taylor is right, others help make us who we are. Aristotle would have agreed, adding that it is only in community that human personhood is really possible at all.[9]

---

[8] *Sources of the Self*, Book I.
[9] Aristotle, *Politics*, Book I.

At first glance the idea that others help make us who we are seems anything but revolutionary. When we consider the usual sort of events that take place in a human life, the formation and dissolution of friendships, attraction, courtship, and marriage, parenthood, professional life, old age and retirement, just to name a few, it seems obvious that our personalities do change in response to all such events and relationships. Taylor's suggestion is a little bit more radical than that. He thinks not only that our notions of *who* we are are shaped by our interaction with others, but that our notion of *what* we are is too. It's not at all clear that we would think in terms of selfhood at all if it weren't for our living in the kind of societies where such ideas have currency. In the same way that it was impossible for most people in the Medieval world to believe that they didn't have souls, so it is impossible for many of us to believe that we don't have a self.

It's also impossible to fully account for the selves we believe we have without including others in the story. It's not just those who are close to us who exert an influence over us either. In terms of *what* we are, our ideas of the self are the product of an ongoing discussion among philosophers, religious leaders, psychologists, neuroscientists, and laypersons too. (Think of the way that Freud's theories changed the way people thought about themselves.)

In terms of who we are, we are influenced by our interactions with strangers too. If we find that others treat us kindly, for example by holding elevators for us, or by returning dropped items, then the natural inclination of most people will be to act in a similar way. A comforting smile, a threatening scowl, averted eyes and a quickened pace—even the small actions of others can change us. The kind words and actions of strangers—or the unkind words and actions, over time, exert a geologic influence over our personalities, as do our relationships with those who are nearer to us. Our identities, as we experience them, are the product of our response to those influences. In the increasingly isolated world in which we live, this is important to remember. None of us can be who we are, or develop into the person we are to be, without others. It should also make us mindful of the roles *we* play even in brief, chance encounters, in influencing others along their paths as well.

Taylor's view emphasizes the interconnectedness of our identities with those of others. We see a bit of this interconnection in

North by Northwest too. Though Vandamm's conviction that Thornhill is Kaplan set Thornhill on the road to becoming more like the fictional Kaplan, it's Eve Kendall who really succeeds in changing Thornhill's character. His boldest moves—such as stepping into the role of Kaplan for the staged assassination in the cafeteria, the rescue attempt at Vandamm's house, and the subsequent escape and chase on Mount Rushmore—are made for her sake. It's when he does these things that he is least like the man he is at the beginning of the film. Certainly we can say that who Thornhill is at the end of the movie has everything to do with others.

As we've seen in this chapter, *North by Northwest* gives us much to think about in terms of our identities both in terms of what we are and in terms of who we are. Thornhill's attempt to prove that he isn't Kaplan leads us naturally to question how anyone could prove it, and that naturally leads us to the quest for a workable criterion of personal identity. This in turn leads us to consider our own natures and how they're formed. The quest to understand the self in all these dimensions is far from finished, and we've looked at only a few of the most popular positions in this chapter. That's alright though. It would be a mistake to draw any one analysis of personal identity from a movie like *North by Northwest*.

Nothing says a great movie has to answer every question it raises. After all, it's not answers that bring us back to this particular movie time and again. It's a desire to believe in our own potential to transform our own identities as successfully as Thornhill transforms his. Most of us aren't spies. Most of us aren't even really good poker players! But that doesn't stop us from being intrigued by the possibility that under the right circumstances, perhaps in the right company, we too could be Mr. Kaplan if the need arose.

11
Ethics or Film Theory? The Real McGuffin in *North by Northwest*

THOMAS E. WARTENBERG

Despite fundamental disagreements about Alfred Hitchcock and his films, one thing that everyone can agree upon is that he is a tricky filmmaker who enjoys putting things over on his audience. We should be wary of assuming that a Hitchcock film makes a straightforward philosophical point, for in any of Hitchcock's movies, things are rarely what they seem.

On the face of it, *North by Northwest* (1959) is a film that pits different ethical perspectives against one another. The temptation is to treat the film as making a philosophical point about which ethical standpoint is valid. However, the film's ending presents not only a surprising resolution to its narrative, but also undercuts the attempt to interpret the film as endorsing any specific ethical perspective. Rather, I suggest, we should see the film's philosophical significance as residing in a dark point about the ability of film—and therefore Hitchcock—to put one over on its—that is, his—audience.

Zealous Patriotism versus Ethical Particularism

To begin, the ethical issue: The first ethical perspective upon which the film concentrates takes threats to a nation's well-being as sufficient to justify treating people in what would ordinarily be seen as immoral. I call this perspective "zealous patriotism," for it takes duty to one's country to override all other ethical considerations. *North by Northwest* presents a criticism of this standpoint as being, to use the language of the film, *callous*, as legitimating acts that are cruel and inhumane. The alternative ethical perspective portrayed in the film is one I shall call "ethical particularism" and it takes our fundamental ethical commitments to reside in our specific personal relationshipships with particular human beings. Here, too, however, the film is critical, presenting the ethical particularist as *headstrong*, tending to act impulsively and thus endanger the very person he cares about and to whom he is committed.

So if we see the film as pitting love of one's country against love for a specific individual, it seems that the film sees each form of love as problematic when it denies the importance of the other. As a result, the film can be seen to suggest that an adequate moral point of view would require the cooperation or synthesis of these two stances.

The Unfortunate Mr. Thornhill

The basic elements of *North by Northwest*'s plot are quite familiar. Roger Thornhill (Cary Grant), the film's protagonist, is an advertising executive who finds himself caught up in a global intrigue when he is mistaken for George Kaplan, a fictitious spy who has been created by the United States Intelligence Agency (USIA) to mislead a group of foreign agents about the existence of a double agent in their midst. Although many discussions of the film focus on Thornhill's personal development from momma's boy to mature male through his liaison with Eve Kendall (Eva Marie Saint), this emphasis obscures what I think is the film's focus on conflicting ethical stances. Instead, I shall emphasize how Thornhill's adventures move him from his self-interested point of view to a confrontation with the conflict between romantic love and patriotism.

When we first encounter Thornhill, we see him leaving a crowded elevator on the fly with his secretary in tow, jostling others, dictating excuses to girlfriends, and elbowing his way into a cab before the man who actually had hailed it.

Thornhill is a man who sees his own interests as more important than those of others and who fails to treat others with the respect demanded by even an ordinary sense of what proper conduct is. His own hedonism—the single-minded pursuit of his own pleasure—is unmediated by any moral concerns. As an advertising man—that quintessentially American profession—his aim is to get others to do what he wants by whatever means

Roger Thornhill Making His Way through the World

possible. Our initial glimpse at Thornhill reveals a man who is amoral and purely self-interested.

Love for a woman prompts his moral transformation. As Thornhill falls for Eve and then tries to understand her apparent betrayals, his basic ethical stance changes. Because he's in love with Kendall, he tries to take care of her, make sure she is not harmed. But in acting to protect her, especially in the final sequence of the film that takes place around and on top of Mount Rushmore (Hitchcock was prohibited from actually filming on top of the monument) he finds himself facing a conflict between romantic love and patriotic duty.

How Cold Is the Cold Warrior?

The conflict facing Thornhill and, more generally, the atmosphere that pervades the entire film are self-consciously inflected by the film's historical context: the 1950s Cold War between the United States and the Soviet Union. *North by Northwest* was made in the penultimate year of Eisenhower's presidency, a time when tensions with Soviet Russia were high. Nixon would make his famous visit to Russia the following year and Khrushchev would reciprocate by coming to the United Nations, shoe in hand. (Readers might recall their famous "Kitchen Debate.") Rhetoric in Washington was high concerning the need to take the threat posed by the Soviet Union seriously. The film adopts a highly critical stance towards official justifications of the Cold War and, in so doing, criticizes what I have called "zealous patriotism." Ironically, despite the passing of the Cold War, our current political climate makes this criticism quite timely indeed.

North by Northwest develops its critique of zealous patriotism through its negative depiction of the head of the United States Intelligence Agency, the Professor (Leo G. Carroll). The Professor believes that Phillip Vandamm (James Mason), a spy for an unspecified foreign power that is clearly meant to be the Soviet Union, poses a major threat to the security of the United States. For this reason, he has recruited Vandamm's mistress, Eve Kendall, as a double agent and, much like a film director, staged an elaborate fiction in which George Kaplan, a non-existent spy, moves from place to place across the country, diverting Vandamm's suspicions from Kendall. Although the film does not go so far as to criticize the spy game as nothing but a house of cards, it does question what sort of sacrifice the Professor is willing to make in his quest to discover the secret Vandamm possesses.

The film's criticism of the Professor is initially formulated in a scene that takes place at the headquarters of the United States Information Agency (USIA).

Thornhill has been abducted by a group of spies who think that he is George Kaplan. As Thornhill attempts to clear his name and discover what really is going on, he wades into ever

The Professor Finds the Going Rough

deeper waters, eventually finding himself wanted for the murder of Lester Townsend, the United States Ambassador to the United Nations. Thornhill seems to be way in over his head in this clash between the intelligence agents of two major powers, a situation that puts him in grave personal peril.

At a meeting of the Professor and a number of his agents who are trying to digest what has transpired, one of the agents, Mrs. Finlay confronts him, citing the likelihood that Thornhill, an innocent man, will be killed as a result of a simple confusion of identities. In response, the Professor reveals his "callousness" towards Thornhill, a callousness that the film thus presents as lying at the heart of the moral perspective of the zealous patriot.

MRS. FINLAY: What are we going to do?
SECOND AGENT: Do?
MRS. FINLAY: About Mr. Thornhill.
PROFESSOR: We do nothing.
MRS. FINLAY: Nothing?
PROFESSOR: That's right, nothing. . . . Oh, we could congratulate ourselves on a marvelous stroke of good fortune. Our nonexistent decoy, George Kaplan, created to divert suspicion from our actual agent, has fortuitously become a live decoy.
MRS. FINLAY: Yes, Professor. But how long do you think he'll stay alive?
PROFESSOR: Well, that's his problem.
SECOND AGENT: What Mrs. Finlay means is that. . . .
PROFESSOR: Oh, I know what she means.
SECOND AGENT: We can't sit back calmly and wait to see who kills him first. . . . Vandamm and company or the police.
PROFESSOR: What can we do to save him, without endangering our own agent?
MRS. FINLAY: Aren't we being a wee bit callous?
PROFESSOR: No, my dear woman, we're not being callous. We didn't invent our nonexistent man, and give him the name George Kaplan, and establish elaborate behavior patterns for our own private amusement. We created George Kaplan and labored successfully to convince Vandamm that this was our own agent, hot on his trail, for a desperately important reason.
SECOND AGENT: Check. Nobody's denying that.

PROFESSOR: Very well, then. If we make the slightest move to suggest that there is no such agent as George Kaplan, give any hint to Vandamm that he's pursuing a decoy instead of our own agent, then our agent, working right under Vandamm's very nose, will immediately face suspicion, exposure, and assassination. Like the two others who went before.

MRS. FINLAY: Good-bye, Mr. Thornhill, wherever you are.[1]

In this scene, the Professor attempts to exonerate himself from the charge of callousness, the moral flaw that Mrs. Finlay lays at his feet. And it certainly is true that, *if* saving Thornhill meant sacrificing someone else, there would be no quick ethical solution to the dilemma. The problem, however, is that the Professor never questions the legitimacy of using human beings—even willing ones—as pawns in his political game. It is he who has created the situation that puts Kendall at risk and he who allows Thornhill to face danger so as to distract attention from her presence. What legitimates this, in the Professor's eyes, is the threat to the United States posed by Vandamm as a spy, for it is this Cold War context that makes it morally permissible for him to endanger and, if necessary, sacrifice individuals for the good of the country.

North by Northwest takes a very critical attitude towards the sacrifice of others justified on patriotic grounds. Instead of seeing patriotism as an unproblematic case of moral motivation—think of the rhetoric that has been applied to those critical of George W. Bush's incursion into Iraq—the film exposes zealous patriotism as justifying the sacrifice of in the name of the public good. *North by Northwest* thus uses the Professor's callousness to undercut our sympathy for the zealous patriot's claim that the Cold War presents such significant dangers to the U.S. that innocent people can justifiably be sacrificed.

This interpretation of *North by Northwest* as critical of the Cold War patriot receives confirmation from earlier films in which Hitchcock portrayed intelligence officers in a negative light, even when they were acting in perilous times. *Notorious* (1946) shows American intelligence agents to be quite callous in their use of Alicia (Ingrid Bergman) in a manner that might even

---

[1] All quotations are from James Naremore, ed., *North by Northwest* (New Brunswick: Rutgers University Press, 1993), pp. 77–78.

be termed sexually exploitative, much like the Professor's use of Kendall. And even earlier, in *Secret Agent* (1936), an assassination plot is presented as morally questionable despite its patriotic justification.

The Professor as Director

North by Northwest further develops its criticism of the ethical perspective of the zealous patriot in a scene that takes place after another elaborate staging directed by the Professor, this time Thornhill's death.

In order to deflect Vandamm's now aroused suspicions from Kendall, the Professor has arranged for Vandamm to witness her shooting Thornhill—albeit with blanks—hoping this will convince Vandamm of her allegiance. After the piece has been acted—apparently with great success—the Professor allows Thornhill and Kendall a brief meeting. As they are about to part, the following conversation takes place:

> **PROFESSOR:** She's going off with Vandamm tonight on the plane.
>
> **THORNHILL:** She's going with Vandamm?!
>
> **PROFESSOR:** Well, that's why we went to such lengths to make her a fugitive from justice. So that Vandamm couldn't very well decline to take her along.

Kendall Shoots Thornhill for Vandamm's Benefit

THORNHILL: But you said . . .

PROFESSOR: I needn't tell you how valuable she can be to us over there.

THORNHILL:: You lied to me! You said that after tonight . . .

PROFESSOR: I needed your help.

THORNHILL: Well, you've got it all right!

EVE: Don't be angry.

THORNHILL: You think I'm going to let you go through with this dirty business?

PROFESSOR: She has to.

THORNHILL: Nobody has to do anything! I don't like the games you play, Professor.

PROFESSOR: War is hell, Mr. Thornhill, even when it's a cold one.

THORNHILL: If you fellows can't lick the Vandamms of this world without asking girls like her to bed down with them and fly away with them and probably never come back, perhaps you ought to start learning how to lose a few cold wars.

PROFESSOR: I'm afraid we're already doing that. (pp. 143–44)

Here, Thornhill clearly rejects the cold warrior's logic: The Cold War poses such a great threat to the nation that standard ethical requirements—such as telling the truth—must be overridden for the sake of national interest. But even more important to the Professor's zealously patriotic eyes is the fact that citizens have an obligation to do what their country requires of them. In Thornhill's case, this means allowing his lover to continue to work for the USIA despite the evident dangers that she faces.

In rejecting the Professor's argument, Thornhill echoes the charge first brought against the Professor by Mrs. Finlay: that he is callous. Although we accept the validity of this criticism, we come to have even greater reason to accept it when we learn in a later scene that Kendall will never have a chance to do what the Professor hopes, for despite the Professor's elaborate attempt to stage a diversion, Vandamm—through the intervention of his assistant, Leonard (Martin Landau)—has come to realize that Kendall is an agent of the USIA. As a result, the two have decided to kill her by throwing her from their plane, once they have left the country with their all-important secret.

Is Love Rash as Well as Blind?

North by Northwest contrasts acting on the basis of zealous patriotism with the ethical framework that I have called *ethical particularism*. For the ethical particularist, moral action stems from his affective or emotional ties to other specific individuals, especially those whom he loves. Actions based on such ties are claimed to be morally worthy because of their basis in an affective relationship. And although it may initially seem that the film endorses this moral framework, I shall argue that it criticizes it as well.

In assessing what the film's criticisms of different ethical stances, it's important not to overlook the fact that it was not the Professor that got Kendall to bed down with Vandamm, but Kendall's romance with Vandamm that gave the Professor the opportunity to employ her. Thornhill's obvious sexual jealousy colors his judgment when he criticizes the Professor for engaging in "dirty business." So the film does not accept his point of view uncritically. Although the Professor may be callous, Thornhill's own emotional involvement colors his judgment in problematic ways, as the film will make clear in the subsequent sequence.

For when Thornhill rejects the Professor's entreaty out of hand—his love for Kendall will not let him view her as simply an agent choosing to sacrifice her own well-being for the welfare of the country—he acts *impetuously* to save her.[2] Indeed, from the perspective of the narrative, Thornhill needs to save Kendall so that they can be together and their romance salvaged. His contempt for the Professor, evident in his accusation, "You lied to me!"—and this from a man who did nothing but lie when we first saw him—leads Thornhill to dismiss out of hand any attempt to persuade him to do what the zealous patriot regards as his patriotic duty, if it means accepting Kendall's death as a necessary cost of doing business. He believes that saving her from the danger she faces is more important than

---

[2] Thornhill's sexism supports his need to protect Kendall. If Kendall were a man, would Thornhill be as upset about her being sacrificed for the good of the country? Most likely not. Yet even if we feel compelled to attribute a sexist outlook to the film—a woman who initially seemed quite self-sufficient is shown to be dependent, requiring a male to save her—it's important not to let that distract us from investigating the ethical dimensions of its own narrative.

revealing Vandamm's secret, despite the significance of the latter for purposes of national security.

At this point in the film, then, Thornhill is no longer the egoist he was at the outset, concerned only with his own needs and desires. But neither is he a Cold War "patriot" who accepts the Professor's outlook in which innocent individuals may be sacrificed for the needs of the nation because of the danger posed by alien powers. Rather, as I have already indicated, Thornhill now embodies an ethical point of view in which one's affective ties to other specific individuals—in his case, his love for Kendall—determine which course of action one will pursue. Thornhill is quite willing to risk his life, but rather than for an abstraction like America, only for the flesh and blood human being he loves.

Thornhill's ethical stance bears important similarities to the feminist philosophical position that has come to be called the *ethics of care*. On this view, ethical actions are motivated by the affective ties an individual has to specific people, rather than by an abstract principle such as doing one's patriotic duty. Although this ethical stance has often been associated with women, who are said to exemplify it in their care-giving roles as mothers, wives, and nurturers, *North by Northwest* presents its romantic male lead as acting in accordance with it. Indeed, the film suggests that such moral motivation marks a man as having achieved an admirable mode of masculine assertiveness.

In order to see why *North by Northwest* is critical of Thornhill's newly adopted stance of ethical particularism, we need look quickly at how the narrative develops: Thornhill ignores the pleas of both Eve and the Professor, and heads off to save her. After discovering that Eve's identity as a double agent has been revealed and that Vandamm plans to kill her by throwing her out of the plane, he manages to free her from Vandamm's clutches. The two then find themselves atop Mount Rushmore pursued by Vandamm and his henchmen. In a terrifying scene on the edge of a cliff, while Thornhill saves Eve from certain death by catching and holding her with his right hand, Vandamm's right-hand man, Leonard, stomps on Thornhill's left hand, threatening to thereby plunge the two to their deaths. Fortuitously, a shot rings out, Leonard is hit, and, as he clutches his wounded arm, the statue he has been carrying shatters, revealing a roll of film—thus disclosed as the object of the Professor's search. With characteristic aplomb, Hitchcock executes a match cut[3] from Thornhill holding the flailing Eve atop Mount Rushmore to the interior of a train. (See the illustrations on the following pages.) Only now, Thornhill is pulling his bride, Eve, onto the upper bunk for a night of lovemaking in their train compartment en route to New York. He manages this startling shift of perspective by first cutting to an extreme close-up of Thornhill atop Mount Rushmore (Shot 2), so that when, after a reverse-shot of Kendall (Shot 3) and a return to a close-up of Thornhill (Shot 4) that is virtually identical to Shot 2, the next shot (Shot 5) shows Thornhill pulling Kendall onto the upper-bunk, there is nothing to distinguish the location of that shot from that of the previous one.

What's the significance of this marvelously daring, breathtaking, and yet tongue-in-cheek sequence? Clearly, Thornhill has been acting so as to save Eve, despite his knowledge that this might jeopardize the Professor's plans to use her to learn what secrets Vandamm has. In love as he is, he seems to care more about the welfare of the woman he loves than he does about the nation's well-being. One might understand this as the film delivering the following message: The goals of the patriot are better realized by the particularistic ethics Thornhill follows than by the adherence to the zealous patriotism endorsed by the Professor.

But this understanding misses the film's implicit criticism of Thornhill for acting impetuously. For while Thornhill's rash actions do bring about the result that motivated all of the Professor's elaborate plans and deceits—the disclosure of secret Vandamm had been attempting to smuggle out of the United States, a role of film hidden in a statue—he succeeds only with the Professor's active assistance.

Indeed, acting on his own, Thornhill had brought himself and Kendall quite literally to the brink of disaster, as they dangled from Mount Rushmore, that most evocative of American symbols, their lives in the balance. Only the Professor's timely intervention resulted in Leonard being wounded and the statue being broken to reveal the film. (See the illustration, bottom of page 153.) Without this, both Kendall and Thornhill would have

---

[3] A match cut is a cut between two scenes that is made somewhat continuous by the fact that certain visual features of one *mise-en-scène*—in this case the position of Thornhill and Kendall—are the same in the two very different circumstances.

Hitchcock's breathtaking Match Cut

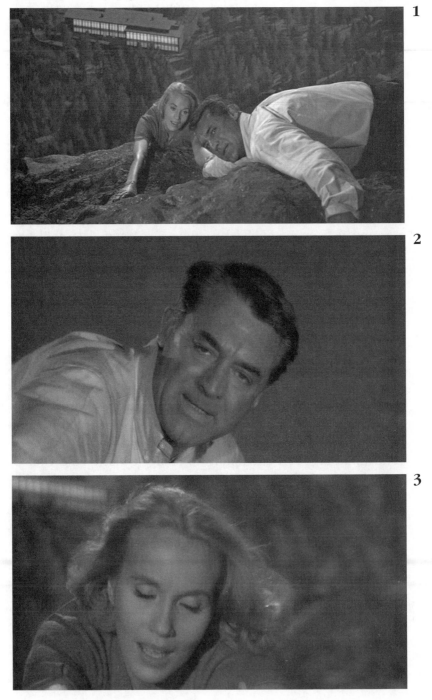

4

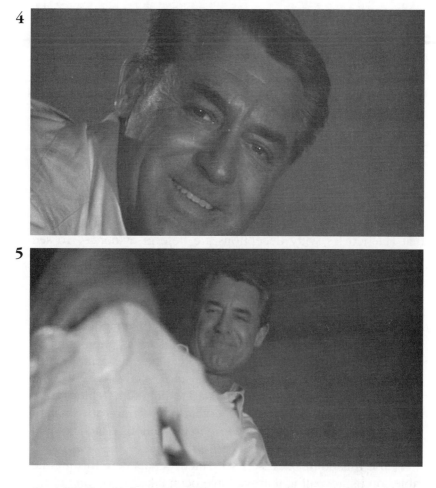

5

One of Hitchcock's famous McGuffins

perished and Vandamm would have succeeded in smuggling the statue out of the country. Only the Professor's foresight in coming to the aid of the rash but heroic Thornhill results in both Kendall's successful rescue and the defeat of Vandamm's plan.

Turning the Tables

What are we to make of the film's apparent muddying the waters of its critique of both these ethical frameworks with this happy ending? Is it asserting the need for a synthesis between the perspectives of the zealous patriot and the moral particularist, of patriotism and romantic love?

Although there is some plausibility to such a claim, I think that Hitchcock's witty deceptions are here in evidence. To see this, we need to acknowledge that *North by Northwest* has a peculiarly light-hearted atmosphere for a Hitchcock film. One feature of the film that contributes to this mood is a series of mockingly self-referential references to film, to acting, and to directing. In the scenes we have examined, this theme emerges in the film's repeated sense of the Professor as attempting to direct and stage actions, most notably when he arranges for Thornhill's staged death. It becomes more obvious when the secret carried by the statue is revealed to be a film. (Critics have conjectured that this might be the very film we are now watching.) And it becomes hard to ignore in the famous match cut that initiates the film's final sequence on the train.

I raise this point because I see Hitchcock as here turning the tables on us, revealing that we have been taken in by one of his famous McGuffins. Hitchcock is known for having his entire film revolve around an element—the McGuffin—that turns out to lack any real importance. So although *North by Northwest* *appears* to be about a conflict between different ethical perspectives, it turns out that it is really about the power of film itself. On such an interpretation, the Professor is ultimately at fault not because he has an inadequate moral perspective—thereby leaving himself open to the charge of callousness—but because he is a bad director whose various attempts at staging don't work out as he intends. Unlike Hitchcock, the Professor doesn't manage a successful deception of *his* audience, Vandamm and Leonard. And even the more attractive Thornhill only manages to escape from his jam atop Mount Rushmore through the creative intervention not only of the character who is a stand in for the film's director—the Professor—but also of the film's actual director, who arranges the daring match cut that results in the film's dramatic resolution and the fulfillment of Thornhill's desires.

So what, then, is the philosophical message of the film if it is not about morality but filmmaking? I take it that Hitchcock is here asserting that it is only *film* that has the power to create the optimistic world in which the commitments of patriotism and of romance will not conflict. The power of the camera—asserted so clearly in that famous match cut to the interior of the train— is that it can reconcile things that are irreconcilable in reality.

For me, then, this is the primary philosophic interest of this film. Going beyond debates about ethical frameworks, *North by Northwest*, in a bold act of self-reflexivity, asserts that it—*film*— has the power to reconcile the apparently irreconcilable, to create a world in which love for one's country will not threaten or be threatened by the love one has for particular individuals. This is the legacy of Hollywood to the world, according to the film. The message, however, is darker than the film's somewhat light-hearted narrative would suggest, for the reconciliations that the film enacts exist only in our imaginations—stimulated as they are by the artifice of Hitchcock's lens—and not in reality as the uncritical viewer might think.

IV

Hitchcock's Ethical Dilemmas

12
Democracy Adrift in *Lifeboat*

RANDALL E. AUXIER

Just about every textbook for introductory ethics courses contains a provocative essay by Garrett Hardin (1915–2003) entitled "Lifeboat Ethics: The Case against Helping the Poor."[1] Hardin was not a "professional" philosopher (whatever that really is), he was rather a professor of "human ecology" (whatever that really is) who became notorious by arguing for extreme positions no one could really stomach. In this case he pictured poor nations as swimmers around a lifeboat, and lifeboats as inhabited by rich nations with their resources and economies and institutions. Hardin argued that rich nations could not help poor nations without swamping their own boats. The best solution was, he claimed, to let the all the swimmers drown.

Arguing in such unpalatable ways is a good method of baiting professional philosophers—seriously try to defend an utterly indefensible position, then wait for their feeding frenzy to begin. Plenty of people wrote articles attacking Hardin, and he became prominent by being so often, so vehemently, and so completely refuted. One reason Hardin's essays are still fed to freshman and sophomore small fry in college is that his arguments are so thin and simplistic that even intellectual *shrimp* can reasonably

---

[1] Originally published in *Psychology Today* 8 (1974), pp. 38–43. Hardin's reasoning has been nicely handled by Michael Patton in "Game Preserve Ethics: The Case for Hunting the Poor," which demonstrates light-heartedly that by Hardin's reasoning one could not consistently stop with not helping the poor, but would in fact be morally obliged actually to *hunt* the poor. See his essay in *Southwest Philosophy Review* 21:1 (2005), pp. 103–110.

expect to dismember the bait. Many ethics teachers think that this sort of thing is good practice for young minds before they have to confront any serious reasoning about ethics.

Hitchcock fans know the lifeboat scenario by other and older means, and indeed, Hitchcock's handling of the scenario is neither simplistic nor extreme.[2] It is challenging to hold in one's thinking the vertiginous complexities of his presentation, but we shall do our best in what follows, using the best binoculars that moral philosophy has to offer.

The Good, the Bad, and the Nazi

Ethics asks the perennial question, "What is the best life?" Even in ancient times people knew that it's impossible to address that question without including politics as a part of the answer—since the best life always includes other people. The companionship of others is essential to living a truly human life, let alone a good one. Hitchcock loved to explore what happens on the outskirts of that need, the pathologies of companionship, if you will. But separating the political and ethical aspects of such difficult questions is tricky, perhaps impossible.

In the history of Western philosophy, the three concepts with which moral philosophers have been most occupied are the "Good," the "Right," and the "Just." The Good is connected to whatever makes a goal or course of action more desirable than some other. The Right concerns what is lawful (whether natural or human or divine law) and how to create or live by such law. The Just concerns the development of character and virtues, socially and individually, that can distinguish the best answers as they relate to and balance the Good and the Right. We have justice when our aims are truly good and our laws are truly right, and we're morally developed enough to recognize that and understand why. Here we have a general way of approaching the best life that is strongly dependent upon the political arrangements of communities. The principles of ethics are crucial to understanding a good, right, and just political order.

---

[2] The script for *Lifeboat* was committee work. Built from a play called "Lifeboat 13" that Twentieth Century Fox had rights to, the script was crafted by John Steinbeck, Jo Swerling, Darryl Zanuck (mainly by complaining about it), Ben Hecht, and throughout the process Hitchcock himself contributed to writing and revising it. Since Hitchcock was responsible for its final form and the dramatization, I will treat the script as his work.

Also, the political ordering of a community sets the context and limits for the moral development of most people who live in it (there are always a few who rise above the standards of their time and circumstances, saints, if you will, and these will not be found in Hitchcock films). Wherever people desire things which only *seem* good to them, but really are not, disorder and unhappiness follow, while wherever the laws are bad, justice is not possible and people are stunted in their moral development. Many such people appear in Hitchcock films; one is tempted to say that *only* such people appear—people who beyond a shadow of a doubt, will mistake what seems good for what really is good, who will not know what is right, and who will have skewed notions of justice and strange character flaws. Even John Milton himself admitted that the devil is more interesting than God in *Paradise Lost* (do they still make kids read that in high school, or has it fallen victim to the separation of church and state? or to the limits of the new shortened attention span—I mean, when is the movie coming out?). The intrigue of the devil may also explain why Hitchcock is more interesting than Stephen Spielberg. In any case, there are no saints in Hitchcock's lifeboat.

Hitchcock's explicit intention in making the film *Lifeboat* (1944) was apparently political, not primarily ethical. The concept for the script presented itself to Hitchcock in 1942, after France had fallen, his native Britain had been daily besieged by merciless Nazi bombers, the allied forces were getting their collective *derrière* kicked by Rommel in North Africa, and Russia was in rapid retreat before the Panzer columns. Things looked bad for the allies, and the outcome of the conflict seemed far from assured. As Hitchcock put it:

> We wanted to show that at that moment there were two world forces confronting each other, the democracies and the Nazis, and while the democracies were completely disorganized, all the Germans were clearly headed in the same direction. So here was a statement telling the democracies to put their differences aside temporarily and to gather their forces to concentrate on the common enemy, whose strength was precisely derived from a spirit of unity and of determination.[3]

---

[3] François Truffaut, *Hitchcock*, revised edition (New York: Touchstone, 1985), p. 155.

So we see that a group of survivors in a lifeboat from a U.S. Merchant Marine vessel, sunk by a German U-Boat, contains a hodge-podge of political viewpoints such as one might find in a democracy. Hitchcock says, "the seaman [Kovac], played by John Hodiak, was practically a Communist, and on the other extreme you had the businessman [Rittenhouse, played by Henry Hull] who was more or less a Fascist" (*Hitchcock*, pp. 155–56). The German U-Boat has gone so far as to fire upon the American *lifeboats*. The Americans in the main vessel have returned fire on their way to the bottom and sunk the German submarine. It is tempting to see the struggle as the snake biting the foot that crushes it, and everyone loses everything, except for an enduring sense of vengeance fully realized.

The political plot thickens when the survivors from the ship drag aboard a survivor from the German U-Boat, known only as "Willy" (perhaps a demeaning and not too subtle allusion to Kaiser Wilhelm II), and must decide what to do with him. To symbolize the political situation, Hitchcock uses as the film's McGuffin a compass. The Nazi sailor secretly has a compass, so he knows where the boat is going, while the others (even the sailors) have no sense of the boat's direction. But the compass is as much a moral as a political direction-finder. Initially it makes a difference to the survivors whether they are rescued by the Nazis or the allies, but this concern begins to fade as they become more desperate and would welcome rescue from any quarter.

Turning Democracy on Its Head

It would be a great task to sort out the political meaning and ethical aspects of this voyage, and such a task would need to consider Hitchcock's other two wartime films, *Saboteur* and *Foreign Correspondent*, not to mention his subsequent Cold War films. A fine study already exists in Ina Rae Hark's work, so I will not pursue this concern further.[4] But I have a point to make about *Lifeboat* that might be overlooked in the political complexities of its plot and conception. No sooner have the survivors dragged the Nazi sailor aboard than a dispute breaks out:

---

[4] Ina Rae Hark, "'We Might Even Get in the Newsreels': The Press and Democracy in Hitchcock's World War II Anti-Fascist Films," in Richard Allen and S. Ishii-Gonzalès, eds., *Alfred Hitchcock: Centenary Essays*, (London: British Film Institute, 1999), pp. 333–347.

KOVAC: Throw the Nazi buzzard overboard.

RITTENHOUSE: That's out of the question and it's against the law.

KOVAC: Whose law? We're on our own here. We can make our own law.[5]

And that's my point. This sabotages the "Right" in our schema of ethics, the place where politics mainly resides, the domain of law. The lifeboat setting reduces the relevance of political loyalties in light of pressing ethical dilemmas—the reason for tossing Willy overboard is for what he has done and what he will do, regardless of whether his political loyalties or his personal judgment were to blame. As the film unfolds, we discover that Willy is in fact the captain of the U-Boat, and has ordered the shelling of the American lifeboats upon his own authority, removing the question still further from politics and making it a war crime for which he would be held morally responsible. This scenario is not about politics, and the lifeboat situation is what eliminates it from consideration.

And I would suppose that this is part of the reason Garrett Hardin uses the same metaphor to focus his own question about helping the poor. He isn't examining the political convictions and systems of wealthy nations at all, simply pointing to a moral fact about them. In fact, a lifeboat scenario effectively turns political questions *into* ethical questions by isolating the actors from what would normally be the legal and political consequences of their actions. As James Agee observed at the time of Hitchcock's film, "the initial idea—a derelict boat and its passengers as microcosm—is itself so artificial that . . . it sets the whole pride and brain too sharply to work on a *tour de force* for its own sake."[6] But what may be a limitation from a filmatic standpoint is an attractive device for a philosophical thought experiment. Or, one critic's trash is another's treasure. Among the many things a philosopher might praise in the lifeboat scenario, I will use only two to illustrate my point about the division of political from ethical loyalties.

---

[5] Quotations from the script for *Lifeboat* are based upon a transcription of the film by Gaye Chandler Auxier and myself. If the script itself is commercially available, I am not aware of the source.

[6] James Agee, *Agee on Film*, Volume 1 (New York: Wideview/Perigree, 1958), p. 71. This essay originally appeared as a film review in *The Nation* (January 22nd, 1944).

First, in the lifeboat there is an equality of condition that would
be hard to achieve in a complex political world, a world in which
a manual laborer like Kovac could have no serious or meaningful argument with a wealthy mogul like Rittenhouse: the power
differential between them determines the outcome of any argument. But in the lifeboat they can have a real dialogue. Second,
since rescue itself is uncertain, since only the *survivors* will tell the
story about was done and how decisions were made, and since
everyone knows that juries will consider their extreme circumstances in determining justice for their actions, even the *idea* of
political and legal consequences is largely neutralized in their
thinking and deciding. The lifeboat may be artificial, but such situations can and do occur, might happen to any of us, and when
they do, it will be our moral rather than political principles tested.

As if making this point intentionally, Hitchcock has the survivors try a hand at organizing themselves politically right from
the start. The businessman Rittenhouse makes this point: "Now,
now, now, we are all sort of fellow travelers in a mighty small
boat on a mighty big ocean. And the more we quarrel and criticize and misunderstand each other, the bigger the ocean gets
and the smaller the boat." After assuming command of the boat,
Rittenhouse begins to issue orders (and he is clearly accustomed
to being obeyed). Here is how the scene plays out:

Kovac: Who elected you skipper?

Rittenhouse: Well . . . I . . . of course if there's anybody else
you'd prefer . . .

Kovac: What do you know about a ship?

Constance: Among other things, he just happens to own a
shipyard, that's all.

Kovac: Has he ever been in it?

Constance: He has thousands of employees. Of course he
knows how to handle men.

Kovac: Not in a lifeboat. What we need is an able seaman
and we've got one.

Gus: Who me? I'm a *dis*abled seaman. Anyhow, I never did
have no executive ability. I . . . I think maybe Sparks there
. . .

Sparks: No, not me. I know a bit about navigation, but . . .
when it comes to taking charge of a boat . . . well . . .
What about Kovac?

CONSTANCE: That klunk? Run this boat? With what? An oilcan? If you're talking about a skipper, we have a skipper right on this boat. (*indicates the German, Willy, who isn't listening*)

RITTENHOUSE: He wasn't the captain.

CONSTANCE: Wasn't he? (*tricks him*) Herr Capitain?

WILLY: Ja?

GUS: Well I'm a monkey's uncle!

CONSTANCE: There. You have a man who's familiar with these waters. He knows seamanship and he knows navigation. What about it?

KOVAC: Do you mean you want to turn the boat over to the man who sunk our ship and shelled our lifeboats?

CONSTANCE: I mean I want *you* to turn the boat over to the man obviously best qualified to run it.

KOVAC: You're crazy.

RITTENHOUSE: Now wait a minute. There are two sides to everything. Let's look at this thing straight, calmly, and reasonably. The German is just as anxious to get to safety as we are. And if he's a trained skipper, why shouldn't he take charge?

KOVAC: Because I'm taking charge.

CONSTANCE: Since when?

KOVAC: As of now, I'm skipper. And anybody who don't like it can get out and swim to Bermuda. What about that?

GUS: I'll buy it.

SPARKS: Suits me. What about you, Miss?

MACKENZIE: I'm for it.

JOE: Yes sir.

RITTENHOUSE: Well, if the rest agree. . . .

CONSTANCE: Alright, Commissar, what's the course?

So much for democratic politics. Faced with the issue of leadership, the democratic method is here turned on its head, and the survivors respond not to leadership experience (Rittenhouse), not to skill (Willy), but to a threat.[7] Kovac's objection to putting the

---

[7] I have no reason to think Hitchcock was aware of it, but Plato describes an uncannily similar scene in *Republic*, lines 488a–489d.

German in charge was not that he was a Nazi, but that he sank the American ship and then shelled the lifeboats from it—this was an objection to his moral fitness, not his political loyalties.

Without necessarily intending to do so, Hitchcock rendered the political issues largely symbolic and allegorical. He motivates the actions and words of the players in accord with their most basic moral and ethical loyalties, not primarily their political loyalties—even Kovac finally accedes to giving control of the boat to Willy when he recognizes that their survival depends on it. This dynamic allows us to examine the action from an ethical point of view without worrying overmuch about the politics. But I should point out that I am not taking Hitchcock's "intentions" blithely. The "Trouble with Alfred" is that it is not really possible to determine what his true intentions were at any given time. One of his biographers pointed out, "Alfred Hitchcock was a master of the red herring, and he told interviewers just what they wanted to hear—a neat psychological explanation, connected to a facile anecdote, to justify a frequent plot device."[8] And Hitchcock was not one to spoil a good story by encumbering it with the truth either.

The Challenge to Ethical Pluralism

One of the first things a person should notice is that any political system can be served for a variety of ethical reasons. One may become a Nazi because one is afraid of the consequences if one refuses, or because one approves of the goals of the Nazis and thinks they have admissible means of achieving them. One may become a Nazi because of a sense of duty to one's nation or race, and the consequences do not really matter. One may become a Nazi because one believes that they are superior people, people who should be imitated, trusted, and looked upon as models of efficiency, intelligence, and insight.

One might become a Nazi out of pure self-interest, or for profit, or fame, or power, or simple survival. The last of these, survival, is Willy's ethical motive, as far as we can ever learn. If he has ethical principles that rise above the intention to survive, we never see them. Each and every act, from saving Gus's life

---

[8] Donald Spoto, *The Dark Side of Genius: The Life of Alfred Hitchcock* (New York: Ballantine, 1983), p. 15.

by amputating his gangrenous leg, to murdering him later, and everything in between, is calculated as means to personal survival. But people also became Nazis on the weight of all of these different ethical judgments and many more. People subscribe to democracies for exactly the same various formal and practical reasons—because they believe a democracy offers the better or best ways of obtaining whatever they value most. Both totalitarian and democratic states can accommodate the variety.

"Ethical pluralism" means recognizing that, as a matter of indisputable fact, in the world we actually inhabit, people embrace the same goals, laws, and balance between them (Good, Right, Justice) for different and often conflicting reasons. On Hitchcock's lifeboat, among the citizens of democracies, we find: a person who thinks that the best life is that of making money (Rittenhouse); one who thinks that fame is the best life (Constance Porter, the reporter); one who thinks that the best life is equality in community (Kovac); one who thinks the best life is to serve God (Joe Spencer, the ship's steward); one who thinks the best life is to help and care for others (Alice MacKenzie, the nurse); one who thinks that romantic love is the most worthy of human pursuit (Stanley Garrett, the radio operator); and one who lives for pleasure—the metaphor is dancing, but Hitchcock makes it clear enough that this is about sex (Gus Smith, the ship's helmsman).

Along with this dizzying array of ideas about the best life comes an equally complex set of reasons for choosing them and ways of pursuing them. These survivors are all more or less committed to democratic principles, more or less patriotic citizens, more or less agreed that Naziism is morally and politically bankrupt. But their problem is that they have spent such a long time pursuing their own ideas about the Good, within the broad limits of Right and Justice that democracy allows, that they are slow to recognize the gravity of their situation and more inclined to have philosophical arguments about what they should do, and why, than to act decisively. As a result, Willy is able to manipulate all of them, not because they lack ethical principles, but precisely because they hold their personal versions of those principles so dearly. Each of the principal characters, apart from Willy, is willing to consider the idea of dying rather than releasing those personal principles. They can always come up with individual reasons satisfactory to themselves (even if in conflict with one another) to allow the German to have his way. And so the German is able to sink their ship, shell their lifeboats, conceal his true identity as Captain, pretend not to speak English, withhold the compass, lie, dissimulate, deceive, and finally even commit murder, all with impunity while the others debate the Good, the Right, and the Just. This is the challenge to ethical pluralism.

A Voyage Down the Hierarchy of Needs

As annoyingly simplistic as it is, the psychologist Abraham Maslow truly put his finger on some facts about human beings and their capacity for moral reasoning. His paper "A Theory of Human Motivation" appeared at the auspicious moment for a pluralistic world, that is, in 1943, just as everyone was beginning to wonder anew, "What is humanity?" I have no reason to think that Hitchcock would have been aware of Maslow's "hierarchy of needs" when he made *Lifeboat*, but in many ways the hierarchy is common sense anyway, and Hitchcock didn't need a psychologist to help him grasp human motives—which is not to say Hitchcock didn't need a psychologist. As time passes on the lifeboat, the survivors descend the hierarchy of needs, and Hitchcock demonstrates to us just how tenacious are those values we seek at the highest and most luxurious perch of self-actualization—and here Maslow lists creativity, problem-solving, spontaneity, lack of prejudice, acceptance of facts, and most importantly, *morality*. Maslow claims that people ultimately seek to be moral as a luxury (which is not to say it isn't a genuine need), when all the more basic needs are satisfied. In the levels below self-actualization we find, in descending order, needs associated with esteem, love and belonging, safety, and basic physiological functioning. In the lifeboat, only Willy recognizes from the outset that their situation must be decided on the basis of the lowest level, that of physiological functioning, and so he gets water for himself, extra food, conceals energy pills and the compass, and knowing he is not safe, feels no compunction about still higher needs of love or esteem or—least of all—morality.

It's a lot of fun to quibble with Maslow about where to place various needs in his famous hierarchy, but what is difficult to deny is that they do all tend to disappear, for most people, as we are reduced to meeting the merest survival needs. And in this domain, well, ethics seems to take a serious holiday. Or does it? If Hitchcock has a single theme in this film, it is that survival can be, and sometimes must be the spring for action and decision. He does not deny that different people will act from different motives, and he does not suggest that they ought to have the same motives, only that they must learn to recognize that survival is a defensible value. So the climactic scene comes when Willy is exposed as having water while the rest are dying of thirst. Let us see what sets them off, finally brings them to kill Willy:

> **WILLY** *(says smugly)*: I took the precaution of filling the flask from the water breakers before the storm, just in case of emergency. And I had food tablets. And energy pills too. Everybody on the U-boat has them. You should be grateful to me for having the foresight to think ahead. To survive, one must have a plan. But there's nothing to worry about. Soon we'll reach the [German] supply ship and then we'll all have food and water. Too bad Schmidt couldn't have waited.

In referring to "Schmidt," Willy is speaking of Gus Smith, whose family has changed the spelling of its name to conceal German heritage. It is clear that, although he "had to" murder Gus, Willy admires only Gus among the passengers, feels a certain solidarity with him, but not enough to alter the uncompromising hierarchy of needs—and after all, Willy has given orders that led to the deaths of many of his countrymen without hesitation, since he views their collective survival as requiring the noble sacrifice of some, a sacrifice he is himself clearly willing to make.

Immediately following the speech above, our democratic individualists suddenly abandon their endless debates and mob Willy, beating him and throwing him overboard. Perhaps the hierarchy of needs has had the last word, but I don't think so. Not only does each "kill Willy" for his or her own reasons, what has actually motivated their action is not a desire to survive but in fact it is moral outrage. Somehow Willy has, in this speech, managed to trigger the moral outrage of the critical mass, and in doing so he badly miscalculated, for the first time. To put it in the vernacular, you actually can rile a group of pluralists to the point of collective action, but it isn't easy. But are they really at the mercy of the hierarchy of needs? It's clear that Hitchcock is saying they are not. In fact, Hitch is saying the opposite. When they killed Willy, as Rittenhouse points out, they actually doomed themselves:

> **RITTENHOUSE** (*says in bemused resignation*): 'Til my dying day, I'll never understand Willy and what he did. First he tried to kill us all with his torpedoes. Nevertheless, we fished him out of the sea, took him aboard, shared everything we had with him. You'd have thought he'd have been grateful. All he could do was to plot against us. Then he . . . he let poor ol' Gus die of thirst. What do you do with people like that? Maybe one of us ought to try to row. Where to? What for? Nah, when we killed the German, we killed our motor.

This sparks a "quitters never win" and "never give up the ship" speech from Constance, but the point is made. The collective action came at the expense of hope for survival, not on account of it. Maslow loses the card game: some people would rather die than curb their personal moral outrage.

E Pluribus Unum?

The motto of the United States means "from many, one," but I think Hitchcock has been careful to preserve that "many" in this ethical situation. He has partly done this by showing the possibility of decisive collective action, simultaneously but for many different reasons, and also by showing that our German antagonist has taken the wrong turn by imagining that survival will be the moral bottom line for his boat-mates. This leaves the Good, the Right, and the Just intact, and even in charge, in Hitch's pluralism. But there are three other altogether crucial features of the film and script that reinforce this pluralistic standpoint.

The first is that Joe, the pious, God-fearing steward, simply refuses to participate in killing Willy. He interprets this as mob behavior, bent upon violence, for which there is never a justification. But he does not stand idly by while the others kill Willy—rather, he makes a sincere effort, even in the heat of the mob, to dissuade Nurse MacKenzie from participating. Yes, Willy will now be killed. But Joe recognizes in MacKenzie's commitment to helping others a kindred soul, someone whose principles, while they are different from his own (being human-itarian rather than theistic) nevertheless overlap. Joe knows she will always regret having taken a life, will not be able to recon-cile it with herself, and tragically, she has no God to approach for forgiveness. But he fails to dissuade her. Humanitarian moral outrage trumps humanitarian impulses to nurture, in Hitchcock's ethical worldview. The others don't actually need MacKenzie to dispose of Willy. She chooses to participate anyway, freely and without necessity (again Maslow takes a hit). Yet Joe not only maintains his peaceable disposition, he will not even look upon the violence, bows his head, and turns away. Hitchcock pre-sents him as neither a coward nor as a hero. Joe embodies a worldview, that of pacifism and genuine piety, which is a per-manent fixture of ethical pluralism—he pleads his case only to the one who has a reason to listen, and leaves the others to their own consciences. And note that Rittenhouse's conscience is not troubled in what he says after he has killed. He is troubled by ingratitude and irrationality, not by his own actions. No one else has a serious bout of conscience, and Joe does not judge them for doing what they have done.

Hitchcock's ethical pluralism cannot only allow this pacifism, but he can present it as a crucial presence in the moral mix. Yet, when the conscientious objectors have made their decisions (and there were certainly still these voices in the US and Britain, even in 1944), still the collective "coalition of the willing" (and I do despise that phrase) will have to act, not for the survival of the democracy, but for the sake of the principles each holds dearly enough to die or kill for their sake.

Second, and more important, is that no character in *Lifeboat* demonstrates any significant moral growth, any basic change of attitude or outlook, any expectation of making a fundamental movement from the principles with which he or she began. We have some serious candidates for moral growth. Constance has every opportunity, as her treasured symbols of success and fame disappear one by one, to come to a new understanding of the best life, but upon realizing that they will be rescued, her first concern is for her appearance, and her second is to make cer-tain that her new love, Kovac, does indeed take charge of the factory he has won from Rittenhouse in a card game—she wants a man of means, even if he is a socialist. Kovac has every opportunity to learn how his collectivism is ideological and how he really isn't a socialist but a disempowered capitalist. Rittenhouse teaches him as much, but Kovac goes along his merry way, collecting a new lover whose grasping worldly values he presumes to despise, and becoming a factory owner himself, with notions of empowering his own workers with weekly meetings and joint decision-making. In short, he learns nothing. Rittenhouse is another well-developed character who does not need to survive and does not fear death, but if he is to live, he will live for the joy of making money. In some ways, the ironic reversal is embodied in the responses of Kovac and Rittenhouse to the circumstances of the group's ultimate rescue.

And the third (and most important) point arises here. The group of survivors is resigned to being rescued by a German supply ship—this had been Willy's plan all along. As the supply ship approaches and sends out a boat to pick them up, a Hitchcock-esque twist follows. An American ship appears and begins to fire on the German supply ship, payback one assumes, and hits the would-be rescue boat and then sinks the supply ship itself. Hence, our many-faceted survivors have a moment of well-earned vengeance, to be followed by a rescue by a friendly vessel. But then two hands appear from the sea and a young German sailor is dragged aboard. Examine closely the dialogue that follows:

CONSTANCE: And a . . . Look!

SAILOR: Danke schön.

MACKENZIE: Let's get his coat off.

RITTENHOUSE: Hey, wait a minute. Have you forgotten about Willy already?

CONSTANCE: Well, Ritt, this is different. The kid's wounded.

RITTENHOUSE: Throw him back!

CONSTANCE: Don't be silly, darling. He's . . . he's helpless. He's only a baby.

(*The German sailor pulls a gun and points it at the survivors; they are completely unafraid.*)

KOVAC: The baby has a toy.

JOE: I should have frisked him.

RITTENHOUSE: See? You can't treat them as human beings. You've got to exterminate them.

(Joe grabs the sailor's wrist; the sailor drops the gun, Constance throws it overboard. Rittenhouse makes a move to throw the sailor overboard.)

KOVAC: Easy Ritt. He'll be taken care of.

(The German speaks.)

CONSTANCE: *(translating)* He says, "Aren't you going to kill me?"

MACKENZIE: *(looking at the wound)* We'll have to tie this up until the ship's doctor takes care of it.

KOVAC: Aren't you going to kill me? What are you going to do with people like that?

We are cued that this is a reprise of their first argument by the German's saying "Danke schön," Willy's first words after he was pulled aboard. Here's an opportunity to see what our survivors have learned. The answer is "nothing" or "not much." But there is a nice role reversal. Kovac is the one who argued for throwing Willy overboard, and Rittenhouse resisted. Now Rittenhouse wants the German thrown out and Kovac resists. This is emblematic of the way in which a socialist and a capitalist are really, for democratic purposes, two sides of the same coin: but for luck and circumstance, one would have been the other, as Hitchcock nicely symbolizes in having Kovac and Rittenhouse play poker all the way through the episode. Only chance and circumstance separate the two ethical viewpoints, but they are what they are: potent, vital, and different.

So what is Hitchcock saying? One does not want to wait upon Sir Alfred for one's ethics, frankly. But there is a certain wisdom in this, and a surprising theme. It is, if I am correct, that there are ethical resources in each of us that demand moral outrage in the presence of those whose only principle is survival. If democracy as a form of life stands for anything at all, it stands for the idea that we may pursue different versions of Good, Right, and Justice, but that we can still act in concert on the basis of moral outrage when we can recognize the need for it. The question that remains is why we are so slow to recognize it. Why do we not learn from having seen it before? Hitchcock doesn't answer that question. If he had answered it, he would be Spielberg. And we wouldn't want that.

13

Why Be Moral? Amorality and Psychopathy in *Strangers on a Train*

STEVEN M. SANDERS

Alfred Hitchcock knew his psychopaths. He featured them in two of his most suspenseful films, *Strangers on a Train* and *Psycho*.[1] Hitchcock knew as well that what fascinates us about the psychopath is not his derangement but his charm. Charming or not, the psychopath is a challenge to ethics, the branch of philosophy dealing with qualities of character and with the nature and justification of our moral beliefs, principles, standards, and actions. Since morality for psychopaths is no more than a set of guidelines to be followed until impulse or self-interest dictates otherwise,[2] the willingness of the psychopath to reject the restraints of morality raises the difficult question, "Why be moral?" Reflecting on *Strangers on a Train* will help us understand how philosophers use the ideas of rationality, self-interest, and psychological health to answer this question.

Family Plot

Strangers on a Train is a blend of Hitchcockian suspense and *film noir* atmosphere, with intricate compositions, dramatic lighting, dazzling special effects, and a hilarious cameo appearance by Hitchcock as the train of the film's title pulls into the

---

[1] Hitchcock liked to say "casting is characterization," and with brilliant performances by Robert Walker as Bruno Anthony and Anthony Perkins as Norman Bates, Hitch found his dictum's finest examples.

[2] Robert J. Smith summarizes and comments on some of the relevant clinical and philosophical literature in "The Psychopath as Moral Agent," *Philosophy and Phenomenological Research* 65 (1984), pp. 177–193.

station and the gray-suited director climbs aboard carrying an enormous bass fiddle.

Two strangers meet on a train—top amateur tennis player Guy Haines (Farley Granger), whose career and love life are covered regularly in the newspapers, and Bruno Anthony, the dapper, spoiled son of a doting and dotty mother (Marion Lorne) and a wealthy father whom Bruno wants killed. Bruno has read that Guy is estranged from his wife, Miriam (Laura Elliott), and is seeing another woman, Ann Morton (Ruth Roman), a U.S. senator's daughter. Guy wants to divorce his wife, marry Ann, and begin a career in Washington politics. Guy's wife, already in the early stages of pregnancy with another man's child, won't agree to a divorce and threatens to ruin his reputation if he refuses to take her to Washington and raise her child as their own. Since both Bruno and Guy have someone they'd like out of the way, Bruno proposes that they "swap murders"—"You do my murder, I do yours. Your wife, my father, criss-cross." Since Bruno and Guy are strangers, there's nothing to connect them. As he explains his "theory of the perfect murder," Bruno offers Guy facile rationalizations ("What's a life or two, Guy? Some people are better off dead") and asks if Guy "likes" his theory, if it's "okay." Guy plays along, telling him "Sure, Bruno, sure. They're *all* okay," just to humor the fellow who's been describing his "theories" all afternoon.

When Bruno calls on Guy to inform him he's *actually* murdered Miriam and expects Guy to keep his end of the agreement, Guy tells him he's crazy and refuses to have anything to do with him. Bruno is furious. He stalks Guy, showing up unexpectedly at Guy's tennis club where he ingratiates himself with Guy's friends, chatting amiably in French. He calls Guy constantly, insisting that Guy carry out his part of the arrangement. When Guy threatens to go to the police, Bruno reminds Guy he's already deeply implicated in his wife's murder. "Who has the most to gain?" Bruno asks with reference to Guy's affair with Ann. "Not me. I'm a stranger." Guy knows he's trapped but clings to the hope that Bruno will go away.

The Wrong Man

Bruno's weirdness is on full display at a party at the home of Senator Morton. He introduces himself to the Senator and tells him he has an idea about "harnessing the life force." "Can you imagine," he asks the puzzled Senator, "being able to smell a flower on the planet Mars?" In the middle of a demonstration of strangulation, Bruno notices Ann's younger sister, Barbara (Hitchcock's daughter, Patricia), whose prominent eyeglasses remind him of Guy's wife, who wore similar glasses. (The scene in which Bruno strangled Miriam was shot as a reflection in her glasses which had fallen to the ground, one of several stunning Hitchcockian visual effects.) As Bruno stares at Barbara, he begins to re-live the killing and gets so carried away he blacks out and has to be carried into the study to be revived. It seems like "nothing's bolted down in Bruno's brain," to use writer Barry Gifford's colorful phrase; "his head is like a trashed pinball machine, with little sparks and bulbs lighting up here and there but in all the wrong places and sequences."[3] But this is not to say he's insane. His motives, at any rate, are quite clear. He hates his father and has good reason to fear him: he's threatened to have Bruno institutionalized. Bruno's behavior, as erratic as it is, is *purposive* in important respects. He wants his father dead. The fact that he's prepared to commit murder to achieve his goal shows that Bruno is *indifferent* to morality, at the very least, and quite likely contemptuous of it. But it doesn't prove he can't tell right from wrong in the first place.[4]

The "Notorious" Question . . .

Most of us believe that Bruno's done something morally wrong. When a person faces a conflict between his own interest and his moral obligation to respect the lives of others, the latter is supposed to prevail. Moral reasons are commonly thought to be "higher" or "stronger" or "better" than selfish ones. A concern for the welfare of, or respect for the rights of, others is normally thought to provide a stronger reason than a selfish regard for one's own interests. Even granting Hitchcock's depiction of

---

[3] Barry Gifford, *Out of the Past: Adventures in Film Noir* (Jackson: University Press of Mississippi, 2001), p. 160.

[4] According to the system of criminal justice in the U.S. a person is not responsible for criminal conduct if, as a result of mental disease, he or she is unable to know or appreciate the wrongfulness of his or her acts.

Guy's wife as a promiscuous shrew and a blackmailer, this does-n't provide Bruno with a moral justification for killing her. Clearly we have good reasons for our commonsense belief that what Bruno did was morally wrong. But the more compelling and difficult question is *why should he be moral?* Can we give Bruno (or anyone else, for that matter) a reason to be moral—especially when there are very strong temptations *not* to be moral? Philosophers since the time of Plato have tried to answer this question and Hitchcock's film helps us to understand the practical implications of a failure to give an affirmative answer. If a generally convincing answer to the question can't be given, why *shouldn't* Bruno make such an arrangement and expect Guy to carry out his end of the bargain? And why *shouldn't* Guy reciprocate? And, by implication, why should *you* refrain from acts of lying, theft, betrayal, and worse if these would be to your advantage (provided you had a reasonably good chance of get-ting away with them)?

. . . And Three Answers

Answers to the question "Why be moral?" can be divided into three groups. One group of views, often associated with the German philosopher Immanuel Kant (1724–1804), identifies moral behavior with rational behavior. For views of this type, it is simply irrational to be immoral. A second group of views is based on the idea that "morality pays." According to this view, which is associated with the English philosopher Thomas Hobbes (1588–1679), life without the constraints of morality would be "mean, brutish, nasty, and short." A third group of views identifies morality with psychological health and immorality with mental illness. We should be moral because the pains and sufferings of others are comparable to our own and only someone who was deranged would think the pain and suffering of others was of no importance to him or her. Representatives of this view include contemporary American philosophers James Rachels, William N. Nelson, and Laurence Thomas. These answers aren't mutually exclusive, of course. One could take all three positions. In fact, it's not hard to find philosophers who hold that morality is rational, that it pays to be moral, and that being moral goes hand-in-hand with psy-chological health.

Morality Is Rational

The writings of Kant are notoriously difficult, but it's surprisingly easy to state his central ethical idea: people are moved by reasons to act in various ways, so their actions are governed by certain rational constraints, the most important of which is a principle Kant calls the Categorical Imperative: "Act only according to that maxim by which you can at the same time will that it should become a universal law."[5] The Categorical Imperative lays down a rational procedure for determining the moral rightness or wrongness of an act. When we are considering what to do, we are to ask whether we consistently would be willing to have *everyone* follow the rule *we* would be following (Kant calls this the "maxim" of our action). If we would be willing, the act is morally permissible; if not, the act is morally impermissible because it is contrary to reason.

Let's return to Bruno to see how this works. The rule Bruno appears to be following (the maxim of his action) is: "If my happiness is in jeopardy, I will take the necessary steps to remove the obstacles to my happiness." Now, Bruno wouldn't be willing for this rule to become a universal law—that is, to be followed by everyone, for at some point Bruno might himself be an obstacle to someone's happiness, and he certainly wouldn't want to be killed for that reason. He wouldn't be willing to be on the "receiving end" of a maxim which made him the "target" in the way he makes Guy's wife (whom he has nothing against) *his* target. Therefore, he can't *consistently* "will the maxim" of his action and yet remain committed to his own happiness and well-being.

Bruno might still somehow accept Kant's procedure. He could insist that the egoist maxim, "People should take whatever steps are necessary to remove obstacles to their own happiness" *can* be universalized.[6] Bruno might be willing to take his chances with everyone's following this rule, believing himself to be clever and resourceful enough to make his way through the minefield of social interactions. He might even mount a vigorous "charm offensive," feigning sympathetic understanding of

---

[5] Immanuel Kant, *Groundwork of the Metaphysics of Morals* (New York: Harper, 1964), p. 67.

[6] Kant assumes there's only one clear maxim in play, but as we see here, this isn't always the case.

people's problems in order to convince them he was no threat to their happiness and that he was in fact quite a decent chap. Far from being irrational, this may be a perfectly rational strategy for achieving his goals. Since there's no inconsistency in Bruno's willingness to universalize his maxim, he would not be acting contrary to reason.[7]

Of course, Bruno might deny the legitimacy of this Kantian procedure for justifying maxims in the first place. Against Kant's approach we can imagine Bruno saying: "What makes you think I have to justify my maxims universally? I can justify them to *myself*, and that's all that matters to me. And if I become a nuisance to others, let them take their best shot. I doubt that they'll succeed."

Defenders of Kant have their responses, but let's consider another answer to "Why be moral?"

Morality Pays

Many philosophers agree that "morality pays," but to give this answer some specificity, let's consider an influential approach that focuses on the pay-offs and trade-offs involved in being moral. This is nicely captured by the idea that everyone will do better if everyone follows moral rules such as "Do not kill," "Do not steal," and so on. As the philosopher Kurt Baier puts it, the moral point of view is a standpoint from which moral rules are adopted "for the good of everyone alike."[8] Developing a connection between morality and self-interest associated with Hobbes, Baier claims that "being moral is following rules designed to overrule self-interest whenever it is in the interests of everyone alike that everyone should set aside his interest" (p. 314). This means that everyone will do better if everyone follows the rules of morality and agrees to accept limitations on the pursuit of their own self-interest.

---

[7] This type of means-end rationality is only one among many ways to understand rationality. It puts no constraints on what one's ends or goals should be, just the effectiveness of the means to achieve them, whatever their content. The Scottish philosopher David Hume (1711–1776), for instance, once wrote that it isn't contrary to reason to prefer the destruction of the whole world to the scratching of his finger. I'll discuss a different view of rationality at the end of this chapter.

[8] Kurt Baier, *The Moral Point of View* (Ithaca: Cornell University Press, 1958), p. 200.

Although limiting your own self-interested actions in this way involves some sacrifice, it pays off because you stand to gain more from the willingness of others to limit their pursuit of self-interest than you lose from your own willingness to do likewise. After all, which world would *you* rather live in: one in which everyone seeks his own advantage (even at your expense), or one in which everyone (including you) is willing to sacrifice some personal advantage for the good of everyone alike? The "morality pays" answer illustrates how it is in everybody's interest to be moral.

Unfortunately, the answer to the question "Why should *everyone* be moral?" is not an answer, for each person, to the question "Why should *I* be moral?" Bruno, for example, seeks his own self-interest by murdering Miriam, thus denying her something that's in *her* self-interest. But that doesn't provide *him* with a reason to be moral, because he knows he can count on *others* to comply with moral rules even when *he doesn't.* It may be true that morality requires each of us to restrain the pursuit of our own self-interest in return for acts of restraint by others. But Bruno will insist *he'll* do *still better* if everyone *except him* follows the rules of morality and restrains their own self-interested actions while he places no such limitations on his own. In ethics Bruno is what is known as a "free rider": someone who exploits the willingness of others to place restrictions on their own self-interested behavior without reciprocating by limiting his own self-interested behavior. The bottom line for Bruno is that "morality pays" as long as everybody *else* behaves morally, but it doesn't pay *him* to be moral.

Morality Is Psychologically Healthy

The answers to "Why be moral?" that make up the third group emphasize our ability to recognize the *similarities* between ourselves and others and to *care about* what happens to them even when this isn't tied to our self-interest. As the philosopher James Rachels writes: "We should care about the interests of other people for the same reason we care about our own interests; for their needs and desires are comparable to our own."[9]

---

[9] James Rachels, *The Elements of Moral Philosophy, Third Edition* (New York: McGraw-Hill, 1994), p. 95.

But it's not obvious that this appeal to the comparability of the needs, desires, and interests of others with our own succeeds in explaining what it's supposed to explain. Rachels's idea that the pain Bruno feels (or would feel if he were in the position of his victim) is comparable to hers doesn't explain *why* he should care about her in the first place. And it surely doesn't give Bruno a reason to treat his victim's needs and interests on a par with his own. The fact that Guy's wife will suffer if he strangles her gives Bruno a reason to avoid causing her suffering only if he *already* cares about her (which he clearly doesn't). Far from *proving* that the suffering Bruno causes others is relevant to the question of what he ought to do, Rachels *assumes* it.

Echoing Rachels's view, William N. Nelson, in a book aptly titled *Morality: What's in It for Me?*, argues that people "are able to adopt the perspective of others and care about what can be justified to them. And so, even when morality requires that we adopt an impartial standpoint, morality can still be justified, at least to most normal people."[10] A more extreme version of this position is put forward by Laurence Thomas, who writes that "it is *because* we are psychologically healthy beings that we are capable of considering the interests of others even when we have no reason to believe that doing so will serve our own interests."[11]

But what do Nelson and Thomas mean by "normal" or "psychologically healthy" people? They seem to have in mind those who consider the interests of others to be no less important than their own interests. But Bruno would not be fazed by the suggestion that he's not "normal" in *this* sense, and he'd rebut the claim that normal people are those who can adopt an impartial standpoint by asking: "Why should I adopt an impartial standpoint? Even if I *can be* motivated to treat others impartially, that's no reason why I *should*. It's only an *option*. Maybe what I *should* do is seek my self-interest at their expense. I think I will!"

Psycho'd

We know enough of Bruno's backstory to establish a pattern found in his whole way of living. He's been kicked out of three

---

[10] William N. Nelson, *Morality: What's in It for Me?* (Boulder: Westview, 1991), p. x.
[11] Laurence Thomas, "Ethical Egoism and Psychological Dispositions," *American Philosophical Quarterly* 17 (1980), p. 78.

colleges for drinking and gambling and he believes "you should do everything before you die." In reality, however, Bruno doesn't know *what* he wants beyond the very things he says he envies in Guy—money, recognition, adventure—and which lead him to believe Guy might accept the "arrangement" he proposes. Bruno knows he *doesn't* want to hold a steady job and "work his way up," as his father thinks he should. As a result, "my father thinks I'm a bum. He hates me. I get so sore at him sometimes I want to kill him." In fact, Bruno has spent a lot of time thinking about how to commit "the perfect murder," so his willingness to murder Guy's wife and to manipulate Guy into murdering his father comes as no surprise.

Bruno's behavior exhibits a number of major symptoms of psychopathy.[12] There's the obvious disregard of Guy's wife; and insofar as Guy is an unwilling accomplice of Bruno's wild scheme, there's Bruno's manipulation of Guy as a means to his own selfish ends. His disproportionate response (murder) to his rage at his father is another example—the father-figure, by the way, is the Freudian representative of a socially conditioned moral order that limits our worst impulses. His superficially clever but erratic plan, which he longs to act out, seems to be based on highly unrealistic expectations. Even if Bruno isn't psychotically irrational, there's a clear enough sense in which he's "mad, bad, and dangerous to know," as Lady Caroline Lamb said of Lord Byron. But do these facts about Bruno undermine the basis of morality, as though the psychopath's form of life might somehow appeal to us as an alternative to being moral?[13] Let's conclude with a suggestion about how we might go about answering this question.

Why Be Moral?

Most of us find Bruno's behavior appalling, but it's troubling that none of the previously proposed answers to "Why be moral?" is

---

[12] I've adapted the general account of psychopathy in Smith, "The Psychopath as Moral Agent," p. 189.

[13] Bernard Williams discusses this general form of the question in *Morality: An Introduction to Ethics* (New York: Harper Torchbook, 1972), pp. 8–10, and at greater length in *Problems of the Self* (Cambridge: Cambridge University Press, 1973), pp. 250–265.

altogether satisfactory. The first answer ("morality is rational") is *too broad*. The psychopath who is willing to universalize his exclusively self-interested maxim might pass Kant's test with flying colors, which is why Bruno can say *he's* rational too (in a sense). The second answer ("morality pays") is *too narrow*. Bruno can enjoy the benefits of morality by free-riding on the willingness of others to be moral even when he's not, which is why Bruno can say it doesn't pay *him* to be moral as long as others are. And the third answer ("morality is psychologically healthy, immorality is pathological") fails to explain why we *should* adopt an impartial standpoint, even if we *can*.

One way to respond to "Why be moral?" is to stop treating the question as a challenge to morality and a demand for its justification and instead to treat it as a problem of decision-making about how we want to live. How *should* we decide between living morally and living a way of life in which we reject morality? If we were to *compare* a way of life in which being moral plays a central role with a way of life in which it plays no part, and then determined which way of life we found *preferable*, that would give us what we want. But *can* we understand the mind-set of someone who rejects morality, so we can make the comparison? Rather than dogmatically insist on the correctness of our own, admittedly non-psychopathic, perspective, we need an impartial standpoint from which to compare the two ways of life. To provide such a standpoint, let's conduct a little "thought experiment," an imaginative device we can use to explore this possibility.[14]

Imagine that you could turn yourself into a Bruno-type: you're incapable of thinking of other people's needs and interests except as extensions of your needs and interests, and even then only when you're fixated on some wild scheme. Now imagine that you can enter a third state in which you can remember both this Bruno-state *and* what you were previously like—a person who had feelings of sympathy, compassion, and benevolence, who was capable of remorse, guilt, and repentance, and who was disposed to care for the needs and interests of others just as you cared for your own. From the perspective of this third state, you could compare the two ways of life objectively and decide which was preferable to you. You could con-

---

[14] In developing this and the next paragraph, I've modified Peter Singer's thought experiment in *Practical Ethics* (Cambridge: Cambridge University Press, 1979), p. 89.

trast the satisfactions of human contact you initially had with those you'd be missing in the Bruno-state, and see whether any compensating satisfactions could be found. If you can make sense of this supposition of finding one way of life preferable to another from this perspective, which would you choose—a life in which the needs and interests of others matter to you for their own sake and are relevant to your decisions about how to act, or a life in which this is not the case?

When you think about it in these terms, you may well discover that far from being appealing, the Bruno-state represents a model of how *not* to live. Here's why. The ancient Greek philosopher Aristotle (384–322 B.C.) suggested that we find the moral life ultimately preferable because it best reflects who and what we are as human beings. It's the path to happiness and the deepest fulfillment of which we're capable. Properly understood, rationality reveals morality's content to us. Some goals, like having friendships, suit our natures better than others, like killing indiscriminately. So following morality's rational dictates is the means of achieving both good consequences and mental health. *Eudaimonia*, or human flourishing, is only possible when we acknowledge these truths about ourselves.

Aristotle's answer, then, goes beyond those offered by the three groups considered in this chapter, incorporating aspects of each. If Aristotle is right, the question of why we should be moral amounts to asking, "Why be happy?," the answer to which, he believes, is self-explanatory. Bruno may think he's rational and happy, but Aristotle would suggest that he simply doesn't know what he's missing. Taking the impartial standpoint described in the thought experiment above, we can see that Bruno is settling for far less than he's capable of, a mere counterfeit happiness, a sad caricature of the real thing. Aristotle's teacher, Plato, would have seen in Bruno's failure to allow his emotions, passions, and desires to be ruled by reason a recipe for disaster and a sure way to lose happiness. It often seems that those people who speak dismissively of rationality have very little of it, and that those, like Bruno, who need reason most want it least. Ultimately, if we wish to attain happiness and express our deepest humanity, we need the guidance of reason.[15]

---

[15] I am grateful to Christeen Clemens for many helpful comments on drafts of this chapter.

14

Rear Window: Hitchcock's Allegory of the Cave

MICHAEL SILBERSTEIN

Hitchcock's *Rear Window* (1954) opens with a long panning shot that takes us on a tour of an apartment courtyard. As the view focuses on the studio apartment of the film's protagonist, we see smashed 8 × 10 camera equipment, a striking photo of a race car accident, other photos of war and disaster, and additional photographic paraphernalia. Eventually we see the resident, L.B. Jefferies (James Stewart), in a full leg cast, fast asleep. When he awakens, he turns his wheelchair to spend his day as he has spent each day for the last five weeks: watching the lives of his courtyard neighbors through his large rear window. With this visual information as background, the opening lines from his recently arrived home care nurse Stella (Thelma Ritter) telegraphs the themes that Hitchcock will explore in *Rear Window*:

> The New York state sentence for a Peeping Tom is six months in the work house. They got no windows in the work house. You know, in the old days, they used to put your eyes out with a red-hot poker. Any of those bikini bombshells you're always watchin' worth a red-hot poker?

The concerns that Hitchcock raises about the dangers of voyeurism (the coveting of and obsession with the lives of others) and the role of popular art (film in his case) in magnifying those dangers are not new. In Plato's Allegory of the Cave (*The Republic*) he likens human existence, prior to philosophical examination by the light of reason, to being perennially chained inside a cave. Imprisoned people mistake shadows projected on the cave wall (sense experience) for the true reality in the world outside the cave (the world of forms). In Plato's allegory, the philosophically unenlightened are captives bound to mistake shadows for reality until they embrace reason. Consider the analogies between the projection of movies on the wall of darkened theaters and the shadows on the cave wall, and that between the bound captives and the film audience. These are analogies that Plato himself would have appreciated, as he held that tragedy (drama) and poetry were mimesis or imitation. If sensory experiences are but shadows of the forms, then films are imitations of the shadows, copies of copies.

Plato criticized all imitations as failing to reveal the forms or eternal realities. Among other things, Plato worried about the seductive power of tragedy to trump reason with emotion. He thought that tragedy pandered to people's base desire for violent spectacle and was in general a poor teacher of virtue, as the good were often punished and the wicked rewarded. He worried that people would confuse poetry with reality. For this reason, in Book X of *The Republic,* he famously excludes tragedy and poetry from the ideal state. Plato's ethical and aesthetic decision to banish this kind of art from the Republic follows from his metaphysical commitment to forms; his epistemological view that reason, not the senses or emotion, provides true knowledge; and his aesthetic view that art is imitation. Plato believed his philosophical view about the corrupting nature of this kind of art was well supported by his observations of its effects.

Aristotle defends art against Plato's attacks in *The Poetics,* arguing that imitation (art) is natural from an early age and is educational and cathartic by appealing to people's minds, feelings, and senses. Aristotle rejected a transcendent world of forms and was more open to sensory experience as an aid to knowledge. Heavy-duty metaphysical and epistemological commitments aside, philosophical debates about the moral and social value of art have continued to rage since the time of Plato and Aristotle.[1]

---

[1] For more on Plato's theory of forms and Aristotle's rejection of the theory, see Anthony Gottlieb, *The Dream of Reason: A History of Western Philosophy from the Greeks to the Renaissance.* (New York: Norton, 2002).

Hitchcock's *Rear Window* is a film about the nature and value of film, and the act of watching film.[2] In *Rear Window*, L.B. Jefferies is the bound captive or film viewer, and his movie is the scene outside the large Rear Window of his New York apartment. *Rear Window* carries on the conversation between Plato and Aristotle and, it will be argued, arrives at the correct conclusion, which is that both Plato and Aristotle are right in a sense. Watching films is neither inherently stupefying nor enlightening; it depends on both the film and the viewer. This is one of the principal messages of *Rear Window*. While some films, such as *Rear Window*, help to awaken the viewer to reality and themselves, other films merely entertain us or numb us into oblivion. *Rear Window* is a film about the great potential for film to do both good and evil. As is so often the case, Hitchcock manages to construct a film in which the philosophical depth, narrative, and other cinematic virtues do not get in each other's way. Instead they complement one another perfectly.

Judging Art: Plato versus Aristotle

While both Plato's and Aristotle's grand philosophical theories may have driven their views about the moral worth of poetry and tragedy, we can still appreciate the basic issues and their differences of opinion. This is especially true in this dark media age of reality TV, journalism as partisan entertainment, and formulaic Hollywood films filled with mindless sex and violence.[3] Plato claims that tragedy is "a harm to the mind of its audience" and its effect on society is that "pleasure and pain will rule as monarchs . . . instead of the law and that rational principle which is always and by all thought to be the best."[4] Plato says the dramatist arouses, rather than checks, emotions. Plato forbids imitativeness, which he defines as the desire and ability to

---

[2] This is a well-worn view of the film; see, for example, John Fawell, *Hitchcock's Rear Window: The Well Made Film*. (Carbondale: Southern Illinois University Press, 2001).

[3] For an excellent defense of Plato's seemingly reactionary views on poetry and tragedy in *The Republic*, a defense grounded in the modern entertainment state and its soul-killing effects, see Alexander Nehamas, "Plato and the Mass Media," in David Goldblatt and Lee B. Brown, eds., *Aesthetics: A Reader in Philosophy of the Arts*, second edition (Englewood Cliffs: Prentice-Hall, 2001), pp. 417–425.

[4] Plato, 1989. *The Republic, Book X* in George Dickie, Richard Sclafani, and Ronald Roblin, eds., *Aesthetics: A Critical Anthology*, second edition (New York: St. Martin's Press, 1989), pp. 20–31.

imitate anything independently of its moral quality and without proper blame or praise toward its object. So for Plato, not only are tragedy and poetry a shadow of a shadow, they imitate for the sake of imitation rather than maximize virtue and provide moral instruction.

According to Plato, "the artist knows appearance and not reality," and "the work of the artist is at the third remove from the essential nature of things." This is not only because tragedy and poetry distract us from the forms, but because "poetry, however skillfully executed, is no evidence that the poet really possessed the knowledge required for the right conduct of actual life."[5] Plato's assumption here is that in order to teach virtue, right conduct, or any skill, the teacher must himself possess this virtue or skill. Plato's question, reformulated for the age of video and film, is what the profession of filmmaker or photographer makes of the practitioner, other than a voyeur or bystander. What virtues does it impart? As we will discuss, several scenes in *Rear Window* suggest that as a photojournalist L.B. Jefferies is himself a fatally detached professional voyeur. Poetry and tragedy (film) are not only harmful to the practitioner but to the patron as well, because they tend to trump reason with unchecked emotion and illusion, and according to Plato, reason is the only hope one has of perceiving the forms.

Because Aristotle rejects the transcendent world of forms, he is much more open to sense experience, emotion, and intuition as means of acquiring knowledge. As well as viewing poetry as providing needed "catharsis, purgation, and purification," Aristotle also sees poetry and tragedy as being more like a science. This is because he holds that, like science, poetry and drama impart "universal, essential, and necessary truths." With their focus on character and action, poetry and drama have greater moral significance than history because they are virtual simulations of ethical conundrums and real-life situations, and can thereby transform us morally. Poetry and drama cultivate and refine our moral sensibilities because "feeling pleasure or pain at mere representations is not far removed from reactions to reality." For Aristotle, imitation is not only

---

[5] For more on Plato's views about poetry in particular, see *Ion* in *Aesthetics: A Critical Anthology*, pp. 10–19.

natural, psychologically cleansing, and stress relieving, it is also highly instructive.[6]

There is much regarding the nature of poetry and drama about which Plato and Aristotle do agree: 1) that they are imitative arts; 2) that they rouse the emotions; and 3) that the rousing of emotions by imitative means has an effect upon the whole personality and behavior of the audience. Furthermore, "Aristotle like Plato thinks that there is a fundamental distinction between artistic creation and discursive reasoning. He does not doubt that theory and art are distinct, or that giving a reasoned account of something is a very different activity from making a poem or play." The essential difference is that, unlike Plato however, Aristotle does not therefore hold that the non-theoretical must belong to the irrational. "Both theory and art are rational, and amenable to rational investigation. Both can result in knowledge, but two different kinds of knowledge, practical and theoretical."[7]

As we will see, in addition to affirming Platonic worries about the effects of film watching, *Rear Window* also supports Aristotelian claims about the insight and wisdom-generating potential of art. That is, *Rear Window* poignantly raises the same worries about film watching that Plato's *Republic* raises about drama and poetry, and so *Rear Window* itself illustrates Aristotle's claims about the potential wisdom in and virtues of art.

Form and Content Unified: *Rear Window* as a Film about Film

There are several formal and content-oriented features that leave little doubt that *Rear Window* is intentionally a film about film. L.B. Jefferies, wheelchair-bound with a broken leg, is an immobilized spectator watching unseen in the dark. From this voyeuristic perspective, he is isolated from others and unable to act on what he sees. In fact, as a photographer and photojournalist, Jefferies is a professional voyeur. His closest friends are his binoculars and telephoto lens. In short, Jefferies represents

---

[6] For more on Aristotle's defense of poetry and drama, see his *Poetics* in *Aesthetics: A Critical Anthology*, pp. 32–47.

[7] Eric Schaper, "Plato and Aristotle on the Arts: From Prelude to Aesthetics," in *Aesthetics: A Critical Anthology*, pp. 48–56.

the quintessential movie spectator alone in the darkened theater. The view framed by his rear window is his movie screen. We become voyeurs along with Jefferies as the film is shot largely from his visual point-of-view.

Among the formal elements that indicate *Rear Window* is intentionally a film about film, the movie begins as the shades on Jefferies's rear window roll up like an old-fashioned movie curtain. In the middle of the film the shades are rolled down and up again like an intermission, and at the end the shades are rolled down into their final resting place.[8] In case the cinematic imagery is lost on the viewer, during the "intermission" when Lisa (Grace Kelly) is rolling the shades down she says, "Show's over, previews of coming attractions."

In addition to the fact that all the action is framed by Jefferies's movie screen-like rear window, his primary view through this window is into other "railroad flats" laid out like individual frames on a filmstrip. The audience cannot escape the fact that they are subjected to "movie-vision" throughout the film. The various occupants of the apartments on which Jefferies spies appear as players on stage or screen. Each apartment is like a different scene from the same movie being played simultaneously instead of serially.

The very staging of *Rear Window* (the picture-box window apartments) suggests the key theme: the viewer as voyeur. As observers of film, we are watching the actions of other people. The form of *Rear Window* is necessarily linked to its content as the story *revolves* around the act of viewing other people "act" in their lives. Indeed, as audience members we are *meta-voyeurs* watching Jefferies watch others.

Rear Window's structure manipulates the very essence of form. The form is like a "mode of presentation" or a way of seeing an object or many objects. The form is the structure within which we "play" with the content, but is bound intimately to the content. How we see things—in movies and in real life—is precisely what's at issue in *Rear Window*. Hitchcock plays on the various structures (the form) of film such that our interpretation of events becomes biased. We are led to believe that Thorwald

---

[8] For a thorough overview and treatment of the formal features of *Rear Window*, see Stefan Sharff, *The Art of Looking in Hitchcock's Rear Window* (New York: Limelight, 1997).

(Raymond Burr) has murdered his wife by watching his actions through the eyes of Jefferies and the "lens" of the picture-box vision created for us by the stage itself. In this way Hitchcock manipulates the viewer into a particular interpretation of events.

The Unifying and Self-Referential Role of Music in *Rear Window*

There are many other clues that *Rear Window* is consciously and self-reflexively about the potential for art to enlighten as well as delude. Perhaps the most obvious clue is the role of music. The entire soundtrack of the film is nothing but incidental sounds and music from around the courtyard. The characters comment on the music at various points in the film as it is the score of their real lives. For example, throughout the film the composer (Ross Bagdasarian) is struggling to complete the score for a song we ultimately find out is called "Lisa." Early in the film the composer sings Nat King Cole's "Mona Lisa." Hitchcock's cameo in *Rear Window* is in the composer's apartment. Lisa herself admires the composer's song and before she knows its title comments that "it's as though it were written especially for us." Later she says to Jefferies, "Where does a man get the inspiration to write a song like that? I wish I was creative." Jefferies's crass reply implies that the composer's real inspirations (or motivations) are sex and greed. The popular song "Lisa" no doubt symbolizes popular films such as *Rear Window* and raises Hitchcock's concern as to whether popular art can be important as well as commercially driven.

This song and the discussion it engenders between Lisa and Jefferies again call into question the value of art—especially popular art. The composer's music is all that connects the isolated and alienated neighbors in the courtyard, analogous to a film and its watchers in the dark. Perhaps most telling of all, it is the beauty of the song "Lisa" that stops Miss Lonely-Hearts (Judith Evelyn) from committing suicide. At the end of the film we see Miss Lonely-Hearts in the composer's apartment telling him that he will never know how much his song means to her. In addition to the composer's music, Jefferies's photography, and Lisa's fashion, *Rear Window* also features a dancer, a sculptor, and a singer, referencing the central role of art in the film, in the lives of the characters and in the lives of the viewers. The composer's creative process throughout the film parallels Hitchcock's, reflecting the state of play in the film's unfolding. The song is completed just at the end of the film when balance and harmony are restored to the courtyard and to the relationships of its inhabitants.

Film and Emancipation

Rear Window raises the Platonic aesthetic and ethical question of whether film watching and the obsession with the visual media are good or bad for the soul of society and the individual. *Rear Window* answers "yes" to both. The claim in this chapter is that *Rear Window* itself is a therapeutic experience from which both the audience and L.B. Jefferies emerge wiser at the end. *Rear Window* is Hitchcock's attempt to free his fellow prisoners from the illusion-engendering cave; a function Plato thought only a philosopher wielding reason could perform. Indeed, the lighting of Jefferies's apartment is quite suggestive in this regard, as everything and everyone projects great shadows on the walls. Hitchcock, himself a voyeur, is both self-critical and sympathetic to our plight. He seeks to bring us back into the light through the very thing that binds us to the dark—cinema. Hitchcock appreciates that film and the filmmaker have a far better chance of "freeing the prisoners" without suffering the Socratic fate of unending "hostility and incomprehension." After viewing *Rear Window*, we are wiser about the dangers and thrills of voyeurism, the wastefulness of *ennui*, and the risks of preferring fantasy to reality. *Rear Window* liberates us from the blinding habitual boredom of our own lives.

Film can have either dormitive or awakening powers. *Rear Window* is a self-consciously self-reflexive film designed to dissolve our unthinking dissatisfaction with reality and bring to light our deep-seated need for dangerous fantasies. Hitchcock indulges voyeurism and dark fantasies as he awakens us to the risks they entail. We're given the opportunity to fall back in love with our own everyday lives and transcend our self-imposed boredom with anything we already identify as our own. *Rear Window* raises the same concerns about the voyeuristic and potentially mind-numbing effects of film watching that Plato's *Republic* raises about poetry and tragedy. Indeed, one can view *Rear Window* as a filmic Platonic dialogue about the moral nature of film, demonstrating that film has the power to teach as well as delude. The very same features of film that make it such a potentially potent pacifier also make it a powerful tool for self-awareness.

Is Film Watching Good for the Soul and Society?

Rear Window is often interpreted as a film about the pitfalls of voyeurism and the theory-dependence of perception, or the precarious nature of interpreting experience and passing judgment on others. At the beginning of the film, Stella, Jefferies's insurance nurse, says, "We have become a race of Peeping Toms. People need to get outside their own house and look in for a change. . . . How's that for home spun philosophy?" and "I can smell trouble right here in this apartment. First you smash your leg, then you get to looking out the window, see things you shouldn't see. Trouble." The following dialogue between Jefferies and his friend, Detective Doyle (Wendell Corey), further sharpens the point:

> **DOYLE:** That's a secret, private world you're looking into out there; people do a lot of things in private they couldn't possibly explain in public.
>
> **JEFFERIES:** Much as I hate to give Doyle credit, he might have got a hold of something when he said that was pretty private stuff out there. I wonder if it's ethical to watch a man with binoculars and long focus lenses. Do you suppose it's ethical even when you prove he didn't commit a crime?

Whereas Doyle probably represents a skeptical "male" brand of reason, Stella represents commonsense and sensible intuition—what Doyle derisively refers to as "woman's intuition." As Stella puts it, "I'm not an educated woman but nothing has caused the human race so much trouble as intelligence." The focus on commonsense intuition over intellect (theoretical interpretation) is anti-Platonic, as is the fact that in *Rear Window* it is the women who exhibit the deepest moral sensibilities and possess the greatest wisdom. Hitchcock suggests that women are much less likely than men to while away their lives as voyeurs, and so live much more in the present moment.

Regarding the state of modern romance, Stella says, "Don't analyze each other to death, just come together. . . . Modern love is over intellectualized. . . . just spread a little commonsense on the bread." What Stella is getting at, and what much of *Rear Window* is about, is the way voyeurism particularly affects our romantic relationships. Stella sees that Jefferies's inability to embrace his own life and his existential boredom are leading him to pass up a great thing in Lisa. Every window that Jefferies peeps into has a romantic or sexual relationship on display for his consideration and comparison. He avoids his own problems and conflicts with Lisa by being a voyeur. Lisa wants Jefferies to settle down in New York and eventually marry her, which to him sounds like torture. Almost all the characters in *Rear Window* are shopping for true love in one way or another. Jefferies's search for ideal love leads him to cruelly reject the real thing, even when it is starring him in the face. Thorwald's search for true love leads to murder, and Miss Lonely-Hearts's search almost ends in her suicide.

Though it may not be obvious at first, Stella is raising the same concerns about voyeurism that Plato was raising about poetry and drama. Since voyeurism *à la* Jefferies represents film watching in *Rear Window*, Stella is taking a Platonic position about our obsession with watching movies. Whereas Plato focuses more on the dangers of emotion trumping reason, *Rear Window* focuses on the anti-social detachment engendered by our voyeuristic obsession. For example, Jefferies is a "window shopper," bored with every aspect of his life except the dangerous assignments abroad and the dark fantasies he envisions spying out his rear window. He cannot take his eyes off other people's lives and other women such as Miss Torso (Georgine Darcy). Jefferies ignores his own day-to-day life and even ignores the beautiful and smart Lisa. He is more interested in Miss Torso than the "too perfect" woman sitting in his own lap. He has more compassion for Miss Lonely-Hearts than he does for Lisa. Jefferies is more interested in everyone else's life than his own, hence his choice of profession, and his total inability to settle down and commit to Lisa, his real life, or anything else.

Jefferies is bored with anything that smacks of the domestic, everyday, or mundane, and is only truly interested in those experiences that bring great risk, excitement, and titillation. Not unlike many of today's entertainment addicts, Jefferies is a peak experience junky. Here we can see that Plato's and Hitchcock's concerns are really one and the same. Voyeurism and unjustified boredom with one's own life are two sides of the same coin. Just as with the overwrought Greek audiences described by Plato, Jefferies's inability to appreciate and embody his own real life leads to voyeurism. This in turn heightens the boredom with everyday life by fueling his dark fantasies, which then drives him to seek out increasingly risky thrills. We learn that Jefferies broke his leg and almost died because he was in the middle of a race track trying to get a shot that was "something dramatically different" when a car flipped over. Jefferies is a tourist in his own life on an endless vacation. In illustration of his dark fantasies, Lisa calls his voyeuristic behavior "diseased" and she comments on their disappointment at discovering that Thorwald might be innocent: "We are frightening ghouls, despairing that the man didn't kill his wife! We should be happy the woman is alive and well. What happened to love thy neighbor?"

In a central piece of dialogue, a neighbor woman (Bess Flowers) says to the entire courtyard when she finds her murdered poodle, "Neighbors speak to each other, like each other, care if we live or die. Did you [Thorwald, as we later learn] kill him [the dog] because he liked you, just because he liked you?" Dogs are good neighbors and "man's best friend," so to harm one is most certainly an act of self-loathing. This scene emphasizes the modern or postmodern themes of isolation, alienation, and self-loathing in *Rear Window*. Unlike sitting around a camp fire telling stories to one another, sitting alone in a dark theater watching a movie can isolate us from our fellow citizens. Cinema and other such entertainment can make us increasingly alienated, apolitical, antisocial, self-centered, and can further erode self-reflection, introspection, and self-awareness. None of the people in the courtyard (including Jefferies) are "neighbors." Instead, they are more like moviegoers sitting next to one another alone in the dark.

Judgment, Voyeurism, and Happiness

The warnings about: 1) hasty interpretation of experience and the rash judgment of others; 2) the dangers of voyeurism; and 3) the promises and pitfalls of film watching, are all inextricably related in *Rear Window*. As we have seen, the primary focus is on how these three elements play out with respect to love and romantic relationships. Voyeurism often leads us to unjustifiably interpret other people's lives and souls as happier or darker than our own. Since our expectations and desires shape what we perceive, we often misinterpret or crudely interpret our experience. Desires and expectations are part of the reason we often perceive shadows rather than reality itself. Hitchcock appreciates that the vehicle of film represents and magnifies our inherently voyeuristic tendencies, and he sees that watching films can either provide us with therapy or deepen our delusions.

In *Rear Window*, perhaps we can even say that each relationship Jefferies spies on represents a part of his psyche. For example, Thorwald and his crime represent Jefferies's dark desire to be rid of Lisa, and Miss Lonely-Hearts represents his deep loneliness brought on by his inability to truly connect with anyone in his own life. Thorwald and the others he sees through his rear window hold up an exaggerated mirror to Jefferies and represent various commonsense lessons such as: "be careful what you wish for," "things are not always what they seem," and "the grass is not always greener." These are the very "necessary and universal truths" Aristotle was lauding poetry and drama for illustrating. The various relationships (or lack thereof) spied on also provide different models of romantic situations for Jefferies to consider for himself. However, as we discover at the film's end, many of his judgments about the people he is watching turn out to be wrong.

Interpreting Film and Experience

Much of *Rear Window* is about the interpretation of experience and the judgment of others. Jefferies, Lisa, Stella, and Doyle provide us with competing interpretations of Thorwald's behavior and the events that transpire in his apartment. Are the knife and saw in Thorwald's apartment household implements or murder weapons? Is the roped-up trunk a piece of luggage or a coffin? Did Thorwald's wife (Irene Winston) disappear because he killed her for being an insufferable "nag" or because she took a train back home? The complexities of interpreting Thorwald's actions and the surrounding events are a perfect analogy with the complexities of interpreting our daily experience and the actions of those around us. *Rear Window* leaves little doubt that Hitchcock intended this analogy, as Lisa says to Jefferies when she finally becomes suspicious of Thorwald, "Tell me everything you saw and what you think it means."

Rear Window illustrates that, just like real-life experience, any good film or work of art will come with its own interpretative mysteries. But *Rear Window* also echoes Aristotle's claim about poetry and drama. Great films will not only raise philosophical or interpretative questions, they will actually simulate, "game," or test various possible answers against one another without forcing conclusions. In art generally, and in literature and film in particular, we often value ambiguity, indefiniteness, and even contradiction. These features can add interest and intensify engagement. In philosophy, however, to call writing ambiguous, indefinite, or contradictory is normally a serious criticism. Similarly, literature and film with a clear, starkly articulated, unambiguous "message" is usually berated as being pedantic or preachy.

Because of their ambiguity and their closeness to real-life experiences, the philosophical interpretation of films is great practice for "real life" philosophical interpretation. Since the film world is fictional, it is much easier to get past the audience's natural defense mechanisms. As Adam Morton puts it:

> What is the special affinity of film and philosophy? The affinity clearly goes deeper than the common concern with illusion. I suggest that one source of the affinity is the ability of film to present very large amounts of information in a way that combines both pictorial and narrative presentation. As a result a film can present many of the beliefs and preferences that would make up a coherent alternative account of the physical or moral universe. We can get into the workings of a proposed set of values, a metaphysics, or an account of human motivation. It is just conceivable that this could be done with words alone, but words alone will not summon the sensory and emotional correlates that in actual human life glue large bodies of belief and value into workable unities. If this is so it can explain why a film can be such an eloquent example to support, illustrate, or rebut a philosophical claim.[9]

---

[9] From his review of Christopher Falzon's *Philosophy Goes to the Movies: An Introduction to Philosophy* (Routledge, 2002) in *British Journal of Aesthetics* 43:3 (2003), pp. 332–34.

The self-reflexive nature of *Rear Window* is such that the riddle of Thorwald's actions and the disappearance of his wife give us a major clue about how to interpret the film. Hitchcock clearly appreciated the potential pedagogical and philosophical value of film and sought to exploit it in *Rear Window* with respect to some central concerns in aesthetics.

Judgment and Interpretation

Jefferies is wrong about so many of his neighbors but right about Thorwald. He judges Lisa to be a soft, pampered snob who is spoiled by wealth and creature comforts. He thinks of her as a lightweight socialite, more concerned with fashion and appearances than anything else. Lisa is "too perfect" in all the wrong ways. By the end of the film we learn that Lisa is more than capable of action and adventure. She is a strong woman, strong enough to face Thorwald and ultimately help save Jefferies from him. He judges Miss Torso to be an opportunistic tease, "a queen bee with her pick of the drones." Yet, at the film's end we discover that she is married to a nerdy nebbish in the military whom she is faithful to and loves very much. Lisa's judgment of Miss Torso, on the other hand, turns out to be the truth: "She's doing a woman's hardest job, juggling wolves. She's not in love with any of them [the drones]." He judges the new-lyweds (Frank Cady and Sarah Berner) to be blissfully happy in their constant state of arousal with their marathon sexual escapades. Eventually, we find out that the groom is unem-ployed and the couple is struggling. He judges the composer to be a drunken letch cavorting "with his landlady for free rent." But in the final scenes of the film we discover that he is a strug-gling artist trying to birth a song called "Lisa" and that he is a soft-hearted romantic who may have fallen for Miss Lonely-Hearts. Again, Jefferies misjudges all these people through the lens of his own desires and expectations, with too little infor-mation at his disposal.

The Moral of Hitchcock's Allegory

In contrast, Jefferies's judgment that Thorwald murdered his wife turns out to be correct. Perhaps part of the reason he got this one right is that he used his journalistic training and the method of eliminative induction, but the primary reason Jefferies is right about Thorwald is a teleological one. Hitchcock needs Jefferies to be right in this case in order to teach him, and by extension, us the viewers, a lesson. If Hitchcock really wanted only to punish us for voyeurism—film watching—he would have made Thorwald innocent. While *Rear Window* is often interpreted as a film about the dangers of voyeurism (film watching as a way of life), Jefferies gains at least as much as he loses as the result of his voyeurism. In other words, voyeurism is not all bad.

Jefferies pays a heavy price for his voyeurism, as he and Lisa are nearly murdered by Thorwald and his other leg is broken in the fall. The message is clear: the film world bites back. There are serious consequences for voyeurism—it is not a passive act, nor an act of innocence. Voyeurism can release us from the mundane and feed our dark fantasies, but at quite a price. Thorwald's attacks and Jefferies's impotent paralysis are our punishment for voyeurism and empty escapism.

Jefferies's voyeurism also leads to many good things. Order and balance are restored to Jefferies's soul and his courtyard-world. A murderer is brought to justice as a result of Jefferies's spying. Jefferies comes to appreciate the depth and strength of Lisa, and their relationship is saved by the events leading to Thorwald's arrest. In the end Lisa becomes the action hero he wants, leading him to intone, "I'm so proud of you." Lisa shows Jefferies "what she is made of" and it has the desired effect of changing his myopic misjudgment of her. As well as the apparent resolution of the conflicts in their relationship, Jefferies becomes a wiser man about Lisa and more generally about the pitfalls of voyeurism. Jefferies no longer views his domestic life as a "swamp of boredom." He is more content and appreciative of his own life. Jefferies realizes that in the end what really saved him from Thorwald (and himself) were not his flashbulbs, but his community and friendships with Lisa, Stella, and Doyle—these three behaved as good "neighbors" and good Samaritans. As we the viewers of *Rear Window* are identified with Jefferies, watching this film makes us potentially wiser, learning all that Jefferies himself did. *Rear Window* is a piece of cinema that has the power to save us from mindless voyeurism and performs the exact functions that Aristotle attributes to good drama and poetry.

Curtain Down

At one point in the film Lisa says to Jefferies, "I'm not much on Rear Window ethics." But fortunately for us, Hitchcock himself is quite sophisticated about "Rear Window ethics," and we are the wiser for it. Unlike standard Hollywood fare, Hitchcock's cautionary tales never have unrealistically happy endings. At the end of the film, we find Jefferies as he was in the beginning, asleep in his wheelchair and carefully turned away from the rear window. Seated next to him, we find Lisa dressed in Safari clothes pretending to read *Beyond the High Himalayas,* when she is in fact reading *Harpers' Bazaar.* Lisa has clearly retained her selfhood and values, and we know that Jefferies will again have to struggle with voyeurism and the essential differences between him and Lisa.

Philosophers no doubt will continue to debate whether or not film in particular and art in general are intrinsically stupefying. Hostility toward the arts has been endemic to some quarters of philosophy ever since Plato banished poets from his ideal city in *The Republic.* This is in large part because the fine arts are perceived by some Platonically-influenced philosophers to be pretenders to knowledge, which they believe to be acquired exclusively by the toil of reason. Though it may have surprised Plato, *Rear Window* is every bit as thoughtful and philosophically engaging as one of his dialogues. Hitchcock allows us to see that art and film are not intrinsically harmful. *Rear Window* illustrates that Plato and Aristotle are both right about the potential vices and virtues of art in general and film in particular.

15

Rear Window: Looking at Things Ethically

AEON J. SKOBLE

I'm not much on rear window ethics.

—LISA FREMONT (Grace Kelly)

Alfred Hitchcock's 1954 film *Rear Window* presents us with the following scenario: a photographer, one L.B. "Jeff" Jeffries (James Stewart), housebound with a broken leg, takes to snooping on his neighbors out of boredom, and discovers what may be evidence of a horrible murder.

Besides being a compelling thriller, this film raises a variety of interesting ethical questions. The film prompts philosophical questions of responsibility—for instance, Jeff seems to acquire responsibilities he ordinarily wouldn't have as a result of activity he shouldn't have been engaged in. How can this be the case? *Does* he have these responsibilities? Is he *obligated* to intervene? Lastly, just why *do* we think it's wrong to snoop as Jeff does? Is it merely an aesthetically distasteful pursuit, as his nurse Stella (Thelma Ritter) seems to indicate? Or is it intrinsically wrong, from a privacy-rights perspective? Or is it only conditionally wrong, depending on the result, which in this case is positive? Can justice be served by doing something otherwise (or generally) wrong? Do the ends justify the means?

Here's Looking at You

To begin with, it's been noted by practically every student of Hitchcock that Jeff's voyeurism parallels the "voyeurism" of the viewer in the cinema. This seems correct, but it's not clear just what the comparison implies in terms of duty and responsibility. In one sense, *all* movies involve the voyeurism of the movie-watcher, and we the audience have no moral duties towards the characters in the film: spectatorship just *is* the essence of our relationship with these people. Within the fictional world of the film, the interesting question is what duties Jeff, *qua* voyeur, might have towards his neighbors.

Hitchcock surely isn't intending to suggest that there's something wrong with watching movies, so whatever moral judgments we make about Jeff would be independent of this analogy anyway. One suspects, though, that Hitchcock *would* be inclined to criticize a totally disinterested voyeurism in which one is entertained by the problems or suffering of those one watches, without caring enough to get involved—as, for example, with "reality TV" programs. And later on, when Lisa and Stella venture over to the other side of the courtyard, they are no longer passive observers, and neither is Jeff. His watching is as far from disinterested as possible, and he is doing more at this point than just watching. When Lisa slips the note under Thorwald's door, when Jeff uses deceptive phone calls to lure Thorwald away from the apartment, they have ceased being voyeurs and have become active participants in the events. Indeed, their active participation with the object of their observations turns out to *affect* the situation, placing both Jeff and Lisa in jeopardy.

Let's remember that Jeff is snooping due to a confluence of factors. It's not just that he is laid up with a broken leg, but it is the middle of a terribly oppressive heat wave, in a time when air conditioning wasn't widespread, so everyone in the apartment block has some reason to have their windows open. Jeff isn't by nature a voyeur, and his neighbors aren't by nature exhibitionists. But the weather has rendered the neighbors exhibitionists and this, combined with the accident, has made Jeff (and later his girlfriend Lisa) into a voyeur. (Not only could the story not have taken place in January, when the neighbors would be more likely to be closed up, but it couldn't really take place today: a contemporary Jeff would be more likely to alleviate his boredom with cable TV or the internet.)

This brings into relief the ethical complexities of the situation: while doing something that he has a sense he shouldn't be doing in the first place, Jeff discovers something that seems to create for him a responsibility to intervene. Actually, he discovers more than one: not only does he come to believe that Lars Thorwald (Raymond Burr) has murdered his wife, he also comes to believe that Miss Lonelyhearts (Judith Evelyn) will commit suicide. But even this second scenario defies easy analysis.

Jeff forms an intention to intervene, to prevent her from killing herself, but before he has the chance to intervene, she hears the composer's music, which causes her to reconsider. We are later left to believe they fall in love. If Jeff had acted more quickly in this case, not only would he have prevented her from killing herself, but, paradoxically, he would have prevented her from discovering the true solution to her problems. But does this mean that Jeff was wrong to form the intention to intervene? That seems incorrect, because he couldn't have known just before she heard the music that she was about to hear the music, or what effect the music would have on her, or that she would eventually become involved with the composer. Even though we can say in hindsight that it's good Jeff didn't have the chance to intervene, he certainly was acting rightly to *decide* to intervene.

Consider an earlier incident: when Miss Lonelyhearts had brought home a date who became sexually aggressive with her. It looked for a moment as though he was going to rape her, or even (depending on how angry or crazy he was) kill her. Jeff might certainly have intervened then—rape in progress! But as it happened, she was capable of dealing with the situation herself: she slaps him and successfully kicks him out. No intervention necessary. The common thread in both incidents is that evaluating them from the point of view of knowing how they turn out in the end is not necessarily an effective way to reason about right conduct as the situations unfold.

This is the moral theory known as consequentialism—the view that the moral value of actions can be found in the end results they bring about, rather than in the motive or character of the agent or any conception of duties or obligations. I am acting rightly whenever my actions bring about the best consequences. Utilitarianism is the most famous example of consequentialism—the view that what is right is what brings about the greatest good for the greatest number, or (less charitably) that the ends justify the means. One problem with this theory is that it's easy to say afterwards, "See, it all worked out okay," but that doesn't tell us whether or not we have done the right thing through our non-intervention. I cannot ask the question, "How should I act in such-and-such a case?" if the answers can only be known afterwards. If, in general, we have an obligation to intervene to prevent a rape, then we have that obligation even if we have discovered the rape attempt through snooping. If, in general, we have an obligation to intervene to prevent a suicide, then again, we'd have that obligation even if we discovered the attempt via illicit snooping. One might reply that we actually do *not* have an obligation to intervene to prevent a suicide, on the grounds that maximal respect for personal autonomy requires us to regard the other person as a better judge of these things. But that objection wouldn't apply to the attempted rape: we surely have no obligation to respect the autonomy of the rapist.[1]

A Race of Peeping Toms

We're inclined to think that Stella is correct when she admonishes Jeff early in the film the he has "no business" looking in on his neighbors' lives. But if your neighbor is chopping his wife into pieces, isn't that your business? The problem arises because Jeff would have no way of knowing that a murder had taken place if he hadn't been snooping in the first place. While it is a good thing that the murderer was brought to justice, we should not conclude that snooping on one's neighbors is a good thing, something we all ought to do so that we're sure to catch any murderers.

We also shouldn't conclude that, since Jeff shouldn't have been snooping in the first place, he has no obligation to intervene. Even if it's true that Jeff was wrong to spy on his neighbors, it could also be true that *if* the spying yields information that would in other circumstances create moral obligations, then those obligations still hold. (So I'm arguing for a conception of moral evidence which is *different* from the usual understanding of legal evidence, on which illegally obtained evidence is generally regarded as inadmissible.)

---

[1] Except perhaps in the sense intended by Herbert Morris, that we express this respect for the rapist's autonomy by affirming his responsibility and inflicting punishment. See his "Persons and Punishment," *The Monist* 52:4 (October 1968).

In other words, there might be such things as conditional obligations. We might say that *anyone* who discovers a murderer ought to help bring him to justice, so all of Thorwald's neighbors might have the obligations Jeff feels, and if they knew what Jeff knows, they would be obliged to act similarly. It's only their ignorance of the situation that might absolve them from pursuing Thorwald. But *given* Jeff's knowledge of the murder, he has an obligation to pursue the matter. Philosophers often say that "ought implies can," meaning that I cannot be obligated to do things I cannot do. So if I don't *know* that a murderer is in my apartment building, I can't have an obligation to bring him to justice. But if I *do* know, then I do have that obligation.

No discussion of moral obligations would be complete without some attention to the related concept of *supererogation.* An act is obligatory when it is both good to do it and bad not to do it. An act is supererogatory when it is good to do it, but *not* bad not to do it. An uncontroversial example of supererogation might be bringing donuts to the office for everyone: it's nice of you to do it, but you're under no obligation to do it, and no one could fairly criticize you for failing to do it. Supererogation is what is captured by the expression "above and beyond the call of duty."

If Jeff hadn't been spying, he wouldn't have known what was going on at the Thorwalds' apartment, and hence would have had no obligation to intervene. Since he does know, is his intervention obligatory, or supererogatory? If the intervention were supererogatory, that would imply that if he failed to intervene, he would be doing no wrong. But surely letting a murderer get away with murder is wrong. So I would argue that regardless of the nature of his acquisition of the information about Thorwald, Jeff has an obligation to intervene. And I would make a similar argument regarding his planned intervention in Miss Lonelyhearts' suspected suicide, although I can see this might be more controversial. Respect for Miss Lonelyhearts' autonomy might be said to preclude the intervention, but I think this is outweighed in this case by Jeff's knowledge of her (likely temporary) despondency.

Jeff thinks he has this obligation too, of course, which is what transforms his guilty snooping into a crusade to bring a killer to justice. His demeanor towards his voyeurism changes at this point: it's no longer a "guilty pleasure" about which he needs to be slightly embarrassed, but a righteous quest to bring a killer to justice, one on which he can enlist the aid of others.

When his suspicions are confirmed by virtue of Lisa's coming to share them, he contacts his friend Tom Doyle (Wendell Corey), a police detective. Doyle does investigate, but his investigation turns up explanations which Jeff and Lisa find unpersuasive, so their sense of obligation leads them to continue on their own, enlisting the assistance of Stella the nurse. Everyone is relieved when Thorwald is brought to justice, and Doyle, who had earlier chastised Jeff for snooping, is pleased at the outcome. It seems, then, that the greater good of bringing a murderer to justice trumps the small bad of snooping on one's neighbors. This would be the utilitarian analysis of the situation.

Doyle's initial investigation seems to show that Mrs. Thorwald is alive and well. Jeff and Lisa are actually *disappointed* that their suspicions were wrong. Lisa characterizes this as "ghoulish," but I think a better explanation is vanity—I mean the intellectual vanity of the puzzle-solver. Another possible explanation other critics have noted might be the disappointed need for excitement, and that may well be part of it, but as I read the characters of Jeff and Lisa, their excitement is as tied to having solved a puzzle as it is to having witnessed something.

They do realize, after a few moments, that they ought to be relieved Mrs. Thorwald is alive, so ghoulishness is perhaps too harshly self-critical. Initially, Doyle doesn't take Jeff's theory seriously, but he does look into it nevertheless. Doyle's alternative explanations, on further reflection, seem skimpy—the real Mrs. Thorwald would not have left her handbag or wedding ring— and Doyle scoffs at Lisa's attempts to deskimpify, mocking so-called "female intuition." And indeed Lisa's observations are both reasonable and correct. At first they accept Doyle's account, and it's easy to see that their intellectual vanity might be wounded by learning that their theory was wrong. Their dissatisfaction in being proved wrong outweighed the actual value of Mrs. Thorwald's life, but only for a moment, and in any case, it's this same intellectual vanity which leads them to reflect further on Doyle's explanation and realize it is inadequate. So even this issue of intellectual vanity is a case where what might be taken to be a character flaw turns out to be instrumental in the larger quest for truth and justice.

Did You Hate Him Because He Liked You?

When Thorwald's murder of a neighbor's dog is discovered, the dog's owner laments that one problem with their neighborhood is that no one cares about anyone else. Indeed, how is it possible to live in an apartment block such as this one and yet remain total strangers? Perhaps Hitchcock means this as an indictment of modern urban life, to demonstrate that if we do *not* care about something, our lives become devoid of meaning. Yet it is Jeff who actually has come to care about his neighbors, who has made the effort to get to know them (albeit in an anonymous and one-sided way). The dog owner's cries bring everyone to their windows, but then they quickly retreat to their own lives, leaving the mystery of the dead dog unexamined, choosing to remain strangers to each other. Jeff, on the other hand, is criticized at different times by Tom, Lisa, and Stella for the very activities that lead him to care what happens to his neighbors. It's his snooping that produces the information, and the information that causes him to care. He feels sympathy, and later concern, for Miss Lonelyhearts, and he feels moral outrage for the murdered Anna Thorwald. He doesn't choose to intervene to help Miss Lonelyhearts until the last minute, when her suicide is imminent. He might have tried to help earlier—is his failure to do so an illustration of the superficiality of his caring, or is it an autonomy-respecting sensibility that prevents him from getting involved until it's literally a life-and-death issue? When it becomes critical, he clearly does care and is moved to act.

Although the movie precedes the incident by a decade, one is reminded now of the Kitty Genovese story: a young woman who was stabbed to death outside her own building while thirty-eight people who were aware of the attack didn't intervene. Was this "none of their business"? Or did they have a responsibility, once they knew she was being attacked, to help her in some way?[2] While most would agree that they did have some responsibility to help, or at least call the police, just as Jeff did once he had reasonable evidence of Thorwald's crime, it's

---

[2] For further discussion of this incident, see my "Superhero Revisionism in *Watchmen* and *The Dark Knight Returns*," Chapter 4 in Tom Morris and Matt Morris, eds., *Superheroes and Philosophy: Truth, Justice, and the Socratic Way* (Chicago: Open Court, 2005).

nevertheless true that Jeff's possession of this evidence was the result of the snooping for which he is criticized.

Doing Things in Private

But just what is it that Jeff is guilty of doing? While he does use binoculars and a telephoto lens to further his investigation of Thorwald, this is only after he comes to suspect him of murder. Initially, all he is doing is looking at the view from out his window, which isn't morally objectionable. The only thing that differentiates Jeff's observations from anyone else's is that he is paying attention to what he sees. While this may be in poor taste, it's not clear just how immoral it is. He isn't going out of his way to gather information, but simply noting what goes on outside his own window. One might argue that Jeff is allowing his curiosity to occupy too much of him, that it's excessive.[3] He's already inclined to distance himself from others—as a photographer, perhaps that comes naturally to him with respect to his subjects—but he's also inclined to keep a critical distance from Lisa. (Jeff also "uses the camera" to keep Thorwald at a distance in the film's climax, although in this case it's clearly a good thing that he does so.)

Perhaps his being housebound has exacerbated his tendency to treat others as "subjects." (Or perhaps it is more accurate to refer to them as his "objects"?) On the other hand, his increased knowledge of these "subjects" ironically makes him care *more* about them, at least in the case Mrs. Thorwald and Miss Lonelyhearts. And of course, the entire sequence of events leads him to see that he was wrong to push Lisa away, that they aren't as fundamentally incompatible as he seemed to think. Jeff learns to see his neighbors as real human beings, he brings a murderer to justice, and he forges a stronger relationship with Lisa. So clearly a lot of good comes out of his voyeurism. And, to continue stretching the analogy, we movie-watchers can come to learn things from our experiences watching movies. Do the ends then justify the means? Perhaps the means don't even require the justification we think they do.

---

[3] If his curiosity about the neighbors is so compelling that it distracts him from Lisa's attempts at seduction, one might infer that he has misplaced priorities, but I leave this as an exercise for the reader.

While our inclination is to think that Jeff is violating people's privacy, everything he saw was on public display. Miss Torso (Georgine Darcy) kisses a suitor on her balcony: that's hardly a private moment. Contrast that with the honeymoon couple: they *do* have a legitimate expectation of privacy, due to their having closed the shades. Or we might argue that, even if there is no actual privacy being formally violated, Jeff is acting badly to look with as much attention as he does, on the grounds that what we consider for ourselves to be private moments deserve reciprocal respect.

In a sense, this just *is* what it means to have a right to privacy: a legitimate expectation that one sphere of your world is indeed private, and that others have good reason to respect this boundary. This might be an account of a moral right. For something to be a *legal* right, it must also the case that violators are subject to legal retribution of some sort. Since everything Jeff observes is in fact on display, and until he discovers the murder he is merely looking out his own window, it's unlikely that he is violating any legal rights of his neighbors—the more interesting question concerns the possibility of ethical wrongdoing on Jeff's part.

Even though my window is open, you should not be watching my dinner date. As Doyle puts it, "People do a lot of things in private they couldn't possibly explain in public"—referring implicitly to Jeff's behavior as much as to that of the neighbors, thus highlighting the need for reciprocity of respect. If Jeff is violating their rights to privacy, it's only in the sense that he ought not to pay attention to the view from his rear window. (Jeff doesn't even *have* a front window. Can we only invade privacy through rear windows, because what we present through the front window is always meant for public consumption?)

The neighbors could gave taken a cue from the honeymoon couple and not offered a view in the first place. (I have so far been assuming that some conception of "reciprocal justified respect" is the grounding of a moral right, but other justifications are possible, for example that regarding people as rights-holders brings about good overall consequences. But this invites the paradox that better consequences might require the violation of the right, which would certainly be the case here.[4] If the ends

---

[4] Utilitarians—those who argue that the criterion for morality is the greatest good for the greatest number—have attempted to resolve this paradox. See John Hospers, "Rule-Utilitarianism," in his *Human Conduct* (New York: Harcourt Brace Jovanovich, 1972).

justify the means, then the same consideration which would lead us to respect Thorwald's privacy would require us to violate it.)

In the final analysis, one can argue that Jeff's curiosity about what's going on outside his window is unhealthy, or a misplaced way to avoid dealing with his ambivalence about getting married, or time better spent reading, but the argument that he's in violation of privacy rights is, on closer inspection, a bit of a stretch. A lot of mainstream criticism of this film is quite negative in its appraisal of Jeff (and by extension the audience) for his (or their) voyeurism, so perhaps the present analysis is nonconformist, but Jeff is more honorable than he is typically given credit for.[5]

One need not argue that "the end justifies the means" to defend the point that, having noticed evidence of a terrible crime, Jeff was obliged to act on it; that doing so was right. In coming to see, really to *see*, his neighbors, he has learned a lot about himself, his responsibilities towards others, the meaning of sympathy. He brings justice to his neighborhood and Lisa into his life. And he has demonstrated something about commitment to truth and getting involved. In a way, Jeff has done the world, himself, and us a favor by looking in, even if some of what he looks at he wasn't meant to see.

---

[5] See Chapter 14 in this volume for a more critical take on this movie where both Jeff and the audience are concerned.

V

What's It All About, Alfred?

16

Plot Twists and Surprises: Why Are Some Things Improbable?

KEVIN KINGHORN

Alfred Hitchcock's movie *Foreign Correspondent* prompted one film reviewer to give this succinct summary: "More twists than a cruller." We could say the same thing about the unfolding plot lines in most of Hitchcock's movies. When you watch one of his films, you might see an ordinary citizen become entangled in international intrigue through a series of improbable events. Or you might come across a surprising revelation that you never saw coming. But one thing is certain. In some form or another, you'll see the improbable, the surprising, the shocking.

But exactly what makes an event improbable? Philosophically, this has become an interesting question in light of the distinctions twentieth-century philosophers have made between different *kinds* of probability. In short, there are different *ways* in which an event can be improbable. And Hitchcock's films are a rich resource of examples of events that are improbable in these various senses of "probability." If we look at the plot developments from a few of his classic movies, we can see how they illustrate the different kinds of probability philosophers have distinguished.

The Science of Frank Fry's Jacket

Much of the modern-day discussion of probability builds on the original work of seventeenth-century philosophers such as Blaise Pascal (1623–1662) and Gottfried Leibniz (1646–1716). Philosophers since that time have not always agreed on how to distinguish the different kinds of probability. Still, by applying

what philosophers have said about probability, we can distinguish three general ways in which an event can be improbable.

First, there is what we might call *physical* probability. This is
the extent to which a particular event is determined by previous
natural events. In past centuries, many philosophers and scientists thought the world worked "deterministically." They imagined the world to be like the internal machinery of a clock.
Once a clock is wound up and begins to tick, the cogs of one
revolving wheel turn the cogs of another wheel. And the cogs
of this second wheel cause the cogs of yet another wheel to
turn. And so on. This scheme allows no room for random or
chance events; everything that happens is completely determined by prior physical events.

Hitchcock at times seemed to hint at the possibility that our
world doesn't operate within such a simple, deterministic mechanism. Consider the bizarre behavior exhibited by the winged
creatures in *The Birds*. While it is *possible* that there are prior,
physical events that cause the birds' behavior, Hitchcock deliberately attempts no such explanation. And so he leaves the door
open to the idea that things in our world sometimes occur due
to mere freakish, physical chance.

Current scientific research supports the idea that there are
some things in our world which are not mechanically determined by prior events. Certain kinds of carbon atoms, scientists
tell us, decay at different rates. And there's simply no way to tell
when they'll decay. The most we can say about any particular
collection of carbon atoms is that it has, for instance, a fifty-per-
cent chance of decaying within the next five thousand years or
so. To cite another example, sub-atomic particles like electrons
can move in ways that, from all appearances, are completely
random. When scientists fire an electron directly at a target on
a screen, the most they can say is that the electron will hit *somewhere* on the screen—with, for instance, a twenty-percent
chance of hitting the specified target.

These kinds of 'indeterminate' events which scientists have
documented are all at the micro-level of atoms and sub-atomic
particles. It's an open question whether our larger, macro-level
world of bowling pins and billiard balls operates deterministically or indeterministically. Our everyday observations of the
world *seem* to suggest that things operate deterministically on
the macro-level. I've never shot a billiard ball toward a corner

pocket only to have it randomly swerve to a side pocket (as much as I'd like to be able to use that as an excuse!). I'm guessing you would say the same. Still, some philosophers of science theorize that the indeterminacy at the micro-level means that the macro-level is also in principle indeterministic—even if it is extremely unlikely that enough micro-particles would ever move randomly in the same direction so as to make a billiard ball suddenly swerve or make a bowling pin unexpectedly spin and topple over.

Because physically improbable events seem only possible at the micro-level, this first kind of probability—physical probability—is of little interest for our larger discussion. In the movie *Sabateur*, Robert Cummings's character Barry Kane grabs the jacket sleeve of the baddie Frank Fry in an attempt to keep Fry from falling from the top of the Statue of Liberty. We then watch the stitches of the shoulder seam of Fry's jacket tear one by one from the weight of the dangling villain. Slowly, agonizingly, the seam finally comes apart altogether and Fry plummets to his death. If, at the macro-level of objects like jackets, the world does in principle work indeterminately, then it will be a matter of probability whether the stitches of the coat hold. Specifically, this will be a matter of *physical* probability. But, again, this is not the sort of probability that is likely to account for the unlikely and surprising events we might witness in the world. So let us turn to the two remaining kinds of probability.

Statistics for Umbrellas?

These last two kinds of probability are given various names in the philosophical literature. Rudolf Carnap (1891–1970), who influentially wrote about the distinction between these two kinds of probability, gave them the names "probability$_1$" and "probability$_2$." Creative, huh? Perhaps we can do a little better! Let's call one *statistical* probability. This refers to the proportion of particular events that are contained within a larger class of events. Suppose in a certain voting district forty-five percent of the people are registered Republicans, fifty percent are registered Democrats, and five percent are independent voters. If you were to conduct a phone survey, how likely is it that you would reach a Republican if you dialed a random phone number? You'd of course have a forty-five percent chance of

218 Kevin Kinghorn

reaching a Republican. And this would be a matter of *statistical* probability. If you happened to reach an independent voter, this would be a statistically improbable event.

In the movie *Foreign Correspondent* a classic scene takes place on a rainy Amsterdam street where a gathered crowd of people are all holding black umbrellas. An assassin shoots a political leader named Van Meer and then disappears into the crowd. Joel McCrea's character, Huntley Haverstock, tries to locate the assassin in the crowd. But there is a sea of identical-looking black umbrellas before him—and only one assassin, who could be hiding under any one of them. Unless Haverstock could somehow search under the majority of the umbrellas, it's unlikely that a simple umbrella-by-umbrella search would yield the assassin. The unlikelihood here is one of *statistical* improbability.

A similar scene takes place in *North by Northwest*, where Cary Grant's character Roger Thornhill puts on a train porter's uniform in order to sneak past the police, who are looking for him. When the police discover that Thornhill has stolen the uniform (well, he actually bribed a porter for it), they begin searching the train station for him. Their "search" amounts to accosting anyone they happen to see in a porter's uniform. But with so many porters at work in the station, it is very unlikely that any single uniform they spot will be the one Thornhill is wearing. And in the end he is able to escape before the police locate him. The unlikelihood of finding Thornhill among the multitude of similarly-dressed porters is again a matter of statistical improbability.

A particularly interesting case of statistical probability occurs in *The Wrong Man*. A villain commits a string of armed robberies. This is particularly bad news for Henry Fonda's character, Manny Balestrero. For the villain looks remarkably similar to Manny, and eyewitnesses to the crimes identify Manny as the one who committed the robberies. Moreover, when the police question Manny and ask him to write down the words used in an original note by the armed robber, they find that Manny has remarkably similar handwriting. Inexplicably, he even makes the same mistake that the robber made in writing the original note. Hitchcock offers a commentary at the beginning of the movie: "This is a true story, every word of it; and yet it contains elements that are stranger than all the fiction that has gone into many of the thrillers that I have made before." The main story line is improbable in the following sense. We ordinarily see many, many people in the course of our lives. And rarely, if ever, do we meet two people (especially two unrelated people) whom we cannot tell apart—and who even have similar handwriting and are prone to the same careless spelling mistake. So, experience tells us that it would be extremely unlikely that Manny would have a "double" in all these respects.

Of course, with a world population in the billions, it is perhaps not that unlikely that *someone* somewhere in the world has a double who could fool multiple eyewitnesses, and who is prone to the same spelling mistakes. And Hitchcock, with his "ordinary man" motif, has a way of reminding us of the unsettling possibility that the next strange coincidence in the world just might throw *our* lives into chaos.

Still, it remains hugely improbable that you, or I, or Manny Balestrero, or any specific individual should have a double somewhere in the world. Perhaps it's not all that unlikely that *a* person somewhere in the world has a double. But it is still wildly improbable that Manny Balestrero would have a double. The improbability here is, once again, a statistical matter.

Show Me the Evidence!

Our third and final kind of probability is what we might call *evidential* probability. This is a matter of how probable a theory is, given a certain collection of evidence. Juries must make probability assessments of this kind. They look at the available evidence and evaluate the competing theories offered by the prosecutor and the defense attorney, respectively. In criminal cases, juries must also determine whether the evidence points "beyond a reasonable doubt" to the prosecutor's theory being true (and thus to the defendant being guilty.) In civil cases, jurors need only determine whether the claimant's version of events is more probably true than the defendant's version.

In the previous section we saw that it was a matter of *statistical* improbability that Manny Balestrero from *The Wrong Man* would be mistaken for someone else. But the jury at Manny's trial was concerned with the *evidential* probability that he was guilty. It's true that the jury might have considered the statistical improbability of physical "doubles" as they reviewed all their pieces of evidence. But it was the evidential probability of Manny's guilt which they were assessing.

What considerations are relevant in assessing evidential probability? This question may draw a mixed response from philosophers, in virtue of an ongoing debate about whether there are *correct* methods of evidence assessment. It seems clear, though, that in our everyday life we assume that there are indeed correct and incorrect ways of assessing evidential probability. Suppose I go with some friends to the movies one evening and I don't bother to lock my car in the parking lot. When asked why I didn't lock the car, I respond by saying that I've already had two cars stolen in the last year. Surely, I explain, the "law of averages" means that it would be extremely unlikely that I would have a *third* car stolen.

In such a case, you would be right to point out to me that I have a thoroughly mistaken understanding of the 'law of averages'. My statements suggest I think it a statistical matter that car owners who experience thefts are unlikely to experience yet more thefts. Yet, it is obvious that this so-called 'law' I cite does not provide the evidential support for my theory (that I won't have my car stolen) that I think it does. My methods for evidence assessment are sadly incorrect. So, there *do* seem to be correct and incorrect methods for determining evidential probability.

What are the correct methods for assessing the evidential support for a theory? Evidence is related to the probable truth of a theory in three ways. So, we must ask three questions about the evidence. It is only by addressing all three that we can correctly evaluate all the ways evidence relates to a theory. Here are the three questions:

(1) Does the evidence fit the theory?
(2) Does the evidence fit *multiple* theories?
(3) Is the theory what we would have expected beforehand?

Jimmy Stewart: Amateur Sleuth or Philosophical Genius?

A concrete example of correct evidence assessment will help us see the relevance of these three questions. Fortunately, we have just the example we need in *Rear Window*. In this Hitchcock film James Stewart's character, L.B. Jeffries (or Jeff), suspects that his neighbor, Lars Thorwald, has murdered his wife. Jeff calls on an old friend, police detective Thomas J. Doyle, to help investigate. Jeff and Doyle then engage in a series of heated discussions about the likelihood that Thorwald is guilty. In their discussions, Jeff shows himself to be quite the amateur sleuth in that he demonstrates an appreciation for each of the questions listed above.

The first question assumes (for the sake of argument) that the theory in question is true. It then asks us whether, on this assumption, we would expect to see the same collection of evidence that we have in fact seen. Suppose the theory is that Thorwald murdered his wife. The first question asks: *If* we assume that Thorwald did murder his wife, would we expect there to be evidential clues of the same sort that Jeff observes? In short, does the evidence fit the theory?

In his debate with Doyle, Jeff wants to focus on Thorwald's mysterious trips at night in the rain, his wrapping up knives and a saw in newspaper, and his wiping down the bathtub. Doyle, on the other hand, wants to balance the discussion by reminding Jeff of such matters as the superintendent seeing the Thorwalds leave the apartment at 6:00 a.m., Mrs. Thorwald being seen on the train to Merritsville, and a postcard that was mailed from Merritsville back to Thorwald later that day. In sum, Jeff is focusing on evidence we *would* expect to see, on the assumption that Thorwald is guilty. Conversely, Doyle keeps bringing up the evidence we would *not* expect to see, on the assumption this theory is true.

At one point, Jeff and Doyle debate the same piece of evidence, but they give it different interpretations. Noting that Thorwald's shades are open and that he's sitting in his apartment, Doyle says, "It's too stupid and obvious a way to murder—in full view of fifty windows—and then sit over there, smoking a cigar, waiting for the police to pick him up. . . . That salesman wouldn't just knock off his wife after dinner, toss her in a trunk, and put her in storage." Doyle is arguing that this is not the kind of evidence we would expect to observe, if Thorwald really had murdered his wife. But Jeff insists that it *is* what we would expect, explaining at one point: "That's where he's being clever. Acting nonchalant." Their debate is precisely on the first question listed above: whether the evidence fits the theory.

The second question asks us whether the evidence fits with multiple theories. Put another way, it asks us how likely it is that we would observe the evidence of the case, *whether or not* the theory is true. To see the importance of this question, think about where we stand so far. In answering the first question, we might conclude that Thorwald is probably guilty because the evidence of the case is very much what we would expect to see if Thorwald did in fact murder his wife. But this consideration loses its force if we would expect to see this same evidence, *even if the murder didn't occur.*

Jeff rightly argues that, on the theory that Thorwald murdered and disposed of his wife, we would expect to find him doing such things as cleaning up a saw and washing down a bathtub. But suppose for a minute that everyone in that community cut up wood for their stoves each morning. In such a case, *most* people might clean their saws every day. So, seeing Thorwald cleaning his saw wouldn't constitute telling evidence that he committed a murder. Or suppose that in their community everyone washed down their bathtubs every day to prevent the spread of a bacterial epidemic. We would expect to see Thorwald washing down his tub *whether or not* he hacked up his wife. Thus, the evidential support for our theory (that Thorwald murdered his wife) stemming from Thorwald's behavior would be undermined to the extent that we would expect to see this behavior *even if* our hypothesis is false. The second question—Does the evidence fit multiple theories?—factors in this point.

Jeff and Doyle come to very different conclusions about how likely it is that the evidence of the case would exist once we exclude the theory that Thorwald is guilty of murder. Jeff insists that there is no reasonable, innocent explanation for Thorwald's observed behavior. He asks, "Why would a man leave his apartment three times, on a rainy night, with a suitcase? And come back three times?" Jeff is emphatic that this is *not* what we would ever expect to observe, if no murder had occurred. He points out that Thorwald's wife is "an invalid who needs constant care." Surely, he reasons, we would expect to see Thorwald taking greater steps to care for her—if we assume for the sake of argument that she is still alive.

Doyle, on the other hand, insists that it *isn't* far-fetched that we would see the events involving Thorwald's behavior, if we consider only alternative theories that do not involve Thorwald being a murderer. Jeff objects to this idea, saying: "You mean you can explain everything that went on over there—and is still going on?" Doyle responds, "No. And neither can you. That's a secret and private world you're looking into out there. People do a lot of things in private that they couldn't explain in public." Doyle's point is that, even though there is an air of "mystery" to Thorwald's behavior, it's still the kind of innocent activity we can expect to see in our varied, complex world.

So, Jeff and Doyle give different answers to our second question related to correct evidence assessment. Jeff thinks it very improbable that the evidence of the case would exist, if we assume for the sake of argument that Thorwald didn't murder his wife. Doyle disagrees. But they both recognize the importance of our second question: whether the evidence fits with multiple theories.

The third question concerns the extent to which our prior, background knowledge leads us to think that a theory is likely to be true. When juries consider whether a defendant is innocent or guilty, they do more than consider the specific evidence of the case (such as fingerprints on the murder weapon, and eyewitnesses to the suspect's whereabouts). Jurors also consider their background knowledge of the defendant. Is the defendant a habitual criminal, who has shown he has no regard for human life? Or is the defendant a model citizen, who has consistently demonstrated strong moral character and an aversion to violence? Our background knowledge of the defendant will affect how much specific evidence we need in order to think him probably guilty of the crime with which he's been charged.

Suppose I told you that I've heard various people report that Hitchcock, before he died, was planning to direct a lavish musical remake of *Gone with the Wind*. Surely you'd be skeptical. Yes, Hitchcock did direct the comedy *Mr. and Mrs. Smith* and the farcical *The Trouble with Harry*. But at no time did he ever show any real interest in directing musicals or in plot lines that resemble lavish soap operas.[1] Surely, you'd think to yourself, this must be some crazy Internet rumor. Your background

---

[1] It's true that, early in his career when he was without a picture to direct, Hitchcock agreed to do *Waltzes from Vienna* so that he could keep working. He also announced to the cast on set that such a movie went against his instincts.

knowledge of Hitchcock is so at odds with my testimony that this testimony is not nearly enough evidence to convince you that my theory is likely true.

The third question of evidence assessment factors in this point and asks us to consider how likely a theory is true, given only our background knowledge. Doyle has no strong views here about Thorwald. His investigation of Thorwald yields only the following: "He has a six-month lease . . . Quiet. Drinks, but not to drunkenness. Pays his bill promptly . . . Keeps to himself, and none of the neighbors got close to him, or his wife." As a detective, Doyle is not naive enough to think that quiet men never murder their wives. But most men don't go around seriously considering whether to murder their wives. And since Doyle sees nothing in Thorwald's background that makes him think Thorwald is different from most men, he doesn't think his background knowledge makes it at all likely that Thorwald is a murderer.

Jeff, on the other hand, thinks there's more to be said about Thorwald's character and his pre-existing relationship with his wife. He says at one point, "I've seen things through that window! Bickering, family fights . . ." When Thorwald seeks advice from someone on the phone, Jeff reasons from his background knowledge of the couple that it couldn't be the absent Mrs. Thorwald: "I never saw him ask for *her* advice before. But she volunteered plenty!" Jeff is saying here that the background knowledge available about Thorwald *does* offer some reason to think he might have a murderous character. Perhaps Jeff wouldn't go so far as to say this background evidence gives a *strong* indication that Thorwald has the kind of vicious character necessary for cold-blooded murder. But considering only background knowledge, he at least thinks the theory of Thorwald being a murderer is not so unlikely as Doyle seems to think it is.

So we've seen that Jeff and Doyle give different answers to each of our three questions about how evidence relates to the probable truth of a theory. It is thus understandable that they reach such contrasting conclusions about the likelihood of Thorwald's guilt. Moreover, there remains the factor—which we've not discussed—that Jeff and Doyle might have particular biases that affects how they answer the three questions. Jeff, for example, by focusing on Thorwald to the point of near obsession, is possibly running away from an issue he needs to confront. Jeff fears his life would be cramped if he were to marry his girlfriend Lisa. He's terrified of the commitment and its implications. Down deep he wants, perhaps, to find confirmation that marriage really is so confining that it drives a man mad.

If this analysis is at least partially correct, then Jeff's reasonable objectivity in evaluating evidence may be compromised. He may really *want* Thorwald to be guilty. And experience shows that people often believe things more readily when they want them to be true.

Still, while these are interesting issues to explore, they involve the ways we might be biased in *how* we answer our three questions. Our main concern, though, has been to identify *which* questions need to be asked in assessing evidential probability. And on this point Jeff and Doyle agree. The fact that Jeff and Doyle debate each of our three questions shows that, though they disagree about how to interpret the evidence, at least their *method* for assessing evidence is correct.

What surprises us in Hitchcock movies is often the occurrence of an event we thought was evidentially improbable. And Hitchcock's characters are themselves frequently surprised by evidentially improbable events. We can think of Patricia Martin's character Priscilla Lane in *Saboteur* being told that Barry Kane, who is on the run from the police and who had virtually kidnapped her, really is innocent. Or Jimmy Stewart's character Scottie in *Vertigo*, who is stunned when the woman whose death he is mourning turns out to be alive. And of course Roger Thornhill in *North By Northwest*, who is surprised and angered when he learns that Eve Kendall is in league with Philip Vandamm—and then subsequently surprised and delighted when she turns out to be working undercover for the CIA. This list could go on and on. And the surprise in each case arises when a character discovers something that all his or her previous evidence suggested was not true. In short, the surprise stems from the occurrence of evidentially improbable events.

One memorable instance of this kind of improbability occurs in *The Thirty-Nine Steps*. Robert Donat's character Richard Hannay is being chased by members of a spy ring, whose leader, Hannay has learned, is a clever and ruthless man with a missing right little finger. A woman, just before she's killed by the spy ring, tells Hannay that a man in Scotland may hold the key to stopping the spies. Hannay tracks down the man,

Professor Jordan, at his Scottish estate. Relieved at having made it to Professor Jordan safely, Hannay is able to relax completely after the Professor shields him from police discovery and then offers him a drink and a cigarette. Finally at ease, Jordan opens up to the Professor and tells him all that has happened and that the leader of the spy ring has a missing little finger. The Professor asks him which hand has the missing finger, and Hannay says it's his left one. Chillingly, Professor Jordan raises his right hand, revealing a missing little finger, and asks, "Sure it wasn't . . . *this* one?" The shock felt by Hannay and by the audience once again stems from the fact that all our evidence seemed to suggest that Hannay, having reached Professor Jordan, is now safe at last. But as it turns out, just the opposite is the case.

Lessons to Take Away

Keeping the different kinds of probabilities straight can help avoid errors that even professional philosophers have sometimes made! One example involves a critique of arguments from design, which purport to show the probable existence of God. Noting the number of highly unlikely events that needed to occur for our evolving universe to sustain life, some believers have argued that a creator God is a more probable explanation for the existence of our universe than are purely naturalistic explanations. However, sometimes philosophers have objected to this line of argument on the grounds that there has only been one Big Bang. And because we therefore don't know how many times Big Bangs naturally produce life, we can't say that life in our universe *is* unlikely. But this is a confused objection. The original line of argument is one that compares the *evidential* probability of life in a purely naturalistic world versus a world where God exists. It looks at the evidence of life in our world, and then compares competing explanatory theories. But the critic's objection is that this line of argument doesn't provide *statistical* data of probability. And this is no good objection.

In criminal trials we would never require a jury to have statistics of how many times the defendant has turned out to be truly guilty when previously put on trial for similar crimes. And this is because juries assess evidential probabilities, not statistical probabilities. Similarly, it is improper to insist of the believer, whose argument is based on evidential probability, that he have statistics about how many times similarly evolving universes have and haven't produced life. So, one lesson to keep in mind from our discussion is that we can make errors of reasoning when we do not distinguish the different kinds of probabilities.

A second lesson worth keeping in mind is that a proper assessment of evidential probability requires us to ask three separate questions. Otherwise, we will fail to appreciate all the ways in which evidence relates to a theory. In our discussion of *Rear Window*, we saw that Jeff, without realizing it, engaged in reflection on all three questions. These questions provide more than guidelines as to how evidence *can* be assessed. They tell us how evidence *should* be assessed. And this is important for anyone sitting at home with binoculars, with suspicious-looking neighbors, and with aspirations of becoming an amateur sleuth like Jeff.

17

The Hitchcock Cameo: Aesthetic Considerations

JASON HOLT

> Hitchcock's cameos are self-publicizing jokes and ironic punctuation marks, no question about it. They also have perkily nondramatic and illusion-breaking qualities. Yet our willingness to point and chuckle at them needn't stop us from seeing them as something more resonant.
>
> —DAVID STERRITT, *The Films of Alfred Hitchcock*

Good evening.

I'd like to discuss a subject of great personal interest, and not without a certain philosophical purchase: Alfred Hitchcock's cameo appearances in his films.[1] The danger of discussing this subject, especially from an aesthetic point of view, is that one may say something both amusing and instructive. However, I'm willing to take the risk.

The Hitchcock cameo is among the best-known, yet one of the least appreciated, elements of his work. Even those who've never seen a single Hitchcock film have some inkling that, *were* they to watch one, they'd be liable to see his unmistakable figure pop up at some point. Those who've seen several of his films can recall a cameo or two, and true fans have their favorites: appearing in a newspaper ad in *Lifeboat* (1944), carrying a double-bass in *Strangers on a Train* (1951), appearing in

---

[1] For an extensive list of Hitchcock's cameos, see Robert A. Harris and Michael S. Lasky, *The Complete Films of Alfred Hitchcock* (New York: Citadel, 2002), p. 248. For a more comprehensive list, go to http://hitchcock.ru/cameos. For better quality visuals, try http://hitchcock.tv/cam/cameos.html.

a reunion photo in *Dial 'M' for Murder* (1954), sitting next to Carry Grant on a bus in *To Catch a Thief* (1955), leaving a hotel room and looking at the camera in *Marnie* (1964), getting up out of a wheelchair to shake someone's hand in *Topaz* (1969). But while a great many know about the cameos, few appreciate them as anything more than a gimmick, part of Hitchcock's signature, yes, ironic and sometimes amusing, but often to the detriment of the films' tension and drama, a superfluous, rather idiosyncratic element with little redeeming value.

Given this impression, the cameos present something of a mystery. What are they *doing* there? What's their significance? What was Hitchcock trying to do? Did he succeed? How could the "Master of Suspense"—of all people—include an element in his work, not once, but time and time again, that detracts, even briefly, from suspense, the very thing of which he's the undisputed master? Is there some other function they serve that somehow redeems them?

Enter a Silhouette in Profile (Stage Left)

The TV show *Alfred Hitchcock Presents* (1955–1961) always began with an introduction by Hitchcock, often a sort of faux lecture. I'll begin with a lecture too, though not a faux one. It will be both dry as Hitchcock's and, if less amusing, reasonably brief. Since we'll be applying an examination of the cameos to theories of how to interpret art, we should start by getting a sense of what such theories are.

Certain aspects of art are *beyond* and come *before* interpretation, *beyond* in that they're matters of evident fact not open to dispute, and *before* in that they're what the interpretations are interpretations *of*: the lines and colors in a painting, the words that make up a poem, the frames and scenes in a film—the data of art. Interpretations are hypotheses about what these data mean, and theories of interpretation tell us how to formulate and justify these hypotheses.

There are three basic theories about how art should be interpreted. According to Intentionalism, an artwork means what the artist intended, and so interpretations should be guided by what we can discover about the artist's intent.[2] Interpretations that

---

[2] See Steven Knapp and Walter Benn Michaels, "Against Theory," in W.T.J. Mitchell, ed.,

don't mesh with the artist's intentions (given by biography or psychology) are dismissed on that basis. According to New Criticism, it isn't the artist but the work itself that fixes its meaning.[3] One way to understand this is by drawing an analogy with the world. Just as the world lends itself to best explanations of the sort achieved in the sciences, so too do the imaginary worlds of art yield best interpretations. Interpretations that don't gel with such quasi-scientific method are discounted on that basis. According to Subjectivism, an artwork's meaning isn't artist- or work-based but audience-based, a function of how the work is received.[4]

Each of these interpretive frameworks has plusses and problems. Intentionalism has appeal because the artist's intentions *cause* the work to be, and to be what it is, in the first place, and if we know what the artist had in mind, if we know the vision, interpreting the work becomes pretty straightforward. On the other hand, it seems we can, and often do, interpret an artwork in ignorance or even violation of the artist's intentions. That's part of the appeal of New Criticism, which maintains an artist-independent, quasi-scientific basis for objective meaning in art. But here's where Subjectivism gets its foothold. Art seems open to a variety of different interpretations, and many interpretive disputes in art seem unresolvable. Maybe there's no fact of the matter about the meaning of art. Let the audience make of it what they will. The problem here is that it seems that *anything goes*, and while art may be open to different interpretations, nothing's *that* open.[5] Something would be clearly amiss if I interpreted Hitchcock's *Psycho* (1960) to mean "Jason Holt rules!"

These options are often taken to be mutually exclusive. The meaning of art is held to be given by *either* the artist's intentions, the work itself, or audience response. One and only one

---

Against Theory: Literary Studies in the New Pragmatism (Chicago: University of Chicago Press, 1982).

[3] See the classic W.K. Wimsatt and Monroe C. Beardsley, "The Intentional Fallacy," in *The Verbal Icon: Studies in the Meaning of Poetry* (Lexington: University of Kentucky Press, 1954), pp. 3–18.

[4] See Roland Barthes, "The Death of the Author," in his *Image-Music-Text* (New York: Hill and Wang, 1977).

[5] I've barely scratched the surface here. For more detail, try my "The Marginal Life of the Author," in William Irwin, ed., *The Death and Resurrection of the Author?* (Westport: Greenwood, 2002), pp. 65–78.

of these can truly ground meaning in art, because whichever is the right one, the other two will, often enough, conflict with it (or so it seems). Using the Hitchcock cameo as a case study, we'll see that this point of view is probably too simple.

The Joke

We'll start with the most obvious interpretation of the cameos—they're jokes. When we see Hitchcock appear in his films, we're often inclined to chuckle, especially when the Master's obviously poking fun at someone, often himself. When we see him in *Lifeboat*, in a newspaper ad for "Reduco," a fictional weight-loss product, or in *Strangers on a Train*, carrying a double-bass, he's the butt of his own body type jokes. He makes fun of his other human frailties in *Blackmail* (1929), being bothered by a child, in *Stage Fright* (1950), staring at Jane Wyman, in *North by Northwest* (1950), missing a bus. Cameos like these can easily be interpreted as Hitchcock trying to establish a rapport with his audience. His more ordinary cameos, walking by or standing in the street, are similarly inflected if not outright jokes.

But the jokes aren't always on Hitchcock himself. His frequent self-insertions, especially the more mundane ones, suggest an almost anyone-can-do-this lampoon of acting. (Hitchcock is reported to have used the word 'cattle' to refer to actors.) Such commentary at times includes remarks on the films themselves. The wheelchair cameo in *Topaz* is plausibly an expression of Hitchcock's dissatisfaction with the slow pacing of the film. In *The Birds* (1963), he walks out of a pet store with two dogs on a leash, the ordinary counterpoint to what's supposed to scare us in the film, the terror of nature *unleashed*. Such thematic and plot tie-ins can also be seen in the *Strangers on a Train* and *Notorious* (1946) cameos.

His cameo behind frosted glass in *Family Plot* (1976) is undoubtedly an allusion to the shadowy profile opening of *Alfred Hitchcock Presents*. As jokes, or commentaries, or allusions *by* Hitchcock, Hitchcock's intent is required. The cameo in *Strangers on a Train* can only be Hitchcock's joke at his own expense if he meant it that way. (It can be at his expense otherwise, but it can't be *his* joke.) To the extent that the cameos can be so characterized, they lend some support to Intentionalism.

The cameos can't, however, be characterized generally as jokes, commentaries, allusions, and such. Of the over thirty-five cameos Hitchcock did, less than a dozen are obvious jokes, and far fewer among the jokes are clear cases of commentary or allusion. Most of the cameos, even if humorously inflected, don't come off that way. They were intended by Hitchcock to be there, but would we be wrong to draw the parallel between Hitchcock's body type and the double-bass if Hitch hadn't intended it? Does the Master hold us hostage? I don't think so. This will become especially clear once we know how the cameos came to be.

Origins and Development

When I first got into Hitchcock I had the impression, as many do, that he did a cameo in every single one of his films. Then I saw one (I forget which) in which I couldn't spot it, and I found the experience maddening. It was only later that I discovered that though he did a cameo in *most* of his films, he did not do one in all. There were many exceptions. Most of Hitchcock's early films are cameo-free. His first (first two, actually) came in *The Lodger* (1926), followed by more, then less, sporadic appearances, until the 1940s, when they became a constant feature of his films. Why?

It's an interesting story.[6] The early cameos were an expediency. One day, they didn't have enough extras on set, and rather than delay production, Hitchcock stood in. As audiences began to recognize him in his pictures, they grew to anticipate his cameo appearance in subsequent films. Hitchcock obliged, and the custom was cemented as a signature move, one that he retained throughout the rest of his career.

The important thing for our purposes is the order of things. The key step in the cameo's progression from expediency to signature move wasn't Hitchcock's intent. He simply didn't envision the function that the cameos would serve, the significance that audiences would attach to them. Once he knew, of course, he took the ball and ran. But the function and significance were there before he knew it. There was something special about the cameos that the audience gathered first.

---

[6] Recounted in *The Complete Films of Alfred Hitchcock*, p. 248.

Of course it's entirely possible that Hitchcock had some foresight into the role the cameos would eventually play. The "expediency" story might just be window dressing, in which case some revisionist film history would be in order. Were that true, though, we'd expect the early cameos to be far less sporadic. The real question, however, isn't whether Hitchcock *in fact* intended the cameos to play the role they do, but whether we can know what role they play without knowing for sure (beforehand or after the fact) what exactly he intended. And so it seems we can. We can view the cameos as a whole (including the early ones, retrospectively) as having a meaningfulness that outstrips, or at least does not depend on, the Master's intent.

This spells trouble for Intentionalism, and one begins to see where the work itself and audience response come into play. As upfront as Hitchcock was about manipulating the audience, he also deferred—he had to—to what makes them tick, whether or not he managed to envision that ticking. Paradoxically, then, out of Hitchcock's respect for the audience he manipulates so well, he's no less our hostage than we are his.

Where's Alfred?

You remember the "Where's Waldo?" kids' books? Spotting Hitchcock in his films is a tougher, adult-level version of the same game. You're watching, say, *Notorious*, and you're caught up in the pivotal party scene, and there he is, screen left, drinking a glass of champagne (and foreshadowing a key turn in the plot). The pleasure one feels at spotting him is akin to that of solving a puzzle, or problem. Where Hitchcock will appear in any given film is a sort of mini-mystery, and one feels, almost, an easy-gotten kinship with Hitchcock's unluckier but more tenacious heroines and heroes in solving it, in getting to the *Eureka!*

But this game is a real mixed bag. On the one hand, looking for it adds, beyond whatever empathy we may feel with the characters, a layer of personal involvement, an extra shot of tension. A link between "Will the hero prevail?" and "Will I succeed?" is set. But the game can go too far, even if one doesn't want it to. One may be tempted or forced to devote too much attention to seeking out the cameo, and not enough to what's happening in the film. Not only does spotting Hitchcock dispel some of the tension that the Master has skillfully built up, looking for it can interfere with the buildup itself. To diminish such distraction, Hitchcock started to put the cameos earlier and earlier in his films. Some are still hard to spot (as in *Rope* [1948], where he walks down the sidewalk, at some distance, during the opening sequence, and possibly later where his silhouette may appear, also at some distance, in an apartment across the street), and even in later movies some of them come well into the picture (as in *Family Plot*, his last film, forty-one minutes in).

When one knows there's a cameo, but fails to spot it, one rightly gets the sense that the richness of the film exceeds what one's taken in, one's contingent appreciation, that the film is more than one's made of it. From a New Criticism perspective, playing the game too much, or perhaps even at all, amounts to missing the point. Even from a Subjectivist viewpoint, the game is somewhat but not entirely legit, since Hitchcock is more rewarding (for the subject) when the cameos, inessential to, and distracting from, the narrative as they are, are given marginal attention. From this perspective, both New Criticism, and to a lesser extent Subjectivism, gain some ground.

The Real Deal

As I mentioned earlier, many people think that the cameos either detract from the films, or are a harmless sort of add-on, part of the artist's signature, but not all that important. Either way, on balance, the cameos don't really do the films any great service. In a way this is true, at least on the surface. However, on balance the films are better for the cameos than they would be without them.

We've already gotten the sense that Subjectivism has its limits, that you can't do just *anything* in how you deal with (how you interpret) art. A good case in point is David Sterritt's take on the cameos as Hitchcock's deliberate (intentional) self-insertion as the master of his domain, as the God-like "presiding spirit" of his films.[7] As evidence Sterritt cites the *I Confess*

---

[7] David Sterritt, *The Films of Alfred Hitchcock* (Cambridge: Cambridge University Press, 1993), pp. 12, 14.

(1952) cameo, in which, I confess, Hitchcock's bearing does suggest such God-like self-casting. But this is a hasty generalization. Not only are many more of the cameos self-deprecating rather than self-aggrandizing, most are quite mundane spots in which Hitchcock presents himself in the near-caricaturish guise of an ordinary person, remarkable only for not being so.

Except on that one occasion (if even then), the cameos just don't function as Sterritt's take on them would lead us to expect. More importantly, the evidence strongly suggests Hitchcock didn't intend them that way either. Just look. The interpretation would have been fine if Sterritt's claim had been merely that *he* finds it pleasing to interpret the cameos that way, irrespective of Hitchcock's intent. But he didn't. The intentional claim doesn't hold, and the work itself doesn't support it.

A better interpretation, I think, focuses on the cameos' mundanity. Hitchcock's walking by or standing in the street, reading a newspaper, playing cards, gawking with the crowd at a crime scene, and so on, adds to the films an appreciable touch of *realism* (in the ordinary sense of realistic, true-to-life, not the philosopher's sense of the term as mind-independence). We willingly suspend disbelief in the improbable, exciting action and plot, but recognizing the real person of Hitchcock in a fictional world (unlike, say, the actors, whose characters obscure their real selves, or the extras, who blend with the background, or even other directors when they do cameos, lacking such iconic status), makes the fictional world seem more realistic, the suspense more plausible. The more realistic the salient context, the more, however improbable, plausible the events. As a mundane but recognizable figure in the context of the cameo, Hitchcock orchestrates a piquant collision between the real and fictional world.

To what extent is my interpretation legit? *I* find it piquant, and the films more enjoyable overall, when I interpret the cameos this way. So far so good, so long as I don't presume anything about Hitchcock's intentions, or the work itself as others will or should take it. Not treading on anyone's toes, neither Hitchcock's nor those of other viewers, my interpretation is legit precisely because it increases my appreciation. This may be so even if Hitchcock didn't intend it, and even if the work itself (as others take it) won't sustain it. At first blush, from the perspective of New Criticism, it may seem that the cameos are unfortunate, practically dispensable elements of the films, as they add nothing to, and often detract from, the work as a whole. However, the work itself may sustain my interpretation as a suitable competitor. On my interpretation, the plot-wise dispensable cameos nonetheless add to and cohere with the films as a whole. They add that touch of realism without which, arguably, the films would be worse off. Even as a signature, an add-on, there's a case to be made that films are better with the cameos than they would be without. Did Hitchcock intend it? An interesting question. But really, who cares? It works for me, does no damage to Hitch, or anyone else, plus there's reason to think it may work for others as well.

Da-dum, Da-da-da-da Dum-da-dum

So where does all this leave us? Interpreting art, and the cameos as an illustrative case study, is a more complex, more involved process than may at first appear. All three of Intentionalism, New Criticism, and Subjectivism hold *within their respective domains*: (1) the history and psychology of the artist, (2) treating the work-as-world or best explanation, (3) facilitating aesthetic experience. For example, the joke cameos lend themselves to Intentionalist interpretation, and the apparent superfluity of the cameos to a reading by New Criticism's lights, although interpreting them as adding a touch of realism, while piquant to me (and so supporting a limited Subjectivism), offers a competing account from the perspective of New Criticism.

In a sense, everyone wins, though it may seem to many a hollow victory at best. Some advocates of Intentionalism, New Criticism, and Subjectivism would have it that *their* approach, and theirs alone, holds the key to unlocking the special meaning of art. But in art, *the* meaning is a fiction, a false ideal. While artists, works themselves, and audience response constrain interpretation, none of them should be held full hostage to another. There are many meanings, as we've seen, not all legit, as we've also seen, but nonetheless there's plenty of room for plurality. Problems arise when an approach that works in one domain is presumed to exhaust the field of meaning.

But intentions don't guarantee results, nor results a best reading. It's best in art as life to keep presumption under wraps.

And now, a word from our sponsor.[8]

―――――――

[8] Thanks to both John Mezey and Monique Lanoix for useful discussion, and to the Philosophy Club at the University of Louisiana at Lafayette, where some of this material was first presented.

18

Knowing When to Be Afraid: Rationality and Suspense

CATHERINE JACK DEAVEL and
DAVID PAUL DEAVEL

Human beings generally assume that our social world and the natural world are coherent wholes. We assume they operate in consistent patterns of cause and effect—that there are reasons why things happen. We further assume that these patterns and reasons are knowable. The trick in Hitchcock's suspense movies is to engage and undermine these general epistemological assumptions.

Philosophically speaking, what makes suspense? Hitchcock plays on and, sometimes, seems to overturn the assumptions of both the characters and the audience about what reality is like and how we know it. The fear in Hitchcock's suspense movies is not just about danger, but about how we can even know what is really dangerous and what only seems to be dangerous. When the possible threat is another person, a character faces twin dangers. If she incorrectly concludes that she ought to fear the other person, she risks betraying this person and destroying their relationship—no small price when the person in question is her beloved. On the other hand, if she incorrectly concludes that she ought not to fear the other person, she may pay for this epistemological stumble with her life. When the possible threat is natural, such as menacing birds, our characters must determine if their belief in the consistency of nature is correct and they are experiencing a series of horrifying coincidences or if their belief in nature's consistency is a sham and the birds are in fact trying to kill them. In both the social and the natural scenarios, the characters can prevail in gaining knowledge and saving themselves only by being persistent seekers of truth and astute interpreters of evidence.

Women in Love and in Danger

In the social world, the suspense is dependent on the question of how we can know another person's character. How do we know that what others tell us is true? How should we interpret their actions? And what if their words and actions conflict, either with our other interactions with this person or with information from another source? Hitchcock builds his suspense movies around the psychological tension of the characters as they—and often we, the audience, as well—try to resolve the seemingly conflicting evidence.

Hitchcock often makes women in love the characters in whom we experience suspense. If the women are wrong about the character of their men, they are in grave danger. The question for our heroines (and, secondarily, for the audience) is how best to interpret the conflicting evidence before them: is a heroine's beloved capable of violent crime, or is there another explanation that accounts for all the evidence and shows her beloved to be innocent? Hitchcock's strategy is ingenious, in part because it raises a second, complicating question about our knowledge of other people. How much importance should we give our own interactions with and feelings for another person, especially in the case of romantic love? As our heroine and the audience try to interpret the information available, we must decide whether our heroine's love makes her a better or worse judge of the evidence at hand. Either love blinds our heroine to the proper interpretation of evidence and the dismaying acceptance of the beloved's guilt, or love provides her with intimate and reliable insight into the beloved's character and, thus, strong and reasonable evidence for his innocence that outweighs competing evidence.

Hitchcock's heroines in *Spellbound, Suspicion,* and *The Wrong Man* all struggle to build a coherent interpretation of increasingly alarming evidence about the men whom they love, but they resolve the conflicting evidence in very different ways. Like the ancient Greek philosopher Aristotle (384–322 B.C.), these women assume that humans are habitual creatures in virtues and vices—that is, our behavior tends to follow patterns of good or bad action, and virtues and vices come in clusters. As evidence mounts, the most plausible theory seems to be that the men are guilty of the crimes they appear to have committed.

On the other side, however, the women's love (or more precisely, the goodness of the men's behavior toward the women) counts as reasonable evidence for their innocence. In each case, the woman in love comes to a coherent interpretation of the conflicting evidence, but the way in which each heroine reconciles the evidence before her is markedly different. At the heart of the struggle to find the truth about her beloved is the question of how much weight to give the evidence of her own love for this man. In these films, our heroines build coherent interpretations of the available evidence in one of the following ways: first, by clinging to the innocence of the beloved despite the case against him (*Spellbound*), second, by losing faith in the beloved in the face of increasing evidence (*Suspicion*), or, third, by building a coherent theory at the price of sanity (*The Wrong Man*).

Spellbound: Amor Vincit Evidentia (Love Conquers Evidence)

Spellbound spins its suspense around the love of beautiful psychoanalyst Dr. Constance Peterson for the troubled amnesiac J.B., who impersonates and may have killed another analyst, Dr. Anthony Edwardes. As the story begins, Constance, "human glacier and custodian of truth," is unrelentingly clinical in all of her human interactions. She considers love dangerous and is happy to observe its effects from afar. "The greatest harm done to the human race," she claims, "has been done by the poets." The poets concoct romantic notions of love that cannot be fulfilled by real-life experience. When experience fails to live up to these impossible standards, human beings become mentally ill. She soon finds, however, that the experience of love might just live up to the poets' promises. When Constance falls in love with the mysterious J.B., she staunchly sets herself to the task of curing him. She is convinced that he did not murder Dr. Edwardes but is instead the victim of a severe guilt complex. The two set out to rid him of his amnesia and solve the murder of Dr. Edwardes before the police can catch them.

One might be tempted to interpret *Spellbound* as a struggle between heart and mind, irrational love and dispassionate reason. The suspense would then be predicated on the question of which aspect of the human person should triumph. As we will see, some of the characters, in particular Dr. Brulov, favor this interpretation of Constance's situation. On this interpretation, she may be in danger precisely because she gives up her commitment to reason for the irrational fancies of love. The plot, however, bears out a more complicated and interesting interpretation.

The question is not whether Constance should abandon reason for love but whether love gives her insight into J.B.'s character and psyche, such that she now has more evidence to which she may then apply her reason and discover the truth. Constance is not irrational in her lonely belief that her beloved is innocent. To the contrary, she is willing to risk her life because she insists that J.B.'s goodness of character is no less true than the other evidence available. Constance holds the quite reasonable Aristotelian position that the moral character of a person is consistent, and J.B.'s interactions with her are evidence that he could not have committed murder. The suspense comes from our sneaking worry that, though love may sometimes provide insight, Constance has instead been blinded by her own desire for her beloved's innocence.

When we first meet Constance in her office, a colleague berates her for work that, he claims, is "brilliant but lifeless: There's no intuition in it." When she asks if he is "making love" to her, the colleague declares he is and attempts to kiss her, only to find her eyes open and her lips unresponsive. Exasperated by her bemused indifference to his passion, the colleague ruefully opines, "Your lack of human and emotional experience is bad for you as a doctor—and fatal for you as a woman." Note that this colleague does not juxtapose reason and emotion. To the contrary, the claim is that emotional experience will make her not only a more complete human being but also a better analyst, that is, reason is aided by insight available only through emotional experience. As she becomes more and more wrapped up in attempting to "save" J.B., these words of her colleague take on an ambiguous meaning. Is the "fatality" for Constance the woman simply a way of saying that she will miss out on life because of her indifference to love? Or is it that a lack of human and emotional experience leaves her naïvely open to falling in love with the kind of man who might kill another and steal his identity?

When on the lam with J.B. this question is deepened. Will Constance be vindicated for trusting her heart, or will she instead learn that her initial assessment of love was, sadly, correct? Constance's mentor, Dr. Alex Brulov, certainly believes it was. When Constance tries to convince Dr. Brulov to help her, he sardonically comments, "Women make the best psychoanalysts until they fall in love; then they make the best patients." And indeed, in her defense of J.B., Constance seems to argue against everything she knows best. To Brulov's convincing argument that J.B. is dangerous, Constance retorts, "You know his mind, but you don't know his heart." Brulov may seem like a heartless misogynist, but there's something identifiably reasonable in his rasping explosion in this scene: "Do not complete the sentence with the usual female contradictions. You grant me I know more than you, but you know more than me. Bah! Women's talk."

Even if the audience wants to sympathize with Constance's declarations of love and trust, accompanied always by the wail of violins, Dr. Brulov's evidence is convincing since his argument with Constance comes after a midnight encounter with a straight razor-wielding J.B. Was J.B. suicidal or homicidal? He was certainly dangerous, and Brulov managed to calm him only by spiking a glass of milk with a sedative. Further, in the original meeting with Brulov, Constance hears her mentor answer, quite testily, police questions concerning his relationship with the missing Edwardes. What Brulov detested about Edwardes was his foolish belief that he could cure his patients with intimacy—taking them skating or for vacations in the mountains. Brulov surmises that this foolish intimacy and trust with a patient was fatal for Dr. Edwardes.

But Brulov's dismissal of Constance is telling. Constance's insistence that she is right and Brulov wrong about J.B. is not a contradiction, even on Brulov's terms. Brulov does know more than Constance insofar as he is a more seasoned and studied analyst; however, Constance knows more than Brulov insofar as she can draw upon her own experiences with J.B. in her efforts to cure him and to assess whether he is truly capable of murder. These two claims can both be true together because the knowledge in question is different. Brulov knows more about psychoanalysis in general, but Constance knows more about this particular case. When Brulov chides, "The mind of a woman in love is operating on the lowest level of intellect," Constance initially replies, "The heart can see deeper sometimes." If she had stopped at this rejoinder, then we might conclude that *Spellbound* does in fact simply pit mind against heart: Constance simply now places her bets with her strong emotional impulses when she seeks to know the truth whereas before she would have sided with her intellectual conclusions. But Constance continues: "A man cannot do anything in amnesia out of his real character. . . . I couldn't feel this way toward a man who was bad, who had committed murder." This line is a key to the story's suspense. On the one hand, Constance offers a reasonable general principle: character is consistent. What Constance knows is that Aristotle is correct when he claims that people's actions will tend to follow patterns of virtue and vice because our moral character is the result of habit. When we deliberately and consistently choose moral or immoral actions, these choices will eventually become second nature. For example, acting patiently now makes me more likely to act patiently in the future. Thus, if J.B. is gentle and moral in the present, then it is highly unlikely that he acted violently and immorally only days ago.

The difficulty comes in the second part of Constance's claim, which amounts to a second premise in her argument: "I couldn't feel this way toward a man who was bad." If we had undeniable evidence that J.B. is indeed gentle and moral in the present, we might happily look back to the principle that character is consistent and conclude with Constance that it is highly unlikely that J.B. murdered Dr. Edwardes. But J.B. recently arrived in Brulov's living room armed with a razor and is given to wild-eyed outbursts and anger. We, like Brulov, have reason to be skeptical that Constance is a clear-eyed judge in this matter.

Constance convinces Brulov to help her despite his disapproval, and J.B. proves to be as innocent as Constance believed him to be. Just as the Empire State Hotel house detective claimed that a good detective must be a good psychologist, Constance proves to be both. Because of her love, she is a better detective. Her insight into J.B.'s character makes her the only one in the movie, even including J.B., who correctly believes in his innocence.

Suspicion: What's Love Got to Do With It?
(the Evidence, that Is)

In contrast to Constance's passionate fight to prove her beloved's innocence, Lina McLaidlaw of *Suspicion* is in the more complicated position of debating against herself about the true nature of her beloved's character and intentions. Lina, too, begins with the Aristotelian assumption that a person's character will tend to follow patterns, but she also stakes her marriage and possibly her life on the belief that we can choose to act against these patterns, especially if motivated by romantic love. The epistemological problem in Lina's case is that her belief in the consistency of moral character and behavior gives her reason both to trust and to distrust Johnnie, depending on which past actions she emphasizes. In *Spellbound*, Constance's experience with J.B. tells overwhelmingly on the side of good moral character, and she can trace his episodes of irritation and anger to his psychological difficulties. In *Suspicion*, Lina falls in love with a man whom she knows to be a playboy, gambler, liar, and unrepentant spender of other people's money. Is it probable—or even possible—that a cad will act against the established habits of his shady past because he has fallen in love with a good woman? The suspense mounts as the evidence pulls Lina between two conflicting interpretations of her beloved's actions. She has evidence both that Johnnie is a mercurial but ultimately loving husband and that he is a deceptive and impulsive man capable of murdering her.

Lina lives a quiet and refined life with her parents on the family's country estate until she catches the eye and then the heart of the charming but opportunistic ladies' man, Johnnie Aysgarth—as much to Johnnie's surprise as to Lina's. The two are disarmingly honest with one another during their whirlwind courtship. Lina says what she thinks and feels because she is guileless. Confiding that she doesn't know how to be coy, she tells him directly that she loves him and asks Johnnie about his romantic past. When he admits to having kissed (at least) myriad admirers, she laughingly inquires if he is always frank with the women he pursues. He is not, he assures her, but he is frank with her because it is "the best way to get results." This scene sets up Lina's bind in interpreting Johnnie's words and actions throughout the film. Johnnie has just been honest that he is a liar. Further, his only reason for not lying to her is self-interested efficiency: honesty will get him what he wants more readily than lying would. Should she take this honesty as a stable feature of their relationship? Will he be a changed man? Or should she take heed that he is a habitual liar and that his honesty with her will last only until deceit becomes the best way to get results?

Lina is inexperienced in love but her belief that Johnnie can change is not simply naive wishful thinking. Johnnie acts out of character by being honest with her about past indiscretions and in pursuing her at all, given his propensity to be a gold digger. Johnnie tells her directly that all of her father's reasons for disapproving of him are well founded, even the ones he doesn't say. But, as Lina notes, though Johnnie initially hopes to live off her income, he couldn't have married her just for her money. Johnnie easily could have won an extravagantly wealthy wife if he had wanted. More importantly, Lina believes that people may act in ways that run against their old habits because she herself has done exactly that. Before the marriage, Lina overhears her parents' speculation that she will be a spinster; she has an intellectual and introspective character, her father claims, that suits her better for unmarried life. Who could predict that quiet, thoroughly respectable Lina would elope with the dashing rogue every woman in the county has been chasing after knowing the man only for a matter of weeks? Lina confides to Johnnie that she had imagined her love and courtship would be far different and comfortingly conventional, but she loves him and is willing to risk her reputation and relationship with her parents for him.

As their marriage begins, however, Lina is horrified to find that Johnnie has not changed many of his old habits. He also begins a pattern of toying with Lina's emotions: Johnnie disconcertingly falls into old vices and then strings Lina along in her dismay before revealing that the imminent disaster has been averted. Upon arriving home after their honeymoon, he informs her that he is penniless and had hoped that they could live off an advance of her inheritance. Shocked and embarrassed, Lina pleads with Johnnie to look for a job, only to have Johnnie finally produce a telegram from his relative Captain Melbeck, who has offered him a position managing Melbeck's estate. Later, Johnnie admits that he sold Lina's set of heirloom chairs to pay his gambling debts and lied to her about it—but he won on a long shot at the races and, at the end of a stream of recklessly expensive gifts, presents her with the receipt from buying back the chairs. Initially, Lina defends Johnnie, even when it seems clear that he is in the wrong. The seriousness of Johnnie's evasion and deceit only grows. By chance, Lina learns from Melbeck that Johnnie was discharged from his position six weeks earlier for having embezzled a large sum. Melbeck will not prosecute if Johnnie can pay back the money in a timely fashion. Johnnie, of course, has not mentioned any of this to Lina, and, when she tells him that she knows he has lost his job, he lies to her about the reason—a clash of personalities rather than his theft.

Some, like Donald Spoto,[1] have argued that the entire movie is simply about Lina's "unbridled suspicion" making her take the "childish" behavior of Johnnie and, on specious evidence, imagine that he is really dangerous. All the suspense is thus a product of a woman's neurosis. But this "boys will be boys" interpretation of Aysgarth does not stand up to scrutiny. Johnnie's behavior and character are objectively untrustworthy and dangerous. In addition to his deceptions regarding his lost employment, embezzlement, and gambling, Johnnie has researched an untraceable poison (soon to appear in the mystery novels of a writer friend) and has contacted Lina's insurance agency behind her back to learn that her life insurance policy can only be converted to cash in the event of her death. Moreover, Lina last saw Johnnie with his dim but wealthy and amiable friend, Beaky. The police visit Lina to report that Beaky is dead, due to an allergy known to Johnnie, and to offer a description of the man seen with Beaky that fits Johnnie all too well. Lina may be a sheltered and conventionally proper young woman, but her suspicion cannot simply be dismissed as wild conjecture.

Further, the suspense of the film works only if Lina's interpretation is plausible. The suspense requires that Lina (and the audience) are genuinely and reasonably troubled by the grow-

---

[1] Donald Spoto, *The Art of Alfred Hitchcock: Fifty Years of His Motion Pictures*, second edition (New York: Doubleday, 1992), pp. 101–08. To Hitchcock's own claims that the ending, in which Aysgarth is portrayed as innocent of designs for murder, was forced on him by RKO so as not to present Cary Grant as a murderer, Spoto claims that this is simply an excuse aroused by critical displeasure. But the conclusion is unsatisfying, if Lina's suspicion was simply the result of neurosis rather than a reasonable reaction to the information available to her.

ing direct and indirect evidence that Johnnie may be dangerous. If, as on Spoto's view, Lina is an obviously muddled and easily frightened woman whose fear of Johnnie is evidently without basis, then the film may be an exercise in the pathetic, or a sad character study of neurosis, but it is not a suspense film because there is no epistemological tension: one interpretation would be clearly correct, and the other clearly incorrect. We have argued that *Suspicion* is indeed a suspense film and precisely because of the epistemological tension. In the face of the evidence, Lina reluctantly but reasonably concludes that she is in danger. In the final scene, as Lina's car door flies open above the cliff and Johnnie lunges toward her, Lina and the audience have their hearts in their throats because the suspense has come to a crescendo and the tension between the competing interpretations of the evidence is about to be dramatically resolved.

The Wrong Man: Stand By Your Man, But "They" Will Get You Anyway

The Wrong Man bridges the movement from the challenge of interpreting human character to the challenge of interpreting the world itself as a whole. Christopher Emmanuel "Manny" Balestrero is neither untrustworthy and unlikable as Johnnie Aysgarth is, nor is he complex and mysterious as is J.B. The first half of the movie, depicting his arrest and interrogation for a string of robberies in his Queens neighborhood, presents a man utterly guileless, trustworthy, even boringly staid. The evidence against him is presented as weakly circumstantial. The identifications made by neighborhood merchants are ambivalent and that made by the life insurance agent who was held-up is untrustworthy—she can only glance at Manny because of fear. Moreover, the whole interrogation takes place under the weight of the movie's title. For the audience, it is impossible that Manny can be guilty. As a detective says, "An innocent man has nothing to fear."

But the suspense comes from the fact that despite this certainty on the part of the audience, the world seems to conspire against Manny. Despite the ambivalence and untrustworthiness of the eyewitnesses, they identify him anyway. During the interrogation, Manny is asked to write out the words of the original hold-up note for a writing sample. On the second time he misspells "drawer" as "draw"—the same mistake made in the hold-up note. All of the people who can corroborate Manny's alibi are either dead or cannot be found. As Manny says to Frank O'Connor, his lawyer, it's like somebody's "stacking the cards against us."

Rose Balestrero, Manny's wife, has no doubts as to her husband's character ("Well, everybody knows Manny can't be guilty," she tells O'Connor) and no doubts as to his whereabouts on the day of the robbery he has been accused of. If it is impossible that Manny is guilty and yet all the evidence keeps turning against him, Rose must account for this. Rose is the locus of the epistemological struggle, and the second part of the movie is in large part her story. Unlike Constance and Lina, Rose does not regain a coherent interpretation by giving up her belief in either the innocence of her beloved or the ominous weight of the evidence against him. Her method of account is to reconcile the evidence by imagining a vast conspiracy—a ubiquitous and undefined "they"—that seeks to punish Manny because of some fault in herself. After being confined to an asylum, she tells a psychiatrist: "They wanted to punish me because I failed Manny. I let him down . . . They'll get me. It's useless."

Hitchcock's method of prolonging the suspense is to keep the pressure on Manny right up to the very end. A man who looks like Manny is caught robbing another store. He is identified by the life insurance agent just as Manny was. And Manny's saga comes to an end only from what seems a lucky break. A Christian, however, might notice that the capture of Manny's double comes immediately after Manny has heeded his mother's pleading to pray. In the scene, the camera stops where Manny's eyes stop: on a picture of Jesus (focusing on his "Sacred Heart"), another "wrong man," who, it is claimed, was vindicated.

Questioning Everything: *The Birds*

Perhaps the work of suspense on the greatest scale is Hitchcock's *The Birds,* where the fear is extended to the entire natural order.[2] In the natural world, the question of suspense

---

[2] Spoto argues forcefully that the attacks of the birds dramatize the broken and disordered human relationships. He further claims that "the film operates completely on the level of symbol," and thus should not be interpreted as a story of "unruly nature"

comes down to whether philosopher David Hume (1711–1776) is right. Hume famously argued that past patterns do not give us a good basis for predicting what will happen, despite the fact that we seem to do so regularly with good success. What we call causes and effects are really simply past correlations that need not carry into the future. In *The Birds*, suspense builds as the characters and audience increasingly face the possibility that we cannot explain the birds' behavior either because the rational structure of nature is inaccessible (at least for the present) or because there is no rational structure of nature (humans incorrectly assume or impose cause-and-effect explanations on data that shows only correlations. We can point to no reason that the birds should continue to act as they have in the past except for our assumption that their behavior is caused and thus should remain consistent).

The opening scene in the highly organized social setting of San Francisco contrasts with the coming disorder in the natural setting of Bodega Bay. (Hitchcock surely intended the irony of beginning a film about homicidal birds in a city named for a saint who talked to animals.) In the social world, information is easily available. After the initial spat in the bird shop, rich socialite Melanie Daniels is quickly able to discover the identity of lawyer Mitch Brenner. With the help of a reporter at her father's newspaper and assorted neighbors, within a day of their meeting, Melanie has used Mitch's license plate number to track down his city address, plans for the weekend, his Bodega Bay address, and the name of his kid sister—not to mention inadvertently learning details of his romantic past from schoolteacher and former girlfriend Annie Hayworth.

The structure of the humans' social world makes such knowledge quite easy to obtain. Not coincidentally, the humans in San Francisco move about freely while the birds are in cages— nature is controlled, knowable, and a pretty object of diversion. In Bodega Bay, the humans will soon be confined to the cages of their buildings while the birds are free.

The most striking feature of the characters' attempts to make sense of the birds' behavior is their stubborn resistance to

---

(p. 330). Spoto would presumably object to our focus on the behavior of the birds, but in order for the birds to operate as effective symbols one presumably needs to consider how the characters react to the birds. Clearly, the characters spend a good deal of time trying to understand why the birds behave as they do.

acknowledging facts that do not fit their previously established theories. Initially, the characters are understandably willing to offer ill-fitting explanations of the birds' actions or just to write off the incidents as random occurrences. When Melanie is attacked by the first gull, she and Mitch are initially puzzled but then let the subject drop. Annie muses that the gull that crashes into her door "probably lost his way in the dark." "But it isn't dark, Annie," Melanie replies. "There's a full moon."

As the attacks escalate, however, some characters' dogged insistence that nature is consistent in its patterns becomes an epistemological failing: when the facts don't fit the theory, the facts are ignored. The local policeman offers several specious explanations for the attack on the children at Cathy's birthday party and for the sparrows' invasion of the Brenners' house, finally telling an exasperated Mitch that "birds don't just go around attacking people without no reason." The prime example of this denial of facts is Mrs. Bundy's speech in the diner. An amateur ornithologist, Mrs. Bundy assures Melanie that birds are neither intelligent nor aggressive enough to launch an orchestrated attack. Melanie points out the obvious: hundreds of crows did just attack the school children. "Impossible," Mrs. Bundy declares. Doesn't it seem odd, she demands rhetorically, after fourteen hundred years on the planet, that the birds would wait until now to "start a war against humanity?" A mother listening to the exchange interrupts, "If the young lady said she saw an attack at the school, why don't you believe her?" The reason seems clear: because the present attacks put the lie to the assumption that Mrs. Bundy's knowledge of birds' past behavior is a good guide to birds' future behavior. Various diners cannot accept that the attacks are anything but random occurrences and still retain a coherent theory; they conclude that there is no good reason to believe in the bird war. Mitch, on the other hand, explodes, "What's happening—isn't that a reason?" After the next onslaught, Mrs. Bundy cowers in the hallway of the diner. Her dialogue in the film has ended.

Clearly, the characters and audience are meant to abandon the comforting claims of Mrs. Bundy and face up to the fact that the birds are, for whatever reason, indeed attempting to kill the humans. The survival of the characters requires that they make this interpretation of the data, regardless of how far-fetched this scenario may initially appear. When Melanie goes to find Cathy at the school, she correctly interprets the massing of the crows on the playground as the prelude to an attack, whereas even the day before she might only have noted their arrival as an oddity and continued with her cigarette. She hurries up to the class-room, and Melanie and Annie begin to evacuate the children. Although the birds attack, the children escape rather than being trapped in the schoolroom during a surprise attack. Melanie does not have a full-blown theory to explain the birds' attacks; she does not have ready answers to the questions Mrs. Bundy will raise. Her epistemological virtue, however, is her willing-ness to base her beliefs about the behavior of the birds on all the data available rather than the most elegant or accepted account. The children escape with their lives because of Melanie's judgment that the birds are a real danger and Annie's quick decision to act on it.

Does the suspense of *The Birds* suggest that the rational structure of nature is inaccessible (whether only for now or in principle) to the human mind or, more frightening yet, that there is no rational structure of nature? Hitchcock leaves it an open question, but the characters still must place their bets on some form of rationality. At the end of the film, Mitch launches the apparently successful attempt to leave the bay on the basis of the radio report: "It appears that the bird attacks come in waves, with long intervals between. The reason for this does not seem clear as yet." This report is humble, stating only *that* the birds attack at intervals without attempting to explain *why* they behave this way. Despite the recent failure of the assumption that behavior in the natural world will follow predictable pat-terns, the characters must still act on some basis. Mitch is forced to rely on the observation of seeming patterns in the birds' attacks. Just as we have seen for Hitchcock's heroines in the social world, so Mitch risks his life and the lives of those he loves on the basis of an epistemological assumption.

19

Shadow of a Doubt and *Marnie*: Entries into a Mind

ROBERT J. YANAL

Shadow of a Doubt (1943) explores the knowledge one can have of *another's* mind, and *Marnie* (1964) deals with the knowledge one can have of *one's own* mind. As it happens, these films by Alfred Hitchcock come down on the side of Ludwig Wittgenstein against René Descartes. How did Descartes and Wittgenstein disagree?

Descartes and Wittgenstein on Mind

Modern philosophy of mind begins with René Descartes (1596–1650). In his brilliant *Meditations,* Descartes put forward two logically dependent ideas. The first deals with certainty about the contents of our own minds, and asserts that a person is necessarily certain both *that* he is thinking and of *what* he is thinking. Descartes arrived at this view through his method of doubt. He thought that it was possible to doubt that there really was an external world filled with material objects and other people, because of the possibility that there was an "evil genius" who systematically deceived him. If you've seen *The Matrix* or watched *Vanilla Sky*—or better yet, Hitchcock's masterpiece of deception, *Vertigo*—you might not find such fanciful speculations too farfetched. Despite widespread and unavoidable possibilities of error, though, Descartes concluded that it was impossible for him to doubt that (and what) he himself was thinking. For even if he were deceived, he had to be thinking to be deceived. Since certain thoughts of his own were immune to doubt, he inferred that he held them with certainty, and that he thereby truly *knew* them.

The flip-side of certainty about the contents of one's own mind is skepticism about the minds of others. Descartes equated certainty with what cannot be doubted, and uncertainty (or skepticism) with what can be doubted. I cannot doubt that I am thinking and what it is I'm thinking of, so the contents of my mind are certain to me. But I *can* doubt whether *another* person is thinking or what he or she is thinking of. Descartes tells us that when he looked out of his window he sometimes saw people. "But in truth what can I 'see' besides hats and coats, which may cover automata?"[1] Descartes knew that *he* was a conscious being—a being that thinks. As for others: well, for all he knew there might well be no other minds, only mindless machines walking around in hats and coats. To generalize the point: whereas the contents of our own minds are known to us with certainty, knowledge of the contents of the minds of others is fraught with uncertainty and so not really knowledge after all.[2]

A bit over three hundred years after Descartes's *Meditations*, Ludwig Wittgenstein (1889–1951) attacked Descartes's two ideas regarding mind, in his *Philosophical Investigations* (published posthumously in 1953). Descartes, a mathematician, proceeded in step-by-step argument. Wittgenstein, a brilliant aphorist, threw out pithy and suggestive challenges.

To counter Descartes's claim of certainty regarding the contents of one's own mind, Wittgenstein demanded: "'Only I know my thoughts.'—How do you know that? Experience did not teach you it." To counter the thesis of skepticism regarding other minds, Wittgenstein asserted, "To say 'He alone can know what he intends' is nonsense: to say 'He alone can know what he will do', wrong. For the prediction contained in my expression of intention (for example, 'When it strikes five I am going home') need not come true, and someone else may know what will

---

[1] Descartes, *Meditations on First Philosophy* (1642), in Elizabeth Anscombe and Peter Geach, eds., *Descartes: Philosophical Writings* (London: Nelson, 1969), Second Meditation, p. 73.

[2] Descartes did have a method for achieving certainty regarding external realities, like the existence of the world and of God. Descartes thought he had accomplished building this bridge from internal to external certainty, but most have considered his effort to achieve the second certainty a failure.

really happen. . . . I can be as *certain* of someone else's sensations as of any fact." And also this: "We also say of some people that they are transparent to us. It is, however, important as regards this observation that one human being can be a complete enigma to another."[3]

In other words, Wittgenstein asserted, contrary to Descartes, that others could know our own thoughts after all, perhaps even better than ourselves. Wittgenstein also insisted that we may be wrong about the contents of our own minds. Alfred Hitchcock turns out to be on Wittgenstein's side.

Enter Hitchcock

Shadow of a Doubt is a counterexample to Descartes's skepticism regarding other minds. This films presents a pair of protagonists who know the minds of one another almost as well as they know their own. *Marnie* is a counterexample to Descartes's claim that we are certain about the contents of our own mind. The principal character in this film has lost touch with important portions of her consciousness. It is left up to others to discover for her lost aspects of her mind.

What is a counterexample? Well, suppose a classic movie buff says, "Hitchcock movies are always great" or "Hitchcock's movies are never bad." A counterexample to the first claim would be a Hitchcock movie that isn't great, and to the second claim, a Hitchcock movie that's bad. The counterexample shows that the thesis is false. Hitchcock himself considered his early *Waltzes in Vienna* (1933) a movie that wasn't great, even if it wasn't entirely bad. So it might serve as a counterexample to the first claim, but not the second.

In *Shadow of a Doubt*, Hitchcock presents a special case in which two protagonists *do* know, at least to a significant extent, the mind of another. Descartes's skepticism regarding other minds can be briefly stated as follows: One person never knows with complete certainty what another is thinking. But the two Charlies in *Shadow of a Doubt* frequently know what's on the other's mind. His claim of certainty regarding one's own mind is: A person always knows the contents of his own mind.

---

[3] Ludwig Wittgenstein, *Philosophical Investigations* II (Oxford: Basil Blackwell, 1953), pp. 222–24.

However, Marnie has an area of her consciousness to which she is denied access.

The films which I present as Hitchcock's counterexamples to Descartes were first and foremost popular melodramas. Hitchcock aimed at popular success, which most of his films achieved, but his popular success was never due to dumbing his movies down or pandering to base instincts. He brought his audience to consider universal themes and insightful analysis of the human condition. Hitchcock was not just a brilliant film-maker, but also a man of high intellect.[4] He was certainly capable of erudite allusions in his films.[5] Hitchcock was not just the master of suspense, but one of the greatest artists of the twentieth century. Hitchcock is certainly not explicitly addressing Descartes or Wittgenstein in these films. Still it is clear that he was thinking about the problems these philosophers raised. In these two Hitchcock films, we get a great mind's views on the nature of mind.

Shadow of a Doubt: **Not Good to Find Out Too Much**

Shadow of a Doubt pits Young Charlie (Theresa Wright) against her Uncle Charlie (Joseph Cotten). Young Charlie comes to discover that her beloved Uncle is "The Merry Widow Murderer," a serial killer of rich widows, something no one else in her family even remotely suspects. In return, Uncle Charlie thinks he can win his niece over to his dark philosophy of life. Both Charlies are equally strong-minded. Uncle Charlie has made attempts on his niece's life, but Young Charlie is prepared to return tit-for-tat. "I don't want you here, Uncle Charlie. I don't want you to touch my mother. Go away or I'll kill you myself. See, that's the way I feel about you." And in their final confrontation, as the train pulls out of town, Uncle Charlie attempts

---

[4] His films are of course the best testimony to Hitchcock's genius. To see some more of the workings of his mind, read the fascinating series of interviews Hitchcock did with François Truffaut in the 1960s, *Hitchcock* (Simon and Schuster, 1966), or delve into the collection of his writings edited by Sidney Gottlieb, *Hitchcock on Hitchcock* (University of California Press, 1995).

[5] To name two: there is a reference to a passage from Hesiod in *Strangers on a Train*, and to the medieval legend of Tristan and Isolde in *Vertigo*. See the relevant chapters in my *Hitchcock as Philosopher* (McFarland, 2005).

to push his niece off the train—but it's she who succeeds in pushing him off.

Hitchcock thus offers a special case of people who know one another's minds quite well. He pairs two characters who are alike in important respects; and their alikeness allows one to be, in Wittgenstein's words, "transparent" to the other. Each, that is, has something like the certainty of one another's thoughts which Descartes attributed only to a solitary individual knowing his or her own mind. And in each film, the plot turns on the knowledge one character comes to have of the other.

On the surface, the paired protagonists are quite unalike. Young Charlie seems a nice young girl, while Uncle Charlie is a ruthless serial killer. And yet Young Charlie is prepared to kill her uncle (and in the end does, though out of self defense). Hitchcock insists on the alikeness of these characters through the patterns of doubles that run through the film. To list just a few, there are two Charlies, each introduced by a camera pan into their bedrooms, he in Philadelphia, she in Santa Rosa, where each is lying pensively in bed; there are two murder suspects, each pursued by two detectives; there are two scenes on a train, and in the end two trains. The pinnacle of doubleness is reached when Uncle Charlie drags his niece into the 'Til-Two bar through double doors each of which has an image of a clock showing two o'clock; inside he orders two double brandies from a waitress who has worked there for two weeks.

What are these similarities that Hitchcock insists on? It is that the "good" member of the pair—Young Charlie—has some of the inner drive or motivation of her other "bad" double. The point Hitchcock is making is that the Charlies' similarities to one another give them privileged access to *one another's* minds. Young Charlie early on realizes that her beloved Uncle is the Merry Widow murderer. To the rest of the family, Uncle Charlie is, to use Wittgenstein's word, an "enigma." For example, Uncle Charlie has large amounts of vaguely explained cash, which arouses no one's suspicions. His brother-in-law and neighbor are fascinated with the case of the Merry Widow Murderer, yet don't remotely suspect the older Charlie. Uncle Charlie may be an enigma to the rest of his family but not to his niece, who knows they are alike: "I'm glad that mother named me after you and that she thinks we're both alike. I think we are, too. . . . I know you. I know that you don't tell people a lot of things. I don't either. I have a feeling that inside you somewhere there's something nobody knows about." "Not good to find out too much, Charlie," her uncle responds. "But we're sort of like twins, don't you see? We *have* to know." Later her uncle will tell her, "Same blood flows through our veins." Wittgenstein would say that Young Charlie and her uncle are "transparent" to one another; Young Charlie says that they have a "telepathic" connection.

Once Young Charlie discovers the awful truth about her uncle, she hides it from the other members of her family as well as from the detectives who question her. In effect, she exhibits some of her uncle's secrecy and cunning. Uncle Charlie senses the similarities between himself and his niece. After he knows that she knows of his murders, he tries to bring her over to his side: "You go through your ordinary little day, and at night you sleep your untroubled, ordinary little sleep, filled with peaceful, stupid dreams. And I brought you nightmares. Or did I? Or was it a silly inexpert little lie? You live in a dream. You're a sleepwalker, blind. How do you know what the world is like? Do you know the world is a foul sty? Do you know if you ripped the fronts off houses you'd find swine? The world's a hell. What does it matter what happens in it? Wake up Charlie. Use your wits. Learn something." Young Charlie foils what appear to be two attempts on her life by her uncle, but meets fire with fire: "I don't want you here, Uncle Charlie. I don't want you to touch my mother. Go away or I'll kill you myself. See, that's the way I feel about you." And in the end, she does just that. Leaving Santa Rosa, Uncle Charlie tries to throw her off the train but after a struggle she pushes him into the path of an oncoming train.

Marnie: An Enigma to Herself

Marnie is a counterexample to Descartes's idea that we are always certain of the contents of our mind. Marnie Edgar (Tippi Hedren), using a series of aliases, steals from one employer and moves on to steal from another. The film opens with her theft from Strutt and Company, and she next applies for a position at Rutland and Co. Mark Rutland (Sean Connery), a client at Strutt, recognizes Marnie as the employee who stole from Strutt, but hires her anyway. We discover that Marnie is terrified of red-on-white and thunderstorms. We're further tipped off that not all is right with Marnie, by a kind of Greek chorus of children who sing-song outside Marnie's mother's Baltimore house:

Mother, mother I am ill.
Send for the doctor over the hill.
Call for the doctor, call for the nurse.
Call for the lady with the alligator purse.
Mumps said the doctor.
Measles said the nurse.
Nothing said the lady with the alligator purse.

After she steals from Rutland, Mark offers her "a choice of me or the police." Marnie and Mark marry, though he is also to discover that besides being a thief and a compulsive liar, Marnie is also terrified of sex.

After the marriage, Mark decides to become Marnie's therapist. He asks her about her past. "What happened to you?" "Nothing," she protests. "Nothing happened to me." When Marnie has nightmares and talks in her sleep, Mark asks, "Who hurt her?" "What noises?" "Who makes them?" Marnie even exhibits a kind of resistance to Mark's amateur psychoanalysis: "You Freud, me Jane." Eventually, Mark hires a private detective who informs him that Marnie's mother had been involved in a killing some years back.

Mark takes Marnie to visit her mother in Baltimore. "Your daughter needs help, Mrs. Edgar," Mark says to Marnie's mother. "You've got to tell her the truth. She has no memory of what happened that night." Mark then knocks to mimic the tapping sounds Marnie hears in her dreams, at which point Marnie recalls the night her mother, then a prostitute, brought home a sailor, whom Marnie beat to death, thinking the sailor was attacking her mother. For Marnie her memory of the murder is as unfamiliar to her as a film she's never seen before, and in fact Hitchcock presents it as a kind of internal film whose principal audience member is Marnie herself. (Hitchcock even marks the recollection as filmic by including the same disorienting shot he famously used to show vertigo in his film of that name.)

Marnie relies on the idea popularized by psychoanalysis that repressed memories of the past can cause all sorts of difficulties in the present; and that recovering such a memory will at least enable us to deal with them. Our philosophical point is that

Marnie has thoughts (memories) that she doesn't know she has, and furthermore has great difficulty gaining access to them. "I know what I am!" Marnie insisted earlier in the film. "I doubt that you do," Mark replied. Until her "therapy session" in Baltimore, Marnie is far from having Cartesian certainty about her mental life. To use Wittgenstein's words, she is an enigma to herself. The film implies that Marnie is at the end, if not cured, at least on her way to full sanity. Indeed, Marnie is not held as "cured" at the end of the film, for the Baltimore children still chant about the sick lady with the alligator purse as Mark and Marnie drive away. Marnie is still an enigma to herself.

Cast and Crew

RANDALL E. AUXIER has no real pathologies that Hitchcock could exploit, is utterly untroubled by Janet Leigh's soggy demise, and his confidence in conventional values is such as to leave him vulnerable only to an accidental glance through anyone's window. He is, however, afraid of heights, and has thus chosen a life on the prairies of Illinois, teaching philosophy at Southern Illinois University, Carbondale. Just North by Northwest of his home, one can stand upon a train car and view the very curvature of the earth, and he admits to being curious about some quiet family-owned motels to the south.

DAVID BAGGETT is Associate Professor of Philosophy at Liberty University in Lynchburg, Virginia. He is co-editor (with Shawn E. Klein) of *Harry Potter and Philosophy: If Aristotle Ran Hogwarts* (2004), and has published articles in ethics, philosophy of religion, and epistemology. His *C.S. Lewis as Philosopher: Truth, Goodness, and Beauty* is forthcoming in 2008. Most of Dave's writings feature big words, small print, no sales.

SHAI BIDERMAN is a Ph.D. candidate in Philosophy at Boston University. His primary research interests are contemporary continental philosophy, philosophy and literature, existentialism, and German philosophy. His recent publications include several papers on reasonability, revenge and determinism, as well as writings on Kafka, Nietzsche, and Heidegger. Shai vehemently denies that chicken-strangling is his favorite pastime. Perhaps *too* vehemently.

SCOTT CALEF is Associate Professor and Chair of the Department of Philosophy at Ohio Wesleyan University. He has published in ancient philosophy, applied ethics, metaphysics, and the philosophy of religion. He contributed to *The Beatles and Philosophy: Nothing You Can Think that Can't Be Thunk* (2006). Scott has a cameo in every

Hitchcock picture except *Family Plot*. By then, Hitchcock had had him arrested for stalking.

NOËL CARROLL is Notorious for being Spellbound by Hitchcock. He lives in South by Southeast Philadelphia where the Rear Window of his apartment overlooks a courtyard. Though he has never been accused of being a Man Who Knew Too Much, he is the Andrew Mellon Professor of the Humanities at Temple University. The Suspicion is that he has written a number of books, including *Beyond Aesthetics* and *Engaging the Moving Image*.

ANGELA CURRAN is Assistant Professor of Philosophy at Carleton College. She is co-editor (with Thomas Wartenberg) of *Philosophy of Film: Introductory Text and Readings* (2005) and author of articles on ancient Greek philosophy, aesthetics, and philosophy of film. Not rich, but possibly strange, she loves topazes and strangers on a train. The lady vanished after she checked in as lodger at the Jamaica Inn, a halfway house for foreign correspondents, the young and the innocent, and philosophers who lead double lives as secret agents.

CATHERINE JACK DEAVEL is Assistant Professor of Philosophy at the University of St. Thomas. She is kept Spellbound by her husband, DAVID PAUL DEAVEL, who is associate editor of *Logos: A Journal of Catholic Thought and Culture*, contributing editor for *Gilbert Magazine*, and a doctoral candidate in theology at Fordham University. Often mistaken for Cary Grant and Ingrid Bergman, the Deavels are kept busy trailing their three young sons (always Thirty-Nine Steps behind), dancing (Waltzes from Vienna, usually), and marketing a mystery-meat sandwich called the Egg McGuffins.

WILLIAM A. DRUMIN is Associate Professor of Philosophy at King's College, Wilkes-Barre, Pennsylvania, where for the past fifteen years he has offered a popular course in the cinematic artistry of Alfred Hitchcock. He is the author of *Thematic and Methodological Foundations of Alfred Hitchcock's Artistic Vision* (2004). Although Bill is a pretty serious guy, he does tend to go a little crazy every now and then, and he needs a lot of watching.

DAN FLORY is Assistant Professor of Philosophy at Montana State University, Bozeman. He has published essays on philosophy of film, race and aesthetics, and classical philosophy. He claims never to have climbed the bell tower steps at the San Juan Bautista Mission and assiduously avoids looking down from high places. Dan also dislikes rain gutters and often feels as though suspended over an abyss.

RAJA HALWANI is an Associate Professor of Philosophy at the School of the Art Institute of Chicago. In addition to numerous philosophical essays, he is the author of *Virtuous Liaisons: Care, Love, Sex, and Virtue Ethics* (2003), editor of *Sex and Ethics: Essays on Sexuality, Virtue, and the Good Life* (2007), and is the co-author of *The Israeli-Palestinian Conflict: Nationalism, Rights, and Terrorism* (forthcoming). Raja always ties his books up in a Rope when he goes to school.

JASON HOLT is Assistant Professor of Communication at Acadia University. He is the author of *Blindsight and the Nature of Consciousness* (2003), which was short-listed for the Canadian Philosophical Association Book Prize (2005), and numerous articles, mostly in aesthetics and philosophy of mind. Often a Stranger on a Train, always the Wrong Man, occasionally he's able to know a hawk from a handsaw.

ELIANA JACOBOWITZ is a Ph.D. candidate at Boston University. She is greatly fascinated by the universe at large and in particular by the history of ideas and the philosophy of religion. She insists that the intensive viewing of Hitchcock movies has had no effect on her life whatsoever. Just to be on the safe side, however, Eliana avoids hotel room showers, rooftops, and other people.

STEVEN JONES avoids the horrors of academia by pursuing a career in architecture at the Chicago firm of Burns + Beyerl Architects. His work includes various residential remodeling and new construction projects and can be seen on HGTV and in recent issues of *Chicago Home*, *Money*, and *Trends* magazines. Currently, Steve is renovating the bathrooms at a family-run motel and designing guest quarters in an anonymous jeweler's home.

KEVIN KINGHORN is a Philosophy Tutor at Oxford University. He is the author of *The Decision of Faith* (2005), and has contributed chapters to *Superheroes and Philosophy: Truth, Justice, and the Socratic Way* (2005) and *The Chronicles of Narnia and Philosophy: The Lion, the Witch, and the Worldview* (2005). Kevin has long recognized that Hitchcock movies provide a rich resource of philosophical examples for the classroom—although he gets exasperated when twenty-year-olds think he is referencing a U2 song when he talks about the developments in *Vertigo*.

SANDER H. LEE is a Professor of Philosophy at Keene State College in Keene, New Hampshire. He is the author of *Eighteen Woody Allen Films Analyzed: Anguish, God, and Existentialism* (2002) as well as other books and scholarly essays on issues in aesthetics, ethics, social philosophy, and metaphysics. He hangs out at the Statue of Liberty, Mount Rushmore, and the mission tower at San Juan Bautista.

STEVEN PATTERSON is Assistant Professor of Philosophy at Marygrove College in Detroit. Steve writes and teaches moral and political philosophy, and he has been an active contributor to Open Court's Popular Culture and Philosophy Series. There are exactly Thirty-Nine Steps from the door of his building to the door of his office.

STEVEN M. SANDERS is a writer and former Professor of Philosophy at Bridgewater State College in Massachusetts. He is the author, most recently, of "Film Noir and the Meaning of Life" in *The Philosophy of Film Noir* (2005) and "Poker and the Game of Life" in *Poker and Philosophy: Pocket Rockets and Philosopher Kings* (2006). His flair for the dramatic, to say nothing of his egotism, is on full display in his frequent cameo appearances at his former colleagues' classes.

MICHAEL SILBERSTEIN is Associate Professor of Philosophy at Elizabethtown College and an adjunct at the University of Maryland where he is also a faculty member in the Foundations of Physics Program and a Fellow on the Committee for Philosophy and the Sciences. He is an NEH Fellow who has published and delivered papers on both philosophy of science and philosophy of mind. His most recent book is *The Blackwell Guide to Philosophy of Science* (2002, co-edited with Peter Machamer). He is currently working on a book entitled *Contextual Emergence: On the Relational Nature of Reality*. He is currently not working on his book *Illuminating Images: Philosophy, Film and Interpretation* but hopes to be soon. He too has a Rear Window and binoculars but as he lives in Lancaster County, Pennsylvania, and not the Village, his voyeurism is confined to the mating habits of deer such as Mr. Antlers and Miss Whitespots.

AEON J. SKOBLE is Associate Professor of Philosophy at Bridgewater State College in Massachusetts. He is co-editor of *Political Philosophy: Essential Selections* (1999), *The Simpsons and Philosophy: The D'oh! of Homer* (2001), and *Woody Allen and Philosophy: You Mean My Whole Fallacy Is Wrong?* (2004), and author of *Deleting the State* (2007). He writes on moral and political philosophy for both scholarly and popular journals, and has contributed to many previous volumes in the Popular Culture and Philosophy series. He wouldn't even harm a fly.

PHILIP TALLON is a Ph.D. Candidate in Divinity at St Andrews University. He has written a number of chapters for volumes in the Popular

Culture and Philosophy series, including *Superheroes and Philosophy: Truth, Justice, and the Socratic Way* (2005) and *Star Trek and Philosophy* (forthcoming in 2008). His interest in Hitchcock goes back to the first time he saw *Rear Window* and immediately fell in love with Grace Kelly. His love of philosophy grew more gradually.

THOMAS E. WARTENBERG has recently edited two books: *The Nature of Art* (2001) and *The Philosophy of Film: Introductory Text and Readings* (2005, with Angela Curran). He is the author of *Unlikely Couples: Movie Romance as Social Criticism* (1999) and *The Forms of Power from Domination to Transformation* (1991). With Murray Smith, he is editing a volume on Film as Philosophy for the *Journal of Aesthetics and Art Criticism*, to be published separately as a book. He is Chair of the Philosophy Department at Mount Holyoke College and teaches in the Film Studies Program as well. Although he likes hiking and riding on trains, he does not speak to strange blonde women.

ROBERT J. YANAL is Professor of Philosophy at Wayne State University, in Detroit. In addition to authoring numerous articles, some co-written with George Kaplan, Yanal is editor of *Institutions of Art* (2004) and author of *Paradoxes of Emotion and Fiction* (1999). His most recent book is *Hitchcock as Philosopher* (2005). He hasn't a Shadow of a Doubt that readers will be Spellbound if not in a Frenzy over *Alfred Hitchcock and Philosophy: Dial M for Metaphysics*.

Index